THE WORLD OF
TACITUS

THE WORLD OF

TACITUS

DONALD R. DUDLEY

LONDON:

SECKER & WARBURG

First published in England 1968 by
Martin Secker & Warburg Limited
14 Carlisle Street, London W 1

Copyright © 1968 by Donald R. Dudley

SBN: 436 13900 6

Printed in Great Britain by
The Camelot Press Limited, London and Southampton

Contents

Contents

Foreword

THIS BOOK IS ONE OF A SERIES whose aim is to introduce the great historians of classical antiquity to the modern reader. Contributors are fortunate in that they are not asked to conform to any brief or pattern—indeed, nothing is prescribed except the title—*The World of Herodotus, The World of Tacitus*, and so on. And since even this might be construed in various ways, I owe a word of explanation as to why I chose to construe it in the way that I did.

The world of Cornelius Tacitus is, in one sense, that of the Roman empire from the last years of Augustus to the early years of Hadrian, roughly A.D. 10–120. His own life spanned the period from Nero to Hadrian. His major historical works cover the years A.D. 14–96, for which they are by far the most important historical source. Of his two monographs, one, in praise of his father-in-law Agricola, takes us to the remote north-westerly province Britannia, and, for a brief while, among the people of the Highlands of Scotland, who never came within the boundaries of the Empire. The other, the *Germania*, also looks beyond the imperial frontiers of the Rhine and the Danube to the unconquered peoples of northern and central Europe.

The period itself is one of the most creative in the whole history of Western civilisation, and many of its consequences are potent in the modern world, though they may not always be generally realised in a society so ready to allow the atrophy of its historical sense. The Jewish Wars of Vespasian, for example, and the capture of Jerusalem by the Romans in A.D. 70, continue to exert a profound influence on the politics of the Middle East. A little earlier, about A.D. 30, the Roman governor of Judaea had put to death an obscure heresiarch, using the form of punishment reserved for criminals of the lowest class. The crucifixion of its Founder did not put an end to the cult. Devoted missionaries spread it through the cities of the eastern provinces and to Rome itself, where by the time of Nero the Christian community was sufficiently numerous to incur persecution from the imperial government, and disapproving comment from Tacitus. Those who imagine that what happened in the Roman world can be of no concern to the twentieth century have overlooked Christianity and all that it has meant for mankind.

Another event of the reign of Tiberius has left an incalculable legacy. Augustus had formed a grand design for the northern frontiers of the empire, which he would have liked to extend as far as the River Elbe, thus incorporating a romanised Germany as a province. Disaster fell upon this momentous plan—first, the unexpected death of Drusus in 9 B.C., in the full flush of conquest: then the massacre of Varus and his three legions in the Teutoberger Wald in A.D. 9. The campaigns of Germanicus revived hopes, but the abrupt recall in A.D. 16 put paid for ever to the Roman conquest of Germany. Henceforward the Roman frontiers ran along the Rhine, and that river has marked the most lasting cultural divide in the history of Europe. But in Gaul and in the Iberian peninsula the seeds of Roman civilisation, planted in the time of the republic, came to full harvest during this first century A.D. As a result, France, Spain and Portugal were stamped forever as lands of Latin speech and culture.

Moreover, quite apart from its legacy to us, the Roman Empire claims attention in its own right. Here is the first attempt by Western man to establish a world-state—the first, that is, that was both substantial and long-enduring. Over four centuries the empire gathered together peoples of Greek, Oriental, Italian, Celtic, Egyptian, African, Germanic and many other races and cultures into the fabric of a common civilisation. It developed a world-wide commerce, a common currency, a common code of law, a common citizenship. There were two international languages, and numerous vernaculars: countless local cults, and a few ecumenical religions. Men of talent from all parts of the empire took part in its administration; soldiers of all nations served in its armed forces. There were emperors from Italy, Gaul, Spain, Africa, the Danube lands, Thrace, Syria, Arabia. Yet local loyalties, to a native city or tribal community, remained strong, and many millions of the empire's inhabitants never knew any other. The story of this extraordinary political experiment—in its failures no less than its successes—must be of great and increasing importance to modern man. Slowly and painfully, the nations of western Europe are trying to re-establish the unity they have not known since the collapse of the Roman Empire. Even more slowly, the peoples of a shrinking but still bitterly divided planet are groping their way towards some sort of world community, only dimly adumbrated as yet in the minds of a few, but, on the material plane, already within our reach. And when those engaged on these vast enterprises turn for help to the past, where are they more likely to find it than in the history of the Empire of Rome, and of China?

Such being the importance of the period, Tacitus would claim our interest even if he were the dullest of writers. But he is not; he ranks among the very greatest of Roman authors: the *Histories* and the *Annals* must be understood, first, as works of art. At this point it may well be asked why any intermediary should be needed? Why should the reader not approach Tacitus directly, either in a good translation or—if he has enjoyed a classical education—in Latin, referring when necessary to one of the many standard histories of the early Roman Empire? For those who can manage it, this will undoubtedly be the best course. But for others—and I take them to be the large

majority nowadays—there are obstacles to be cleared out of the
way before they can appreciate an ancient historian—and,
especially, one so complex and so individual as Tacitus. (Herodotus might be another matter.) And since we can only take
what Tacitus has to give, we must first understand what that is.
The first obstacle is that his idea of the nature and purpose of
history is so very different from ours. The concept of history
dominant in our own time is that of an academic discipline,
whose techniques were first formulated in the universities of
nineteenth-century Germany, but which have now been adopted
and further refined in the universities of the whole Western
world. It has turned history into a highly specialist, highly professional discipline, pursued as a life-long avocation by scholars
who work for their own satisfaction and the approbation of
their peers. It cares little for moral values, or the instruction of
the public, or the edification of posterity. It is happier with
limited fields than broad horizons: it honours research, and
deprecates synthesis. There are, of course, historians who do not
share this outlook, but I believe it to be dominant, and it is
wholly alien from that of Tacitus. He is concerned, above all,
with moral purpose, he believes that human character shapes
events, rather than events human character, he writes as pro-
secuting counsel at the bar of posterity. To understand the kind
of historian he is, we have to think back to Macaulay and
Carlyle, to Gibbon and Clarendon.

But, after all, that is not so very far. A further difficulty is
Tacitus' choice of themes. He would write much of the wars in
Germany, and their failure, but very little about the romanisation of Gaul and Spain: the campaigns of Vespasian and Titus,
but not much about Christianity, and only error and prejudice
about the Jews. For what Tacitus is writing is, primarily, the
annales populi Romani, the historical record of the Roman
people, and not a general account of the Roman world. And
that record itself is seen largely as the affairs of the *res publica*—
the state and its institutions. The relations between the Emperor
and the Senate, intrigues at the imperial court, campaigns

against foreign enemies, civil wars, important trials, debates in the Senate, the deaths of famous men—these are what interested Tacitus and the men of the senatorial class for whom he wrote. The scene is most often in Rome, or else in the army camps on the frontiers, or with some expeditionary force in Parthia or Armenia, in Germany or Britain. To use Tacitus is to use some powerful and delicate instrument—a telescope perhaps, whose magnification is high and whose definition clear, but so set that it will only bear on certain fields. These fields make up what I understand as the world of Tacitus—a personal world, the amalgam of his experience, outlook, and interests. To interpret this is the object of this book.

In the chapters that follow I shall begin with his life, of which all too little is known, and go on to his writings, whose dates have (with one exception) been pretty well established by modern scholars. I have tried here to say something about the lost books of the *Histories* and *Annals*. There follows a section devoted to his outlook on history, and to the main characteristics of his historical style—narrative, speeches, and character-study. Thence to the institutions of the Roman state, the most important being the emperors and the imperial court. The Senate and the Army appear as collective characters, never long off the stage. From institutions to peoples and places. First Rome, which Tacitus both hated and loved, and its polyglot, cosmopolitan population, which he loathed. Then to the provinces, some prominent, some almost neglected in his pages. Next, the external peoples with whom Rome had to deal, divided into Parthia and the East, and Germany and the North. Finally, a brief account is given of the rediscovery of Tacitus in the fourteenth and fifteenth centuries, and of the vicissitudes of his influence and reputation down to our own day. Notes amplify certain points in the text, and there is a bibliography for further reading.

Any book on a classical author is wasted if it does not win new readers—and send back old—to the original. I shall assume that my readers will keep a translation of Tacitus at hand for reference, and shall be pleased if they are encouraged to read his historical works as a whole. I should be best pleased if some at least turn back to the Latin text. I must further say that all passages quoted are in my own translation, and that I am grateful to the B.B.C. for permission to use some material that I first wrote for two talks on Tacitus which were broadcast in the Third Programme.

CHAPTER ONE
Life and Writings

MOST OF WHAT IS KNOWN of the life of Tacitus depends on statements, direct or indirect, in his own writings. These are neither frequent nor copious. Tacitus belonged to a tradition of historiography that did not encourage an author to obtrude his own personality. For those who wished to do so, whether by way of reminiscence or apology, the memoir was available as the appropriate literary *genre*. But the historian was expected to stick to his proper theme—the narration of public affairs. The most important personal statement of Tacitus is found in Book I of the *Histories*. 'I must not deny that my public career was launched by Vespasian, promoted by Titus, and still further advanced by Domitian' (*Histories* 1, 1, 3). Book XI of the *Annals* gives an invaluable date—the year 88, in which he was Praetor and a member of the College of Fifteen.[1] To hold the Praetorship in the year 88 would argue for birth in 55 or 56. A passage in the *Annals* cannot have been written earlier than 115.[2]

In the *Agricola*, which was written from a sense of family duty, there was less need for reticence. Hence we are told of Tacitus' marriage in the year 77 to Agricola's daughter, 'a girl of rare promise' (we are not told her name, but in all probability it was Julia). The details given of his father-in-law's family origins and political outlook have a bearing on Tacitus.[3] Gnaeus Julius Agricola was a member of the provincial nobility from the ancient colony of Forum Julii (modern Fréjus) in Gallia Narbonensis. His father Julius Graecinus was the first of the family to reach senatorial rank; a well-known orator and a man of independent views, he opposed the Emperor Gaius, and lost his life in consequence. The lesson was not lost on his family. The young Agricola, sent to be educated at Massilia, showed an intemperate interest in philosophy, but was restrained by his mother Julia Procilla from drinking of it more deeply than 'was suitable for a Roman and a senator.'[4] Later in life, when his military reputation might have qualified him to set up as a focus of opposition to the Emperor Domitian, he refused to do so, and held aloof from those senators of stoic views who posed as the champions of freedom. A man so worldly wise would hardly betroth his daughter to a social inferior, and indeed all we know of the origins of Tacitus suggests that he came from just such a *milieu* as Agricola himself. We further learn that Tacitus and his wife were absent from Rome between 89 and 93, though the nature of his employment is not stated.[5] Several passages of the *Agricola* emphasise how deeply he was seared by personal experience of the tyranny of Domitian's last three years, 93–96.

These personal statements can to some extent be supplemented from other sources. We know that Tacitus was *consul suffectus* in the latter part of 97, and in that capacity delivered the funeral oration for the famous Verginius Rufus.[6] His friend and close contemporary, Pliny the Younger, provides some interesting details in the eleven letters which are addressed to Tacitus. Both were concerned in the prosecution of Marius Priscus for mis-government in the province of Africa in the year 100. Both distinguished themselves by the speeches they made in that rather unsatisfactory affair. Early in the reign of Trajan, Tacitus is shown as the patron of a group of serious young men engaged in the study of law and oratory.[7] About 106 he seems to have been at work on those books of the *Histories* which dealt with the reign of Titus, and Pliny sends him an account of the eruption of Vesuvius in the year 79, in which his own uncle lost his life.[8] In the *Natural History* Pliny the Elder had mentioned a certain Cornelius Tacitus as procurator in Gallia Belgica; it is almost certain that this man is the father of the historian. An inscription from Caria records that Tacitus himself was governor of Asia in what appears to be 112–113.[9]

These sources can be combined into an outline biography, leaving some notable gaps. Though we can date Tacitus' birth very closely, we can only make conjectures about his family origins. Certainty on this important matter is very narrowly missed. There is a well-known anecdote in one of Pliny's letters (Book 9, 23, 2). Tacitus finds himself seated next to a knight at the Circus and is asked 'Are you an Italian or a provincial?' His reply is (unfortunately for us), 'You know me, and it is through my public speeches.' To which the knight replied, 'Are you Tacitus or Pliny?' Understandably the incident brought pleasure to Pliny, however tantalising for posterity. But Tacitus' marriage, and the intimate knowledge he displays of Narbonensis and its people, argue strongly for his origins in that province. The alternative is northern Italy, as with Pliny himself. Whichever it was, Tacitus was clearly a *novus homo*, one of the provincial nobility who found new prospects of public advancement open to them in the service of the empire.[10] It is a class of men for whom he has repeated words of admiration, contrasting their thrift, virtues, and old-fashioned morality with the decadent aristocracy of the capital itself. As a young man, in the years around 75 Tacitus will have studied in Rome with the leading orators of the day, and have acquired that life-long expertise and interest in oratory which is so clear in his historical writings.

Where Tacitus was between 89 and 93 we do not know. It has been suggested that he held the command of a legion, perhaps in one of the German provinces. Alternatively, he may have governed a province.[11] However that may be, he returned to Rome to find Agricola dead, and the tyranny of Domitian entering into its final phase. 'When Domitian no longer allowed intervals and breathing spaces, but drained the blood of the Roman state by a never-ending succession of blows, fused together as in a single fatal stroke.'[12] To his shame and regret, Tacitus did nothing to withstand the tyrant. He was part of that servile senate 'for whom a major part of our miseries consisted in watching and being watched. Our very sighs were noted down against us, and the savage countenance of Domitian, and the blush which sheltered him against all shame, were in clear contrast to the blenched faces of so many senators.' Unable to act or to write during those years, Tacitus was still free to think, and it is likely that it was then that he formed the design of turning historian and arraigning Domitian at the bar of posterity. In 98, immediately after his consulship, he published two monographs, the *Germania* and the *Agricola*, the latter a belated tribute to his father-in-law. At the same time he announces a project 'of recording, in however unskilled and untrained a voice, a record of our former slavery and a grateful acknowledgement of our present blessings.'[13] This project is undoubtedly a design for the *Histories*, which set out to tell the story of the Flavian dynasty from the death of Nero to that of Domitian (69–96). The 'unskilled and untrained voice' is not mock modesty; Tacitus is announcing his transfer of interest from the field of oratory, where he already had a major reputation, to that of history. The most likely date for the publication of the *Histories* is 107–108. Pliny, who saw individual volumes before they were given to the public, was confident that they would procure immortality for their author.[14] The next stage, according to Tacitus' original scheme, was to have been for a history of the reigns of Nerva and Trajan 'which I am reserving for my old age.'[15] But Tacitus was not yet done with public service. In 112–113 he served as governor of Asia, one of the most important of the provinces under the control of the Senate. He returned to Rome in his late fifties with little more to expect from politics. The reigns of Nerva and Trajan seemed a less promising subject than once it did; even under a good emperor, the writing of contemporary history was full of pitfalls and dangers. Perhaps, also, Tacitus had come to realise that the central problem of the first century A.D. was not so much the moral characters of individual emperors as the nature of the principate itself. The Flavian emperors could not be understood without an account of the Julio-Claudians, and the development of that unhappy dynasty had been conditioned by the legacy bequeathed to them by Augustus—hence the last great project of Tacitus' life, the history of the period from the death of Augustus to the death of Nero, which now goes under the title of the *Annals*. This seems to have engaged him fully (as well it might) from his return to Rome until shortly after 120, when it was published. As a kind of coda, he had thought of writing briefly on the reign of Augustus; this project was never realised. Tacitus did not long outlive the publication of his greatest work; his death may be set with some confidence about the year 125.[16] There followed a long period of oblivion, until in the third century the emperor Tacitus (275–276) who claimed descent from him (not, it would seem, on good grounds) tried to popularise the historian by providing copies of his works in all the public libraries.[17] A more substantial tribute was paid in the fourth century by Ammianus Marcellinus, himself an historian of all but the first rank, who deliberately set up as the heir of Tacitus and wrote a history of Rome which began where Tacitus left off.[18]

It is clear that the *Histories* and the *Annals* must have been the main preoccupations of the last twenty years of Tacitus' life. They form a single grand historical design, whose structure and proportions have long been a matter of argument.[19] Inevitably so, because what has come down to us amounts to no more than a torso in either case. To be precise, we possess of the *Histories* Books I to IV, and a part of Book V, which complete the narrative of the year of the civil wars, A.D. 69, and introduce the war against the Jews under Titus. Of the *Annals*, we have Books I to IV, part of V, and VI; a second sequence of complete books runs from XII to XV inclusive, and we have parts of XI and XVI. The key to the total number of books is to be found in Jerome's statement that they amounted to thirty in all.[20] How these were divided between the *Histories* and the *Annals* has long been disputed. It is now widely accepted that both works were designed in groups of six books, or hexads, giving twelve books for the *Histories* and eighteen for the *Annals*. Syme has pointed out that the hexadic structure is also to be found in the *Aeneid* of Virgil and the *Annals* of the Roman poet Ennius. Such a division would also fit on chronological grounds. In the *Histories* I to IV would give us the year 69, V and VI the reign of Vespasian, VII that of Titus and (in all probability) VIII to XII the reign of Domitian. In the *Annals*, I to VI as we know, covered the reign of Tiberius (twenty-three years) VII to XII those of Gaius and Claudius, with presumably two books for Gaius and four for Claudius, covering seventeen years in all for this hexad. The third hexad, devoted to Nero, covered fourteen years. The historian worked on the annalistic scheme, dealing with the events year by year. Such a method, with all its inconveniences, had deep roots in Rome, going back to the *Annales Maximi* maintained by the Pontiffs. It might seem an inflexible framework, but Tacitus felt himself free in the selection of themes and the scale on which they were to be treated. These changes of pace and of proportion are made with the utmost skill, and frequently escape the observation of the reader. It will thus be seen that between them, the *Histories* and the *Annals* provide a narrative of public events under Rome's first two imperial dynasties, covering the reigns of eleven emperors. Had the project of a work on Augustus been completed, they would have given a narrative from 37 B.C. to A.D. 96. It was designed to be a final verdict, for men of Tacitus' class and outlook, on the first century and a third of the Roman Empire.

CHAPTER TWO
The Writing of History

'AS I SEE IT, the chief duty of the historian is this: to see that virtue is placed on record, and that evil men and evil deeds have cause to fear judgement at the bar of posterity.'[1] Here Tacitus defines the purpose of his calling. It is one which would be repudiated by the modern professional historian, who would regard it as more important to establish an accurate record of events than to pass moral judgements. But Tacitus' view informed, to a greater or lesser degree, all the major classical historians. Herodotus wrote 'so that time may not blot out the memory of human achievement, and so that the great and remarkable deeds of the Greeks and Barbarians may not lack their meed of honour.'[2] Tacitus did not share the universal sympathies and large optimism of the Greek. He saw the world as a Roman and a senator, proud of his country's past, cynical about its present, doubtful about its future. The importance of perpetuating the memory of famous men to posterity is stressed again at the beginning and at the end of the *Agricola*. It filled a need which the Romans seem to have felt with peculiar poignancy; avid in the pursuit of *gloria* during life, they were no less concerned with their reputation or *fama* after death. Lacking as they did any firm belief in life after death, such *fama* (whether good or bad) was the only kind of immortality to which they could aspire. The wax portraits or *imagines* of famous men, kept in the family mansion, the funeral speech, the commemorative monument with its inscriptions (*tituli*) all gave expression to this desire. At its most impressive, we find it in Augustus' great programme for his Forum, which he turned into a kind of Hall of Fame.[3] In it were displayed the statues of all the *triumphatores* from Romulus to Julius Caesar, each with an inscription recording his deeds. In the view of Horace, poetry gave a more secure claim to immortality. And in the last chapter of the *Agricola*, Tacitus explicitly says that, while he would not wish to put an end to statues of bronze or marble, none the less imitation by example, and incorporation in the record of history, is the surest way to posterity's regard. 'Agricola's story has been set down and told to posterity. He will survive.'[4]

Tacitus had set himself a double task. Yet as we read his account of the years between the death of Augustus and the death of Domitian, the impression grows that he has shown more zeal in the indictment of evil than in the recording of virtue. He would no doubt observe—he often does—that this was due to the nature of the times. Where Livy could display virtue, Tacitus has to rebuke vice. But when we are told that one man alone—Vipstanus Messalla—played an honourable part in the civil wars of 69, it is fair to ask how this prevalence of evil might be due to the predisposition of the historian.[5] According to Tacitus 'the gods care little for our wellbeing, but greatly for our proper chastisement.'[6] If it is true that men tend to make gods in their own image, one may ask whether these avenging deities are not cast in the mould of the historian himself?

A second motive for the writing of history is for the profit of the reader, in that it affords examples of moral and, especially, of political behaviour. It was on this basis that Thucydides counted on his *History of the Peloponnesian War* to be a possession for ever—or, at least, for so long as human nature remains the same. Polybius, too, was concerned with the practical applications of history to the conduct of politics. He wished, as Walbank[7] has said, to reassert 'a concept of history as a training school for politicians and as a form of instruction for the ordinary man on how to bear those blows of Fortune, which can be seen illustrated in his pages as they befell others in the past.' For example, 'at the end of a long interlude on the Gallic invasions of Italy, he expresses the hope that it will help Greek statesmen to cope with similar attacks.' Again, 'in Book III his discussion of the difference between causes, pretexts, and beginnings, in the analysis of such occasions as the outbreak of a war, is intended for the edification of statesmen. For, he asks, what is the good of a statesman who cannot reckon how, why, and from what source each event has originated?' Again, it is for the use of statesmen that he has given his detailed account of the Roman constitution.

Tacitus mentions the utilitarian aspect of history, but without undue stress. His most explicit statement is to be found in the famous apologia for the nature of the account of the reign of Tiberius (*Annals* IV, 32, 33). Few men, he says, have the intelligence to discern the good from the bad, the expedient from the harmful: most have to learn these lessons from the experience of others. So, 'since conditions have changed, and public affairs are virtually under the control of one man, there is some point in the inquiry and report I have to offer.' The inquiry, is, in effect, into the politics of despotism. As to its nature and object— 'profit it may afford, pleasure it can hardly give. Descriptions of new countries, the shifts of fortune in great battles, the deaths of famous generals—these are what grip a reader's mind, and bring him recreation. I have to recall harsh edicts, prosecution following prosecution, false friendships, the rule of innocent men, trials, all ending in the same way. It is a plethora of monotony, and the reader can only balk.' We have been warned. One should not go to the *Annals* for pleasure or recreation, but from a desire to understand the worst.

The *Histories* might be very different. In the prelude to Book I, Tacitus writes: 'I now approach a theme prodigal of disaster, fearful in its battles, seething with revolution, and cruel even in peace. Four emperors died by the sword. There were three sets of civil wars: more against a foreign foe: usually they raged simultaneously. In the East we met with success, in the West, with disaster. . . . Italy suffered new forms of catastrophe, or such as had not been known for long ages. Volcanic eruptions buried or overwhelmed cities in the most fertile regions of Campania. Rome was devastated by fires, which destroyed its most venerable shrines. The Capitol itself was fired—by the hands of Roman citizens. . . .' And the long list of disasters goes on: informers, and the hatred and terror they caused, false slaves, corrupt freedmen, a society where, if a man lacked an enemy, he could be betrayed by a friend.

But there was a credit side. 'The age was not so barren of virtues that it could not produce some good examples. Mothers followed the flight of their sons: wives went into exile with their husbands . . . slaves remained faithful in the face of torture: great men endured their going hence with fortitude, so that there were death-bed scenes as edifying as the most famous of antiquity.'[8] Human disasters were accompanied by portents and prodigies on an unprecedented scale. . . . 'Never was it made so obvious that the gods care little for our well-being, but greatly for our chastisement'—(the quotation will bear repetition, for it is of prime importance for Tacitus' outlook on the world). Here's matter indeed! If the reader of the *Histories* should balk, it would not be from monotony. But if he finds enjoyment, perhaps he has no right to do so: the theme is too serious for that. At any rate, Tacitus does not openly profess to be catering for the reader's pleasure.

Personal claims, too, for the regard of posterity and the *gloria* that it conveys, are something he eschews. In the *Annals*, indeed, he explicitly renounces them, as excluded by the nature of his theme. 'I am very conscious that a good deal of what I relate—and still have to relate—can only seem trivial, and unworthy of being placed on record. But it would be wrong of anyone to set this book of mine alongside the earlier histories of the Roman people. Then, the historians were dealing with great wars, cities captured, kings routed and taken prisoner: in internal affairs, they had the disputes of consuls and tribunes, land laws and corn laws, the struggle between the orders—all themes of ample scope. I labour in a narrow field, and shall reap no glory.'[9] *Nobis in arto et inglorius labor:* the plea is not wholly valid. For if evil men and evil deeds are brought to judgement at the bar of posterity, will not posterity have regard for the historian who has arraigned them?

It was common form for classical historians to avow impartiality in their approach to their theme, and to undertake to observe veracity in its treatment. Such claims are duly advanced by Tacitus, nicely differentiated between the circumstances of the *Histories* and the *Annals*. In the *Histories*, there is a frank avowal of the benefits he has received from the Flavians: 'my public career began under Vespasian, advanced under Titus, and reached high office under Domitian. But those who profess strict historical veracity must handle every character without partiality or jaundice.'[10] From adulation, the ruling vice of the Flavian historians, he promises to stand aloof: in any case, 'it is always easy to discount a historian's self-interest, denigration and envy find a ready audience.' Galba, Otho and Vitellius present no problem, since from them he received neither favour nor injury. '*mihi Galba Otho Vitellius nec beneficio nec iniuria cogniti.*' This would seem the starting-point for the famous and much disputed phrase in the *Annals*, that he will deal with the history of the Julio-Claudians, *sine ira et studio, quorum causas procul habeo,* 'without prejudice or partisanship, having no motives for either.'[11] Tacitus had been a contemporary of the events recorded in the *Histories*, but the reign of Tiberius was almost a century in the past. So much is obvious. But, further than that, Tacitus was a 'new man,' a *novus homo*: no ancestral memories or grudges could distort his account, as they might with those who belonged to older families—'there are many descendants alive of those who were punished or disgraced under Tiberius.' His claim to impartiality then, rests on a highly practical and personal basis—the absence of benefits conferred or injuries inflicted on his own family. It takes no account of personal prejudice nor of settled convictions, and Tacitus, more than most people, seems apt to credit these with an objectivity they can hardly possess.

It remains to show what qualities Tacitus could bring, from his own talents and experience, to his task as historian. Here it was of first importance that he was a senator, and that he had risen through the regular stages of the official career to the highest post open to him, that of consul. He had governed a province, and thus knew at first hand the problems of provincial administration. We cannot give any detailed account of his travels, but his service had taken him to the eastern and the western parts of the empire. He may have commanded Roman troops; we do not know whether he saw action in the field. But his knowledge of military affairs could well have been greater than that which Gibbon acquired with the Hampshire Militia, and which he found of service to the historian of the decline and fall of the Roman Empire.[12]

Tacitus had practised in the courts, had appeared with success in at least one famous trial, and shows a keen interest in the origins and history of law. His selection to the Commission of Fifteen gave him an insight into the organisation of Roman public cults, of which the celebration of the Secular Games of 88 was a splendid occasion, comparable to a sovereign's coronation in our times. It gave him a lasting interest in religious affairs, as shown by his digressions on the cult of Serapis in Egypt, the origins, temple ritual, and cult image of Venus at Paphos in Cyprus, the sanctuary rights of the temples of Asia, the reported appearance of a phoenix in Egypt, and many more. Such an interest was, be it said, purely formal and legalistic, without any moral or spiritual overtones.

As a member of the Senate, Tacitus was in a first-rate observation and listening post. Devoid—or nearly devoid—of political power it might be, but the Senate was still the embodiment of the political tradition of the state. Collectively, its members knew at first-hand every part of the empire, and had filled every office of state except those reserved for the imperial family or its nominees. In this sense, it was an unrivalled school of political experience, as the British House of Lords is still said to be, even when its political powers are so curtailed. Moreover, the Senate was successful to a remarkable degree in imposing its own values and traditions on new members. These were, in the main, conservative and backward-looking: they had been formulated in the days of Senatorial supremacy, which had effectively ended as early as the First Triumvirate of 60 B.C. But they lived on in the minds and affections of senators, not a little assisted by the claim of Augustus to have 'restored the Republic' at the settlement of 27 B.C. And when, in the first century A.D., and especially from the time of Claudius onwards, the 'new men' came flocking in from Gaul, Spain and the municipalities of Italy, they took over the political outlook and values that had once been held by the aristocratic families of the old Republic.

This neo-republicanism was something that went far deeper than that of Lucan and the Stoic opposition, the men who observed the birthdays of the tyrannicides Brutus and Cassius, and regarded Cato the Younger as the model of political wisdom. (This latter attitude was, at base, emotional and sentimental, akin to the Jacobitism that in Britain so long survived the disaster of 1745.) It was not derived from political theory, for which Romans had scant regard. Tacitus has a dry comment on political Utopias: 'All nations and cities must be ruled either by the people, by the aristocracy, or by a single man. Blends and compounds of these forms of government are hard to establish: if established they seldom last.'[13] So much for the Mixed Constitution of Polybius and Cicero, by which they sought to explain Rome's rise to world supremacy! Nor did it formulate a political programme. There was no thought of abolishing the Principate, though from time to time the attractions became obvious of removing a bad emperor. Its causes ran deeper. Most of these senators of the first-century Principate were prepared to devote all their energies to the service of the state, as men had once done in the old Republic. The trouble was that they expected the same rewards—honour, dignity, high office, great commands.[14] Such, in essence, was Tacitus' concept of political freedom, or *libertas*. These, at the highest levels, the Principate could not afford to let them have. Agricola's career came to a stop, Domitius Corbulo was forced to commit suicide, precisely *because* they were highly successful generals. But the highest honours in politics, and still more in war, must belong to the imperial house: the Principate was, of its nature, hostile to *virtus*.

So men like Tacitus served the Principate and acknowledged its necessity, but judged it by the values of the Republic. It was a strange situation. The poet Horace, it seems, had shown an unusual degree of political prescience in warning against any restoration or longing for the old Republic—if the old Republic is indeed represented by his warning against rebuilding Troy.[15]

> sed bellicosis fata Quiritibus
> hac lege dico, ne nimium pii
> rebusque fidentes avitae
> tecta velint reparare Troiae.

(On this condition I pronounce their destiny to the warlike people of Rome—let them show no undue piety, nor count on their prosperity for the hope of restoring the buildings of Troy from which came their ancestors.)

Troy—the old Republic—was rebuilt in the minds of many Roman senators: still in its ashes lived its wonted fires. It is this ambivalence which accounts for much of Tacitus' settled pessimism about the Principate: it also affects his claim to write of its affairs *sine ira et studio*.

Last among these endowments is what Tacitus' historical writings derive from his training as an orator. We owe to Pliny a picture of Tacitus in action: in the trial of Marius Priscus he spoke 'with great eloquence and—an outstanding feature of his style—on a note of grandeur.'[16] Such virtuosity was the fruit of long practice, wide reading, and a deep interest (very manifest in the *Dialogues*) in the theory as well as the art of rhetoric. And, since rhetoric is the art of speech and Tacitus spoke Latin, of a deep knowledge of the resources of the Latin language and of what had been achieved in Latin literature. From oratory, too, he will have derived the concept of forging, like a specialist tool, a prose style appropriate for the task. This was no mere matter of literary aesthetics. To have such tools at command could, in the ancient world, be literally a matter of life and death—in the courts, for example, or on an embassy, as when Claudius Cossus, a delegate of the Helvetii, saved his community from destruction by working on the feelings of Caecina's soldiers.[17]

So Tacitus set himself, over many years, to perfecting the style most suitable for historical narrative. As part of this process, he made himself familiar with the whole corpus of historical writing in Latin, and perhaps, also, with much of that in Greek, though he mentions the Greek historians in critical terms, and never refers to any by name. His admiration went out to the historians of the Roman Republic, those '*clara ingenia*'—(great intellects): and, above all, to Livy and Sallust. How he ranked them against each other is uncertain: Livy is once called 'the most eloquent of ancient writers,'[18] but on another occasion Sallust is 'the foremost historian of Rome' (*rerum Romanarum florentissimus auctor*).[19] But that his personal preference was for Sallust is clear from his greater readiness to draw on that historian for allusions or parallels. This high estimate of Sallust was not peculiar to him; it was the general critical opinion of the age, to judge from Quintilian's remark that he would not hesitate to compare Sallust with Thucydides ('*nec opponere Thucydidi Sallustium verear*').[20] It is not a judgement that would be endorsed today. Nor can a modern audience respond with the same perceptivity to the many Tacitean echoes of Sallust, Livy, Virgil, and other Latin authors.

We owe much to those modern scholars who have collected and analysed these passages; they have added notably to our knowledge of the range of response that Tacitus was able to evoke.[21] So an echo of Sallust will suggest a parallel between the arch-favourite Sejanus and the arch-revolutionary Catiline, or between Poppaea and the infamous Sempronia. Or a whole passage may have a Sallustian prototype, such as the famous digression on the origins of civil law (*Annals* III, 26–28). An echo of Livy will suggest that the demoralised Roman troops trapped by Civilis are on the verge of another disaster like that of the Caudine Forks.[22] Especially subtle are the effects of some of the Virgilian allusions. As the Roman Army approaches the scene of the massacre of Varus' legions, we hear the tones used of Aeneas' descent into the underworld in the Sixth Book of the *Aeneid*.[23] An echo from the same source supplies, at the death of Augustus' wayward daughter Julia, the nuance that she might join the dead lovers in the Fields of Mourning—'*quos durus amor crudeli tabe peredit.*'[24]

Such, in brief outline, was the combination of experience of affairs, political judgement, historical acumen, and literary genius, that Tacitus brought to the writing of history. No Greek or Roman author was ever more splendidly equipped. If he has a peer, it could only be Thucydides—*nec opponere Thucydidi Tacitum verear.*

The problem of the sources used by Tacitus is a difficult one, though its elements may be set out quite simply.[25] On a number of occasions, Tacitus mentions the sources used for individual topics, both documentary and narrative. If these are not numerous, it must be remembered that an ancient historian was under no obligation to give his sources in detail, nor even to mention them at all. Modern scholarship can produce a much wider list of sources which could have been available to him for the periods with which he dealt. Unfortunately, practically the whole of this material, whether primary or secondary, is a total loss. Indeed, in some cases, Tacitus' reference to his source is practically all we know about it. The problem for modern research has always been to find out exactly how he used this source material. Did he follow a single authority over long periods, or several? Which did he regard as the most trustworthy? What did he do when he found his sources in conflict? Not very much headway has been made in resolving these

problems, though it may be said with some confidence that the
view that Tacitus followed a single authority no longer commands support.[26] It is in conflict with statements of his own
about seeking a consensus of his sources, and only naming them
individually when they differ. Nor has much of value come out
from comparing Tacitus with Suetonius and Dio when they are
dealing with the same themes.

Two documentary sources are to be noted. Much the more
important was the official record of the Senate—the *acta
Senatus*.[27] This contained an account of debates in the Senate
(probably not *verbatim* as in Hansard) and also resolutions
taken. Other official documents, such as letters from emperors,
from the governors of senatorial provinces, from allies and client
kings, and the *memoranda* of visiting embassies, are also known
to have been recorded. Presumably the files were kept in the
Chalcidicum or Senate Record Office, where they were available
for consultation by members of that body. It will be seen how
this gave an advantage to senatorial historians over others. The
acta diurna[28] was the nearest equivalent of a daily paper in
Rome, and was a kind of gazette, though it included a good
deal of unofficial and indeed trivial news items. It was one of
Julius Caesar's innovations, and began publication in 59 B.C.
Apparently it circulated widely in the provinces and among the
armies. Both these sources will have been used with caution. The
acta Senatus was edited by a senator specially chosen by the
emperor, who presumably exercised a kind of censorship. The
acta diurna was of limited value because of the nature of its
contents.

Memoirs and biographies must have been an important
source. Tacitus mentions that in the memoirs of the younger
Agrippina he found material which was not in the standard
histories, and it is likely that he drew on them largely for
information about the imperial families in the reigns of Claudius
and Nero. Tiberius wrote his own biography; Corbulo's
memoirs are certainly drawn on for the accounts of his eastern
campaigns. The biographies of members of the stoic opposition,

mentioned below, must also have been useful. Tacitus must also have used a large number of special informers. The best known instance is the account of the eruption of Vesuvius in 79, written at his behest by Pliny the Younger.[29] It would have been most interesting, had Tacitus' account of this episode survived, to compare it with the elaborate composition with which he was furnished. Agricola will of course have told him much about the campaigns in Britain of himself and his predecessors. He could have had many such private informants about the Civil War and the later years of the Flavians.

Tradition, as preserved verbally, or in written form in the great historical houses, must also have been valuable. Members of such houses were *dilettanti* (in a good sense) of Roman history. We hear them at work in the first book of the *Annals*, debating the merits and defects of the reign of Augustus immediately after his death. Then there were the writers of narrative histories, for most of whom, it would seem, Tacitus had no high regard. But, in the *Histories* he does mention Vipstanus Messalla, who wrote on the Civil Wars. There is also Pliny the Elder, whose *German Wars* are mentioned in both the *Annals* and the *Histories*. One should also mention Aufidius Bassus, whose history appears to have dealt with the period from the death of Caesar to the death of Gaius, and Fabius Rusticus, who certainly wrote on the reign of Nero.

While Tacitus quite certainly built up his own *corpus* of source material, he may also have worked in the public libraries with which Rome was so well provided. The senior of these was the Palatine Library,[30] established in the temple of Apollo by Augustus, and containing two great collections of Greek and of Latin authors respectively. Dual libraries, on the model of this one, were also founded by Vespasian in the Temple of Peace, and by Trajan, housed in his Forum and flanking the famous column. These two libraries were established about 113, and it is fascinating to think that Tacitus may have worked there when he was engaged on the *Annals*. It should be added that Pliny[31] writes to him on the pleasure of working 'among the

woods and groves,' which suggest that some of his writing was
done at a villa in the country, whether his own or a friend's.

A comparison with the sources available to a modern historian may be illuminating. The three-volume centennial history of
the American Civil War, by Bruce Catton, could serve admirably
as an example. That project was launched by the publishing
firm of Doubleday and Company, in conjunction with the *New
York Times*, and its object was 'to constitute a modern history,
drawing on extensive research into traditional and recently discovered material.' A research team, under a separate Director
of Research, put in ten years' work on collecting and sifting
source material. This involved consulting manuscripts at several
hundred collections throughout the United States, and in
addition, the investigation of private papers, historical journals,
newspaper files, books, pamphlets and periodicals. Every major
battlefield, and many of the secondary ones, were visited. Several
distinguished historians gave advice, or read the manuscript during preparation. There were several hundred private informants.

The main result of all this huge research project—more akin
to what is associated with the natural sciences than the humani-
ties—is the narrative itself, contained in three large volumes of
between 450 and 500 pages each—Volume One, *The Coming
Fury*, Volume Two, *Terrible Swift Sword*, and Volume Three,
Never Call Retreat. Each volume can be read independently, or
as a part of the series, and contains maps and plans of the main
campaigns and battlefields. (In Volume Three, for example,
there are thirteen such maps for the battles fought between
December 13th, 1862, and April 9th, 1865.) In addition, there is
to be an 'Almanac' or factual reference book, as well as an
illustrated book with a narrative by Bruce Catton, which can be
read as a companion volume to the series. Quite clearly, the
amount of source material is vastly greater, and the whole
infrastructure much more complicated than could ever have
been conceived by Tacitus or any other classical historian.
But Catton belongs, essentially, to the same genus, since his

narrative is the work of a single man, and makes its impact (to quote one judgement) by a combination of 'narrative vigour, literary grace, freshness of view, independence of judgement, and a catholic spirit which embraces the whole vast and tumultuous scene.' Other critics rank the trilogy with the work of Carlyle, Macaulay, Motley and Churchill, and predict that it will become one of the historical classics. If it does, and if its vigour and freshness remain unimpaired to a reader two thousand years hence, it may then stand comparison with the writings of Tacitus.

CHAPTER THREE
Narrative

THE EARLIEST LATIN PROSE known to us is represented by the works of Cato, dating from about the first half of the second century B.C. They reveal a vigorous but clumsy language, adequate for the presentation of facts, but with limited resources of syntax and vocabulary. There is little in them to suggest that Latin prose would ever be able to challenge Greek, and indeed to become the most enduring of the international languages, so far, of the Western world. But the dramatists had already shown that Latin possessed rich resources for tragedy and comedy. Its development as a vehicle for prose was the work of the orators and statesmen of the time of the Gracchi and the succeeding generation. Prompted by the demands of the political and legal life of the Roman republic, they were able to establish Latin prose on a high level of sophistication, from which the works of Cicero—written between 81 and 43 B.C.—carried it to a peak of excellence.

This was in oratory and philosophy—not, as yet, in history. Indeed, Cicero himself comments on the bald and jejune style of the histories so far written in Latin. His comment was soon to be rendered out of date by the historical writings of Sallust, Caesar and Livy. But it is interesting to see how each of the three wrote in a style which deliberately diverged from Ciceronian Latin. Sallust evolved a harsh and discordant prose, well

BT

suited to the portrayal of violent and revolutionary scenes, and destined to be the major influence on the style of Tacitus. The historical works of Caesar are written in that apparent artlessness which is one of the most subtle disguises for propaganda. The 'creamy abundance' of Livy is well suited to his roseate and patriotic view of the Roman past.

As with poetry, Latin prose entered into a new phase in the post-Augustan age. It was the product of changed political conditions, of a systematic education in the art of rhetoric, and, to some extent, of the widespread influence of philosophy. The characteristic products of this Silver Latin prose (the metaphor is not very helpful) are the works of Seneca. Quintilian might plead for a modified Ciceronianism, but he was swimming against the tide. In the writings of Tacitus imperial Latin prose touches its highest eminence. There was a barren period after the death of Hadrian, and it must have seemed unlikely that there would be a third great master of Latin prose. But the new stimulus provided by Christianity gave rise to a series of major Latin writers in the fourth century—such as Jerome, Tertullian and Lactantius. From this *milieu* arises the third truly great writer of Latin prose—Augustine. He does not, of course, move always on the highest levels, for he was an exceedingly prolific author, and in his own words 'my tongue cannot live up to my heart.'[1] But in his greatest works—*The Confessions* and *The City of God*—he shows himself one of the undisputed great masters of the Latin tongue.

Two things united Cicero, Tacitus and St. Augustine across the centuries. One was a common interest in the art of rhetoric. Both Cicero and Tacitus were among the great orators of their day; both wrote works on the subject. Augustine taught rhetoric professionally in Carthage, Rome and Milan. All three stress the allegiance and love we owe to the community of which we are members—the *res publica*. But while for Cicero and Tacitus the *res publica* was Rome, for Augustine it was the City of God. When, in Renaissance times, a standard model for Latin prose was required, the choice fell rightly enough on

Cicero. This has had unfortunate consequences for Tacitus, in so far as he has been looked upon as a deviation from the classical norm. The great Victorian edition of Furneaux, for example, devotes no fewer than thirty pages to setting out the characteristics of Tacitean grammar and syntax. Lesser editions are apt to refer to Tacitus' 'peculiarities of style.'

It is doubtful whether this approach contributes much to an understanding of Tacitus. It has, in the past, encouraged the *virtuosi* of the classical sixth in British public schools to suppose that they could write prose 'in the manner of Tacitus.' This may be a harmless delusion. More serious, the approach is a static one, allowing no scope for the evolution of Tacitus' prose style. The work of Lofstedt, Syme and others, has shown that the style of Tacitus underwent as marked a development as did that of Shakespeare, and reached its high point of intensity in the first hexad of the *Annals*.[2] But we are concerned with style only so far as it contributes to an understanding of the historian. Here most can be gained from a general consideration of his narrative style, noticing the architecture of individual books (especially in the *Histories*), the selection of certain longer epi- sodes (especially in the *Annals*), and the use of that device, so unfamiliar to the reader of histories in our own times—speeches which are known to be the work of the author.

The stylistic claims of Tacitus have never been put more succinctly than by Henry Savile,[3] whose translation of the *Histories* was dedicated to Queen Elizabeth I: 'for Tacitus I may say without partialitie, that he hath written the most matter with the best conceite in the fewest words of any Historio- grapher ancient or moderne. But he is harde.' There is the case for the historian, and the problem for the translator, and in words that have a Tacitean—almost a Churchillian—ring. They rightly stress his foremost asset—a unique and splendid Latin style. Complex, subtle and sustained, it gave him an instrument unequalled by that of any other historian—save Gibbon, and the organ voice of Gibbon lacks Tacitus' wide range of tone. It is here that the common estimate of Tacitus' style is inadequate, in so far as it concentrates on brevity and wit as his two distinctive marks. 'He writes,' I used to be told, 'as though every word would be charged at the full rate of Cable and Wireless.' Why, so he does, if the occasion calls for it. At other times he can be involved, elaborate, even prolix, never using one word where five will do.

So Davanzati, the author of the great Florentine translation published in 1600, was wrong in seeking brevity at all costs: 'I have done in nine sheets,' he boasts, 'what took ten in Tacitus.'[4] As for wit, we should never suppose that it is confined to the famous and memorable *sententiae* or epigrams—'capax imperii, nisi imperasset,' and the rest. As early as the sixteenth century it was realised that no other classical prose author offers such rich hunting to the collector of aphorisms. As part of the cult of Tacitus at that time, collections of these *sententiae* were published in French, Italian, Spanish and English as political maxims for the use of statesmen. But they occur in their context and depend on it for their effects: they cannot be appreciated in isolation, any more than the smash in tennis can be understood without the rally it concludes. The metaphor is not inept, and may be extended. Like a great games-player, Tacitus evolved his style over many years of thought and practice, cultivating his strong points and cutting out weak ones, to reach maturity in the first six books on the *Annals*.

It must be repeated that before he took to writing history, Tacitus had been one of the leading orators in Rome. That is to say, he had attained excellence in a highly sophisticated art, and won acclaim from an audience of connoisseurs. This demanded a combination of mastery of the spoken word and knowledge of the resources of language to which there is no parallel in modern life. Quintilian shows how the training of an orator was based on a wide knowledge of Greek and Latin literature. So it is that Tacitus can repeatedly draw on Horace, Virgil, Lucan or Livy to evoke a parallel or suggest a mood: here is a major difficulty for the English translator, who can only faintly shadow forth the effect by a phrase from Shakespeare or the Bible.

But above all, Tacitus echoes and exploits his model, the Republican historian Sallust, who also lived in corrupt and violent times. In range and intensity the mature style of Tacitus far excels Sallust, but it belongs to the same school. It can strike a sledge-hammer blow or make a rapier-thrust, yet it can achieve precise and delicate effects, especially in parody. Thus it can catch the pomposity of the medical reports delivered when Vespasian was asked to heal the sick in Egypt.[5] 'The doctors discussed the issue from several points of view. In the one case, they reported that the power of vision had not been totally lost: it would return if obstacles could be removed. In the other patient, the limbs had suffered atrophy and degeneration, but the application of some healing measure might offer a possibility of cure.' Lightness, too, is within its compass, as in the description of the delights of Capri *'caeli temperies hieme mitis obiectu montis quo saeva ventorum arcerentur: aestas in favonium obversa et aperto circum pelago peramoena: prospectabat pulcherrimum sinum, antequam Vesuvius mons ardescens faciem loci verteret.'*[6] ('The winters are mild because a mountain gives protection from the fury of the gales; it is delightful in summer, facing south-west, with the open sea all round. It looks out on a most beautiful bay—beautiful, that is, before the eruption of Vesuvius changed the whole face of the landscape.')

But it is a style most at home with the lurid, the fearful, the supernatural—with all that is covered by that favourite Tacitean adjective, *'atrox.'* Such were the scenes encountered by a Roman army that ventured across the Rhine into the swamps and forests of Germany, with their savage warriors and memories of Roman disasters. We have seen that as the army of Germanicus approaches the scene of the massacre of Varus there are echoes of Virgil's description of the underworld in Book Six of the *Aeneid*. 'So they trod that unhallowed ground of evil memory and hideous aspect. . . . In the middle of the battlefield the bones lay white, scattered where the men had fled, piled up where they had made a stand. . . . By them were broken weapons, horses' limbs, skulls fixed to tree-trunks. . . . So a Roman army, six years after the disaster, came to this place and buried the bones of the men of three legions. No one knew whether he was casting earth over his own kindred, or those of another. All were regarded as kinsmen, all as blood-brothers, their anger was against the enemy, fury mixed with sorrow as they worked at the task of burial. . . .'[7]

It will be clear that the translators of Tacitus face an almost impossible task, and that their readers must not expect them to convey the full flavour of the original Latin. Here again Savile's words come to mind, 'I present here to your Majesty's view my imperfections in their own colours, and the excellencies of another with much loss of their lustre as being transported from their natural light of the Latin by an unskilful hand into a strange language. . . .'[8] But the translator can at least hope that the sweep and splendour of the Tacitean narrative will come through, and the reader will gain from considering how these effects are achieved in the diverse contexts of the *Histories* and the *Annals*.

The salient fact about the surviving books of the *Histories* is the scale on which they are composed. No fewer than three books are devoted to the single year 69—*longum et unum annum*, or, as we may prefer to call it, the Longest Year. Of these, Book I, deals with events from January 1st to March 15th: Book II moves a very little faster to take us to the end of August; Book III goes to the death of Vitellius on December 23rd. The first three books of the *Annals* by contrast, go from the accession of Tiberius in 14 to the end of the year 22. Bearing in mind that each book of the *Histories* is longer than the corresponding books of the *Annals*, the time scale is greater by something like a factor of ten. Fortunately, the events of 69 made it possible for Tacitus to compose with large elements. There were four contestants for the imperial throne in that year; three of them were killed by their successor. It is like the ancient contest for the priesthood of Diana at Nemi:

The priest that slew the slayer,
And shall himself be slain.

A simple formula for the first three books of the *Histories* would have been AB, BC, CD; the first letter standing for the incumbent, and the second for his supplanter. Tacitus was more subtle. In Book I, after a general survey of the Roman world, a large block of chapters (28–50) deals with the reign of Galba, and his death on January 15th. Next, twenty chapters are devoted to the mustering of the forces of Vitellius in Germany, and their advance by two routes to North Italy. Another twenty chapters deal with the reign of Otho in Rome. By the end of the book we have thus met three of the four rivals.

The first sentence of Book II is a dramatic introduction to the fourth: 'Meanwhile, and in an opposite part of the world, fortune was already laying the foundations for a new dynasty, which brought in its varying destinies both joy and disaster for the state, and to its own emperors, success and doom.' We have looked ahead to Vespasian, and beyond him to his successors Titus and Domitian. From this time onwards the Flavian cause will not be long out of sight. Meanwhile, twenty-five chapters describe the struggle between Vitellius and Otho in North Italy, the first battle of Bedriacum, and the death of Otho. This is followed by Vitellius' march to Rome. In twelve chapters we hear of the mustering of the forces of the East, and the final choice of Vespasian as their candidate for the throne. The book ends with the entry of Vitellius' northern army to Rome.

Book III has been rightly described as 'a miracle of speed and splendour.'[9] First, thirty-five chapters deal with the advance of the Flavian army to northern Italy, their clash with the forces of Vitellius, the second battle of Bedriacum, and the sack of Cremona. Thirteen chapters are now devoted to events in Rome. In chapters 49–63 the Flavians advance to the capital. In 64–86 Flavian armies enter Rome, and in the ensuing fighting the Capitol is destroyed and Vitellius killed.

The Longest Year is over, and in Book IV there is a change of scale and tempo to suit the coverage of events from the beginning of January to the end of November in A.D. 70. The narrative moves between Vespasian's doings in the East and those of his sons and supporters in Rome. Meanwhile, there are two major but detached episodes 'at opposite quarters of the world' —the rebellion of Civilis in Gaul and the Jewish War. The Civilis rebellion has been given two detached sections of twenty-five chapters each in Book IV. In what remains of Book V, it is run in parallel with the Jewish War, each being given thirteen chapters. The treatment here foreshadows the use of longer episodes which is so marked a feature of the *Annals*. There is a significant ending—the retirement of Domitian from public affairs for private study. The Roman reader will not fail to have noted the analogy. Tiberius, once, retired to Rhodes. But he came back. So will Domitian.

In any consideration of Tacitus' narrative style, the longer episodes in the *Annals* are of high importance. In these Tacitus has selected for special treatment certain themes which he believes will hold the readers' attention and are worthy of his own full powers. These are twenty-one such episodes in the *Annals* as we have them. Eight of these run from six to ten chapters each: a second group of eleven are between ten and twenty chapters long; three are over twenty chapters, including the exceptionally large-scale treatment of the conspiracy of Piso, which runs to no fewer than twenty-six chapters (XV, 48–74). Fourteen of these episodes—two-thirds of the whole—are concerned with military affairs, the campaigns of Germanicus in Germany or Corbulo in the East, rebellions such as those of Florus and Sacrovir in Gaul, or of Boudicca in Britain. This agrees well with Tacitus' views of the interest his public will find in battles and sieges.

Of the political episodes the first (I, 17–14) is on the debate in the Senate at the accession of Tiberius; another (III, 1–18) describes the return of Agrippina to Rome and the subsequent trial of Piso. The other five are concerned with the deaths of

various eminent personages—Germanicus (II, 69–85), Messalina (XI, 26–38) Agrippina (XIV, 1–16), and Thrasea Paetus
and Barea Soranus (XVI, 21–35). They are by no means evenly
distributed as between books. For example, Book I contains no
fewer than four, and Book XII contains three. On the other
hand, they are almost absent from Book IV unless we count the
six chapters (46–51) on the rebellion in Thrace. It is interesting
to note that this is the book in which Tacitus complains of the
monotony of the history with which he has to deal, as compared
with that of the glorious days of the Republic. Book XIII, which
corresponds to Book IV in so many ways, also has a single
longer episode of six chapters. Book XV is exceedingly complex,
and to its architecture we shall have to return. It is possible to
suggest, with more or less certainty, the longer episodes that
must have found a place in the last books of the *Annals*. Under
Tiberius, the fall of Sejanus is certain, and the death of Agrippina probable. Under Claudius we should expect the invasion
of Britain to balance the two long British episodes which do
survive; perhaps, also, the events by which Mauretania became
a province. Under Nero, that emperor's Hellenic tour, the
rebellion of Vindex in Gaul, and the death of Nero, are highly
probable. In short, there may well have been upwards of thirty
of these longer episodes in the *Annals*.

A fair sample of the military episodes is the account of the
rebellion of Boudicca (*Annals* XIV, 29–39). The rebellion is
given as the first event of 61, and is characterised as a terrible
disaster (*gravis clades*). The first chapter, in a few quick strokes,
sketches its prelude on the Roman side. In a sequence of three
governors of Britain, Didius Gallus had done no more than
maintain the *status quo*, Quintus Veranius had shown promise
cut short by death, but in Suetonius Paulinus Britain had a
governor able to rival the exploits of Corbulo in the East. He
had planned an assault on the island of Mona, stronghold of
the Druids. By the end of the chapter, we have been rushed to
the Menai Straits, and planted, with the Roman Army, on the
Anglesey shore. The next chapter is an exotic—a description of

the 'mob of women and fanatics' who for a brief while terrorised the Roman Army by their outré appearance. Rallied by their general, the Romans cut to pieces the British forces: the Druids are consumed in their own fires, and the sacred groves cut down. But the note of triumph is cut short before the end of the chapter, when news is received of a sudden rising (*repentina defectio*) in the province itself. Chapter 31 concerns the grievances of the Britons, and the faults of the Romans. There is the widowed queen of the Iceni, Boudicca, and the injuries inflicted on her. There are grievances of the Trinovantes against the insolence of the veterans at Camulodunum, and an account of the neglect of the colony's defences by Roman governors in the interests of amenity. Chapter 32 is an account of British successes. Camulodunum goes down in flames; a relieving force under Petilius Cerialis is cut to pieces, and he himself barely escapes with his cavalry to 'a legionary camp' (where?). The procurator, Catus Decianus, whose greed has been largely responsible for the rebellion, flees to Gaul.

In the next chapter the spotlight is turned on Suetonius Paulinus. With remarkable steadfastness, he marches to Londinium (London), which here finds its first mention in history. But the place is untenable and he has to retrace his steps. Londinium is abandoned to the enemy, Verulamium (St. Albans) also. The chapter closes with the atrocities practised by the triumphant Britons. In Chapter 34 Suetonius has concentrated his forces to the number of ten thousand men, and seeks a decisive engagement (where?). Boudicca's speech takes up the whole of the next chapter, a moving recital of British wrongs. A balancing chapter is given to Suetonius. His speech is short and professional: 'Keep together: throw your javelins: continue the slaughter with your swords and the points of your shields. Don't give a thought to booty: once you've won the victory, it will all be yours.' The victory is duly won in the chapter that follows. British casualties are enormous, eighty thousand British dead as against four hundred Romans. Boudicca poisoned herself (where?). And there is an eminent casualty on the Roman side, singled out by Tacitus for words of disgrace: 'as for Poenius Postumus, camp commandant of the Second Legion (where?) he fell on his sword when he heard of the honours won by the Fourteenth and Twentieth Legions—for he had cheated his own men of a like distinction and disobeyed his commander's orders in defiance of army regulations.'

Two chapters narrate the sequel to the rebellion. First, the energetic steps taken by Suetonius to bring his forces up to strength, and to lay waste rebel territory by fire and sword. Secondly—to the disapproval of Tacitus—a commission of inquiry suggested by the new procurator, Julius Classicianus. What is worse, it is conducted by the freedman, Polycletus, sent out by Nero as investigation commissioner. The Britons—simple barbarians—cannot understand how an army and a commander who could complete so great a war should obey the command of slaves. But so it was under Nero. The commission finds that Suetonius is unduly protracting the war (and he had certainly had a hand in provoking it): he is superseded. Petronius Turpilianus, a man of milder outlook, is sent to replace him; his governorship 'confers the honourable name of peace on what was really sluggish inaction.'

The narrative compels admiration for its dramatic quality. But this has been purchased by an economy in the mention of names, places and the lapse of time, that is infuriating to the investigator. To begin with, it is almost certain that the events in question spread over two years, and that Tacitus has given the wrong date for their outbreak.[10] Again, we would give much to know exactly how long Suetonius took over his dash from Anglesey to London. And how long after that was the decisive battle fought? The vague geography is almost worse. Where was the final battle? All that modern research has been able to suggest is that it must be somewhere along the line of Watling Street, north of Towcester. Where was the base of the Second Legion? Gloucester? And what precisely were the instructions which Poenius Postumus disobeyed? As for Petilius Cerialis, we can deduce with confidence that the legionary base to which he escaped was Lincoln; but where did he suffer his defeat at the hands of the Britons?

All these questions are very properly posed by modern scholars; it will be seen how few of them can be answered. But Tacitus was not concerned with providing the kind of narrative we now ask. He aimed at a distillation of the rebellion of Boudicca which would convey its essential qualities. In that, beyond doubt, he has succeeded.

For a political episode, I choose the story of the fall of Messalina, and its sequel (*Annals* XI, 26–38).[11] The scene is Rome; the setting and persons are familiar to Tacitus' audience, justifying a more detailed treatment. We have had earlier warning (XI, 12) of the new and almost lunatic love affair of the Empress and Gaius Silius. It quickly became public property to all but the Emperor 'who was busy exercising his powers as censor.' Building aqueducts, checking disturbances in the theatre, and inventing three new letters for the Latin alphabet, Claudius was in happy ignorance of the wreck of his marriage. The longer episode is prefaced by a foretaste of its outcome: 'soon Claudius was compelled to take note of and to punish his wife's scandalous immoralities, though as a result he would himself conceive a desire for an incestuous marriage' (with Agrippina). The first chapter is devoted to the adulterous pair. Messalina is becoming bored with the ease of her adulteries, and urging Silius on to new vices. Driven on by a fatal lunacy (*fatalis vaecordia*) Silius urges that a desperate situation calls for a desperate remedy—marriage. Messalina's response is at first unenthusiastic. Once Silius won the throne he might turn against her. But the name of wife was attractive 'for the sheer enormity of the scandal—depravity's most lasting thrill. Waiting no longer than for Claudius to go to Ostia to perform a sacrifice, she performed all the solemnities of marriage with Silius.'

Tacitus now proceeds to anticipate his readers doubts: 'here, I am well aware, we seem to be entering the realm of fantasy. . . . Here is the consul designate, marrying the wife of the Emperor, on a duly appointed day, in the presence of witnessess, "for the procreation of children": here is the Empress, hearing the auspices, taking the bridal veil, sacrificing to the gods. Together they take their place at the wedding feast among their guests; there is an exchange of kisses and embraces, the night is passed in the delights of honourable marriage. But I invent nothing, I recount, and shall recount, what an older generation heard and wrote.'

We next hear of the confusion that reigned in the imperial household—or rather in the only important part of it—the freedmen. There is a council of the most important freedmen— Callistus, Pallas, Narcissus—a parody of the family councils of the great days of the Republic. The problem is how to bring the affair to Claudius' notice, and to prevent him from giving a hearing to Messalina. In the event, it is Narcissus who keeps his nerve and finds a way. The scandal is leaked through Claudius' concubines, acting as a pair; 'Calpurnia (that was the girl's name) flung herself at Claudius' feet and cried out that Messalina had married Silius. She turned for confirmation to the other girl, Cleopatra, who stood waiting for her cue and when she nodded asked that Narcissus should be sent for.' Narcissus drove the point home. 'Do you know,' he explained, 'that you are divorced? The Roman people, the Senate, the Army, have all witnessed the marriage of Silius; act quickly or this new husband will seize Rome.'

In the next chapter, Emperor and Empress are juxtaposed. In a panic, Claudius summons his loyal friends, repeatedly asking, 'Am I still Emperor? Is Silius a private citizen?' Messalina, utterly at ease, was holding one of her famous parties. 'It was autumn; she was holding a mock wine-harvest on her estate. The presses were at work, the vats brimming; women clad in skins capered like frenzied bacchantes at a sacrifice. The Empress, hair unbound, brandished the thyrsus; Silius, ivy wreathed, wearing the buskins, stood by her, rolling his head. Around them yelled the lewd crowd. Vettius Valens is said to have climbed a huge tree as a joke, and when asked "What do

you see?" answered, "Dirty weather coming up from Ostia!"
The sky may indeed have betokened it, but perhaps this casual
remark was taken as a prophecy.'

The dirty weather appears in the next chapter. 'Messengers
kept pouring in, saying Claudius knew everything, and was on
his way to exact vengeance.' Messalina now tries a last desperate
throw. Her children, Britannicus and Octavia, are ordered to
seek their father's arms. Vibidia, the senior Vestal Virgin, was
exhorted to speak to the Emperor, as Pontifex Maximus, and
beg for mercy. 'Meanwhile, with no more than three attendants
—her retinue had already shrunk to that—she walked on foot
the entire length of Rome. Then, in a cart used for removing
refuse from gardens, she set off along the road to Ostia. No man
pitied her; all were overwhelmed by her fearful crimes.' The gay
party has been left far behind. On the other side, the problem
was how to control the Emperor and the troops. Narcissus
offers to take command of the soldiers for a day—'he also
asked for, and was granted, a seat in the Emperor's carriage,
lest on the journey to Rome his friends Lucius Vitellius and
Largus Caecina might have an opportunity of persuading him
to change his mind.'

The coach journey from Ostia to Rome finds Tacitus at his
most sardonic. Claudius is garrulous: 'there are many reports of
the Emperor's contradictory remarks, as he passed from reproaching his wife's scandalous conduct to recollections of their
marriage and the infancy of their children. Vitellius said nothing
but "how scandalous! how disgraceful!" His purport was not
clear; Narcissus pressed him to be less oracular. But, like an
oracle, Vitellius did nothing but give vent to hesitant remarks
which could lead to any interpretation.' Largus Caecina followed
his example. The friends of Caesar were playing a waiting game.

Now comes a short but passionate scene, the encounter with
Messalina, which is the core of the whole drama. 'By now
Messalina was in sight. She called out that a hearing must be
given to the mother of Octavia and Britannicus. Her accuser,
Narcissus, shouted her down, bringing up Silius and the marriage;

then he handed over a detailed inventory of her vices, so as to attract the gaze of Claudius.' (A well-timed memorandum is the trump card of the Civil Service!) 'Soon after, they entered the city. Here, the two children they shared were brought forward. Narcissus ordered them to be taken away. Vibidia (the Vestal Virgin) he was unable to remove before, with many reproaches, she had demanded that Claudius should not condemn his wife unheard. Narcissus replied that the Emperor would give her a hearing and an opportunity to clear herself; meanwhile, the Vestal Virgin should take herself off and attend to her sacred duties.'

All the time, Claudius had been strangely silent, and Vitellius seemed unaware of what was happening. 'All obeyed the freedman's orders.' He saw to it that Claudius was conducted to the mansion of Silius. There Claudius was roused to anger by the sight of a statue of Silius's father, executed for treason, and by all the gifts from the imperial house that Messalina had heaped on her new 'husband.' Thence to the Castra Praetoria, where the principal conspirators were in custody. Narcissus addressed the troops. Claudius could only stammer a few words in shame. But the Praetorians had raised him to power, and they meant to keep him there. They clamoured to know the names of the guilty and their punishment. Silius was pushed forward. He did not attempt to defend himself or play for time. His example was followed by several Roman knights. They thus earn the approval of Tacitus, always extended to those who make a good end.

The punishments given to the other conspirators are then recounted. They are neatly varied. The case of Mnester occasioned some delay. He was the ballet dancer who had been a lover of the Empress, and pleaded that Claudius himself had assigned him to Messalina, with instructions that he was to do exactly as she ordered. He had done just that. The plea had a logic of its own which appealed to Claudius. Fortunately, the freedman were able to trump it with another. They urged him 'not to spare a ballet dancer, after the deaths of so many men of rank; in a crime of this magnitude, the question whether participation was enforced or voluntary was unimportant.' The appeal to social considerations carried the verdict against Mnester. Traulus Montanus, 'a modest young man, but physically handsome,' pleaded that he had spent only one night in Messalina's bed 'for she passed with caprice from lust to disdain.' This argument also carried no weight. But two of the conspirators escaped the death sentence—Plautius Lateranus, through family connections, and Suillius Caesoninus, 'thanks to his own vices, for in that rabble of perverts he had played the woman's role.'

Messalina remained. She had not yet given up hope. Indeed she was compiling a petition in which anger was an ingredient, for she preserved her arrogance till the last. The chance that she could even now turn the tables on her accuser appeared. Claudius returned home, dined late, and became maudlin and sentimental. He was actually heard to use the phrase, 'let the poor woman know that she should come tomorrow and plead her case.' This was something Narcissus could not risk. It was necessary to arrange at once for Messalina's despatch. A task force was sent to carry it out, with the freedmen attached to see the deed done.

The last scene of Messalina's life was played out in the Gardens of Lucullus, with her mother at her side. 'When Messalina had been in her glory, they had quarrelled; now, moved to pity, Domitia had come to be with her daughter in her last hours. She urged her: "not to await the assassin's blow: your life is over, all you can now hope for is an honourable death." But honour found no place in that lust-besotted heart. There were tears and useless complaints, until the doors gave under the weight of the assailants. Then there was the officer, looking down on in her in silence, and the freedman hurling his slaves abuse.' Even now, Messalina cannot kill herself. Her end is told in short phrases of disgust. 'She moved the steel in useless panic from her throat to her breast. A blow from the officer ran her through. Her corpse was turned over to her mother.' Claudius' insensitivity persisted to the end. 'He was still at dinner when he

received the news that Messalina was dead, whether by her own
hand or another's was uncertain. He did not bother to inquire.
Asking for wine, he went on with the feast. In the days that
followed he gave no sign of hatred or pleasure, of anger or
sadness, nor of any other human emotion. . . . The Senate
helped him to forget by ordering Messalina's name and statues
to be removed from all public and private places.' The Empress
had suffered *damnatio memoriae*. As for Narcissus, the only
person to gain from the affair, he is given the status of *quaestor*,
which he affects to despise. None the less, he emerges clearly
more powerful than his rivals Pallas and Callistus.

The dramatic quality of this episode is clear; it also excels as a
piece of social satire. Tacitus' powers of character drawing are
seen at their best. Messalina appears as she does in Juvenal—
meretrix Augusta, the nymphomaniac Empress.[12] But the portrait is more subtle, with more light and shade. All of Claudius
is there—irresolute and inconsequent, under the influence of
freedmen and of women, in the last resort, inscrutable. The
friends of Caesar are impotent. Narcissus, the freedman, is full
of resource, ingenuity and perseverance; he deserves to succeed.

> 'The best lack all conviction, while the worst
> Are full of passionate intensity.'

Only two people appear to any credit—Messalina's mother and
the Vestal Virgin Vibidia. And Vibidia is told to go away. Once
again, it is hard to reconstruct the chronology of the episode.
Only the reference to the wine harvest makes clear that it was in
the autumn. It can have spread over a few days only, at the
most—but exactly how many? Three days seem a minimum
from the mock marriage to the death of Messalina. But Tacitus
has not chosen to be precise.

There is yet another device which Tacitus employed in the
interest of liveliness and variety—the use of speeches and of
letters. Nothing can have been more congenial to a Roman
audience. Nothing is harder to accept on the part of the modern

reader, with our standards of historical veracity, and against the
ingrained contemporary dislike of oratory. The very frequency
with which Tacitus employs this device is surprising. Miss B.
Walker[13] has given a very useful list of the speeches in the
Annals (though it must be said that it is incomplete, and that the
speeches and letters are not always correctly described). She
lists more than sixty speeches in the surviving books on the
Annals, of which some twenty are singled out for being remarkable for length or unusual brilliance of style. They are put in the
mouths of a wide range of persons—emperors, empresses,
senators in public debate or in private conversation, generals of
the Roman Army and also rebellious private soldiers, defiant
barbarian chieftains, prisoners of war, slaves and freedmen.

Tacitus' historical characters are highly articulate, but, then,
so was the world in which they lived. Moreover, the speeches
themselves are of very various kinds. Some were actually
delivered and recorded—for example speeches in debates in the
Senate. But we can never be confident that Tacitus has recorded
the actual words of the speaker rather than re-worked in his own
fashion the gist of what he found in the *acta senatus*. The one
case which we can actually check is not reassuring on this point.
The words used by the Emperor Claudius in the debate on
extending the citizenship to the Gauls, and recorded on the
famous Bronze Tablet of Lyon differ very widely from the
speech Tacitus has given to Claudius (*Annals* X, 24). Others are
plainly fictitious. How can Tacitus have known what Poppaea
said to Nero in the privacy of (presumably) the imperial
bedroom (*Annals* XIV, 1)?

To consider a little more closely. On a battlefield somewhere
in the Highlands of Scotland (perhaps at Culloden Moor itself)
a Roman and a Caledonian army confront each other.[14] Before
the battle they are addressed by their leaders. Calgacus delivers
a fiery and eloquent speech on the evils of Roman imperialism.
Agricola speaks to his troops in terse and soldierly terms, calling
on them to put an end to all their hardships on that day. How
much of this could conceivably be historical?

We may accept that speeches were made on both sides. It is just faintly possible that Agricola may have given Tacitus an outline of the words he actually used, although the historian had not seen him for some nine years before the *Agricola* was written. What we have in Agricola's speech is the traditional address of the Roman general to his soldiers, modified by Tacitus' knowledge of Agricola's character and of the circumstances of the day. There may be a small residual kernel of words actually used. This can hardly be the case with the speech of Calgacus, unless we are to suppose that Caledonian prisoners of war were cross-examined as to what he had said. In fact, Tacitus uses formulae which attempt to indicate different degrees of veracity. Calgacus is said to have spoken to this effect (*in hunc modum locutus fertur*): Agricola 'spoke in these terms' (*ita disseruit*). But these are no more than plausible formulae. In fact, Calgacus employs the commonplaces of the free barbarian defying Roman imperialism, modified to suit the time and circumstance of the actual battle. But, after reading the contrasting pair of speeches, we understand better the minds of the two sides, and the causes for which they fought.

Again, consider the pair of speeches[15] given to Nero and to Seneca, when the latter begged for retirement at a private audience. Glib and insincere, they show the nature of the relationship between the two men. Nero's irony is noteworthy. His speech begins: 'the first debt I owe you is that I know how to answer impromptu your carefully prepared speech,' and at the end of his speech he clinches the matter with the words: 'if you give back your wealth, if you desert your emperor, they will not praise your moderation. No, they will all speak of my greed, and of your fear of my cruelty. And whatever praise your self-denial wins, no true philosopher can gain credit from a course of action that brings his friend into contempt.' The familiar stories of the dishonest rhetorician bested by his more dishonest pupil are here echoed at a higher level. And the final scene is this: 'with these words, Nero clasped Seneca to his embrace. Nature had endowed him, and practice had perfected him, in the art of concealing his hatred under deceitful endearments. Seneca returned thanks—the invariable end of all conversation with tyrants.'

We know much more about Seneca and Nero after reading these two fabricated speeches. Indeed, it is not too fanciful to compare the speeches in ancient historians with the myths in the dialogues of Plato. Plato, it is well known, employs the device of the myth to hint at or to express some inner reality which could not be brought out in the dialectical exchange. So may the historian express character, motive or principle, in a way that could not properly be done in the straightforward narrative of events.

Let us again turn to Bruce Catton for a parallel. The last 300 or so pages of his third volume, *Never Call Retreat*, take us from the battle of Gettysburg (July 1st–3rd, 1863) to the surrender of the South in May, 1864. In that period, President Lincoln delivered two famous speeches—the Gettysburg Address and the Second Inaugural. Neither is quoted in full. As for the Gettysburg Address, it is known (let us hope) to every American child. Bruce Catton[16] contents himself with describing the impression produced by the two hours' address of Edward Everett. Of Lincoln he says this: 'He was very brief; perhaps what had to be said here was phrasing itself in men's hearts and needed only to be touched lightly in order to be brought alive. He spoke of liberty and equality instead of victory, as if these words alone could give meaning to what had been done here, and instead of dedicating the ground he called upon those who stood there to dedicate themselves to something that might justify all that Gettysburg had cost them; and after two minutes he had done with it, and the Associated Press man wrote that there was "long-continued applause." Then the crowd broke up and people began their long journeys home, and by eight o'clock that night Gettysburg was quiet again.'

Secretary John Hay, who had spent a pleasant twenty-four hours in the town, put an entry in his diary: 'Mr. Everett spoke as he always does, perfectly—and the President, in a fine, free way, with more grace than is his wont, said his half-dozen words of consecration, and the music wailed and we went home through crowded and cheering streets. And all the particulars are in the daily papers.' At the Second Inaugural, Lincoln's speech is briefly summarised; some details are given of the ceremony itself, of which the most impressive is a kind of *sors Biblicana.* 'When the oath was given, Mr. Lincoln bent, as by ancient custom, and kissed the open pages of the Bible. Chase noted the precise point the lips had touched, marked the place, and later gave the Bible to Mrs. Lincoln. The marked verses were the 27th and 28th verses of the Chapter of Isaiah, "None shall be weary or stumble among them; none shall slumber nor sleep; neither shall the girdle of their loins be loosed. . . ." '

How Roman all this is! Thoroughly Roman again is Lee's last order of the day to his army after the surrender at Appomattox. But the narrative is constantly enlivened by the interjection of short quotations from soldiers' letters and diaries, official telegrams, newspapers and comments of the major military and political figures. The above may suggest that the gulf between Tacitus and Catton in the use of speeches is not so wide as it might have seemed. Tacitus used his speeches as literary set pieces, and his Roman audience enjoyed them all the more as such.

Here it would be as well to remember another impediment with which we have shackled ourselves. Good writing, 'mere literary skill' as it is sometimes called, is an art which few can command. And for that reason it is at something of a discount among contemporary historians. One sometimes sees it stated in the review of a book: 'there is no attempt at fine writing'— and this is meant in praise. We should do well to emancipate ourselves from such anaemic pruderies, and to enjoy fine writing for its own sake when we come across it in the pages of Tacitus. And if, in so doing, there is an occasional protest from our sense of strict historical veracity, then there is the advice given that poetic faith requires that we should practise a 'willing suspension of disbelief.'

CHAPTER FOUR
Characters

SELECTIVE IN HIS CHOICE OF THEME, Tacitus was no less so
in his choice of characters. His art has been compared to that of
the dramatist, or the painter—'the finest painter of antiquity,'
as Racine called him: it is odd that he did not claim him as a
fellow tragedian. The first comparison may help us to understand the care he shows for the exits and entrances of his
characters, and also for the dialogues they conduct with each
other—either directly or in the course of the action—Germanicus and Piso, victim and rival; Roman general and native
patriot, Agricola and Calcagus; tyrant-Emperor and virtuous
senator, Nero and Thrasea Paetus. Like all great painters, he is
a master of scale and arrangement. Sometimes he will give no
more than a sketch, boldly but economically drawn at the
moment of action. Towards the other end of the register major
figures, such as Germanicus, Agrippina and Sejanus, develop on
an ample scale in which narrative and comment are combined:
there may be the final tribute of an obituary.

Some of the best effects are seen in characters not of the first
historical importance. Such are those two exponents of *la dolce
vita* at the court of Nero, the Empress Poppaea and the elegant
voluptuary Petronius Arbiter. Poppaea makes her entry immediately before her greatest amorous triumph—the seduction of
Nero. In no more than two chapters, (*Annals* XIII, 45–46) we

are brought to understand the lady and the part she is to play.

'There was another notorious example of lust in that year, and one which marked the beginning of much evil for the state. There was in Rome a lady called Poppaea Sabina. . . . This woman had every gift—except virtue. Her mother had been the greatest beauty of her day, and she inherited her looks and her distinction: her wealth was equal to her birth. Her conversation was charming, her mind lively; her outward behaviour was dis-creet—her life depraved. She seldom appeared in public, and then with part of her face veiled. She meant her beauty to have a scarcity value—and found the fashion suited her. She cared nothing for her reputation, and took married or single men as lovers indiscriminately. Her own affections, and those of others, counted for nothing with her: her passions were adjustable, as expediency called. . . . A Roman knight had married her and she had borne him a son: but Otho seduced her by his youth and extravagance, and also because he was thought to be Nero's most intimate friend. Their liaison soon turned into marriage.

'Otho was always praising her beauty and graces to Nero. It may have been a lover's indiscretion, or it may have been a wish to arouse his interest, so that sharing the same woman would be bound to increase Otho's power. He was often heard to rise from table at the palace with the words, "I am going to Pop-paea. She has brought me beauty and nobility—all men pray for such gifts, a fortunate few attain them." Under such prompt-ings there was no long delay. When she was admitted to the palace, Poppaea made her way with a practised flirtatiousness— she found Nero's looks as irresistible as her own desires. But as the Emperor's passion grew she became haughtier. If she were kept for one or two nights in the Palace, she would insist that she was a married woman, and had no desire to destroy her marriage. "I am devoted to Otho," she would say. "No one else lives in such style: wealth and culture are united in him, he is equal to any fortune. Nero has a slave-girl for a mistress: he is tied down by Acte's company; an intrigue with a servant is a mean and squalid affair!" Otho lost his intimacy with the

Emperor, then he was expelled from court. Finally, lest he should stay in Rome as a rival, he was sent to govern Lusitania. This post he held up to the Civil Wars, and discharged it honourably and well, quite out of keeping with his earlier habits. A playboy in his private life, he showed self-discipline in his public office.'

Petronius Arbiter was just such another gifted playboy as Otho. He, too, made a good end, in his own way, and gets this tribute from Tacitus.[1] 'For Gaius Petronius, a brief retrospect will be in order. His days he passed in sleep, his nights in the pleasure and duties of life. The reputation that others acquire by energy, he won by idleness. Others who waste their substance are thought of as profligate or spendthrift; in Petronius it seemed a refinement of luxury. His deeds and sayings bore the mark of unconventionality and insouciance, and people were glad to accept them as unstudied and sincere. Yet as Governor of Bithynia, and subsequently as Consul, he had shown himself active and fully equal to his duties.[2] Later, relapsing to vice, or to a pretence of it, he gained admittance to the exclusive circle of Nero's intimates in the capacity of Arbiter of Elegance. Nothing was thought smart or amusing, unless it had Petronius' approval. Tigellinus grew to detest him, as a rival with a greater expertise in vice. . . . So he accused Petronius of intimacy with Scaevinus. A slave was found to denounce him; most of his household were arrested: he was given no chance of defence.

'Nero was then in Campania; Petronius had reached Cumae when he was arrested. He could not tolerate the hopes and fears of delay, though he made no headlong escape from life. Severing his veins, he bound them up again as fancy took him, and talked with his friends, but not on serious topics, nor to win a reputation for stoicism. He heard them reciting, not the doctrines of the philosophers nor on the immortality of the soul, but flippant songs and light verse. Some of his slaves were lavishly rewarded, others were whipped. He went in to dinner, dozed off to sleep— his death might be forced, but he wanted it to seem natural. Even his will, which so many dying victims used to flatter Nero or Tigellinus . . . was handled in his individual manner. For he wrote out a long account of the Emperor's perversions, naming all his bed-fellows, male and female, and categorising the speciality of each, and sent it under seal to Nero. He also destroyed his signet-ring to prevent it being used to incriminate anyone else.

'Nero was at a loss to know how this detailed research into his sexual refinements could have been compiled. Silia seemed the leak: her marriage to a senator made her a person of note, she had been Nero's partner in every lubricity, and was also an intimate of Petronius. She was sent into exile for not keeping quiet about what she had seen and known. So Nero paid off his score.'

A third example shows a diffuse treatment. Petilius Cerialis figures in the *Agricola*, the *Annals*, and the *Histories*. First, as commander of the Ninth Legion at Lincoln he marches to relieve Colchester from Boudicca's rebel forces, is disastrously defeated, but manages to get back to base with his cavalry.[3] There is no comment on his conduct: later, we learn that lucky escapes are his *métier*. In the Civil Wars of 69 he makes his way through hostile country disguised as a peasant, to join the Flavian army. Given a cavalry command, he advances on Rome with such recklessness and dash that he suffers a shameful defeat.[4] The fact that he was later given the major task of suppressing the rebellion of Civilis in Gaul would seem due to his relationship to the new emperor Vespasian rather than to anything we have so far learned of his military record.

But in Gaul he brought fresh hope to a desperate situation, in which it seemed that Roman rule was to be superseded by an upstart Empire of the Gauls. Dismissing the forces sent to his help by the loyal Gallic states, he tells them: 'once Rome starts a war, it is as good as won.'[5] After defeating the forces of the rebels by a brilliant assault on a mountain position, he summons the nobles of two disloyal Gallic states to the Senate-house in Trier. 'You who love words so much,' he tells them, 'I shall speak to you for your own good . . .' and proceeds to the most eloquent defence of Roman imperialism in Latin literature,[6] ending with these words: 'The good fortune and discipline of eight hundred years have built the framework of this empire, which will overwhelm its destroyers if it is destroyed. You stand in the greatest danger, who have gold and wealth, the principal causes of war. So, cherish and love peace and the city of Rome which we both, conquerors and conquered, possess with equal rights. Take heed of the lessons of good and bad fortune: do not choose defiance and ruin rather than obedience and prosperity.'

Nobly spoken, but let us not get too solemn. A little later, the rebels still in arms make a night attack on the Roman Rhine flotilla, and cut out the flagship. Cerialis should have been on board, but luckily he wasn't; he was off visiting his mistress, a lady from Cologne![7] Good fortune, perhaps: but discipline? In the end he defeats Civilis: and the last time we see this thrustful commander is in Britain once more as Governor, and at the head of a grand offensive that subdued all northern England, and may have penetrated as far as the Lowlands of Scotland. Briefly mentioned in the *Agricola*, it may have been described at length in a lost book of the *Histories*.

A special interest attaches to Tacitus' portrayal of that small group of senators who have been called 'the Stoic opposition.'[8] They provided martyrs in three reigns—Thrasea Paetus and Barea Soranus under Nero, Helvidius Priscus under Vespasian, and Arulenus Rusticus and Herennius Senecio under Domitian. They formed a small, tightly knit, homogeneous group. Many of them came from North Italy, they were closely connected by origin and marriage, and they (and their wives) showed a common devotion to republicanism and to the stoic philosophy. Both were expressed in their choice of exemplars from the history of the late Republic—the tyrannicides Brutus and Cassius, and Cato and the Stoics of his day. Their lives tended to follow a common pattern. Opposition to the emperor would turn to defiance. This would draw down persecution, followed sooner or later by a scandalous trial and the death sentence. The last act (and they were good at last acts) would be an edifying death, with memorable last words. The martyrs' crown would be conferred in the writings of their followers. Throughout, these men impress by their personal rectitude and courage; usually, they dismay by their political futility.

It so happens that in the writings of Tacitus they appear in the reverse of chronological order. First, in the *Agricola*, come the Stoics martyred by Domitian. Withstanding the tyrant, they are a reproach to those who did not. Tacitus expresses regret for their fate, and honours their memory. But the dominant emotion is that of horror and shame at the part the senate was forced to play in their conviction. Moreover he has a stern rebuke for their thoughtless admirers. 'Let it be made clear to those who persist in admiring unlawful courses, that good men can exist under a bad emperor, and that obedience and moderation, if supported by hard work and ability, can reach that high point of honour that many have tried to capture by dangerous paths, and in the blaze of a melodramatic death that has done no service to the state.'[9] That is Tacitus' earliest judgement on the Stoic martyrs, written from first-hand knowledge and within some fifteen years of their deaths. He will have had to treat of them again in greater detail in the last books of the *Histories*, but it is unlikely that this judgement was modified. There may have been some force in Domitian's jibe at Arulenus Rusticus— that he was no more than *simia Stoicorum*—the ape of the Stoics.[10] None the less, his ghost haunted Domitian's dreams before the Emperor's death.

But Helvidius Priscus[11] was a more important figure than these *epigoni*. The warm terms in which he is introduced in the *Histories* (see p. 127) are due to the fact that he was one of the very few good men who played a part in politics at the time of the Civil War. In a later chapter, I show how he tried to re-assert the rôle of the Senate in the political vacuum of the year 87. Helvidius Priscus had had a remarkable career. His father had served in the Army as a centurion, and risen to the rank of *primipilaris*. The son studied philosophy and entered politics. When he was *quaestor*, Thrasea Paetus chose him to marry his daughter. He went into exile at the time of his father-in-law's death in 66, but was recalled by Galba in 69. It was in the reign of Vespasian that he had time to indulge 'that passion for glory' which Tacitus singles out as something of a weakness. It is a pity that we lack Tacitus' account of how he came to break with Vespasian, and was finally put to death. It would have been interesting to see whether Tacitus offset in any way the tradition preserved in Suetonius[12]—that Vespasian was extremely lenient towards Helvidius, but was finally provoked beyond endurance by his insolence. The death sentence passed against him was not, according to Suetonius, intended to be carried out; indeed, a reprieve was written, but it miscarried. A harsher tradition about Helvidius is preserved in Dio Cassius. There he is shown as an agitator, 'always currying favour with the mob, always abusing monarchy and praising democracy. . . . He would band men together as though it was the proper business of philosophy to insult authority, to stir up the mob, to overthrow the established order and to foment resolution.'[13] Dio explicitly contrasts his behaviour with that of Thrasea Paetus: 'he took his father-in-law for a model, but he fell far short.'[14] It seems that a much more sympathetic picture will have been presented by Tacitus, and indeed it also appears in the isolated references made by Pliny.

Tacitus wrote of Thrasea Paetus almost fifty years after his death. He was thus able to give a balanced judgement on undoubtedly the greatest of these Stoic senators. On the moral side, the verdict is unqualified. Thrasea Paetus was *virtus ipsa*—virtue incarnate—which was why he drew down on himself the attack of Nero in 66. As Dio Cassius was later to write, he was attacked, not for what he did, but for what he was.[15] But Tacitus allows more doubts to be seen about his political rôle, and these can only be understood in the light of his whole career, so far as we know it. Publius Clodius Thrasea Paetus[16] came from a wealthy family in Patavium (Padua, the birthplace of the historian Livy). Like Tacitus, he seems to have been a *novus homo*, the first of his family to enter the Senate. We do not know where he learnt his Stoicism, but it must have been acquired early in life, for we find him married to Arria, daughter of the lady of the same name who shared her husband's death so bravely under Claudius. It seems that his political advancement in the reign of Nero was due to the influence of Seneca and he was *consul suffectus* in 56.

He first appears in the pages of Tacitus in 58, when he intervenes in a debate on a trivial subject, gladiatorial shows in Syracuse. This gave a handle to his critics. 'Why,' they demanded, 'if Thrasea thinks the state needs a free Senate, does he waste time on such trifles? Why not speak on peace or war, on tariffs or laws—the really decisive issues?'[17] Already, it appears, Thrasea Paetus has his enemies in the Senate, and already he is known as the champion of senatorial freedom. Already, too, he has a following of friends, who are disturbed by criticism and ask for an explanation. His reply is that he assumes the Senate will realise that those who concern themselves with minor matters were likely to hide their interests in what was more important. Such issues arose in the following year, in the debate in the Senate after the murder of Agrippina. Thrasea Paetus was so disgusted at the servile attitude of the Senate towards the matricide that he walked out of the House. Tacitus' comment is interesting—'this endangered his own life, but did nothing to advance the cause of public freedom.'[18] He made another dangerous abstention in the same year—from the *Ludi Juvenales* or Festival of Youth, at which Nero made his first public appearances as an artist. This gave all the more offence because Thrasea Paetus himself had appeared on the stage at the festival held in Patavium every thirty years, and founded by the Trojan Antenor. Moreover, Thrasea is known to have been the friend of the distinguished tragedian Pomponius Secundus. His critical approval would have been worth having.

Thrasea is not mentioned again in the *Annals* until the year 62, when he plays the decisive part in the Antistius affair. Here his boldness induced the Senate, much against Nero's wishes, to vote against the death penalty. Again Tacitus' comment is notable: 'Thrasea showed his usual resolution of mind—and did not wish to miss his hour of glory.' His next appearance[19] did not involve open confrontation with the Emperor. This was in 63, at the prosecution of the Cretan Claudius Timarchus. This wealthy provincial had not only tyrannised over his fellow countrymen, but also insulted the Senate by repeatedly asserting, 'it depends on me whether the Roman governors of Crete get an address of thanks or not!' This Thrasea Paetus was able to turn to the public advantage. Proposing the defendant's expulsion from Crete, he dwelt on the need 'to correct this example of provincial arrogance as befits the honour and dignity of Rome.' The reputation of the Roman citizen should depend on the judgement of Romans, not on that of provincials. 'I know,' said Paetus, significantly enough, 'certain virtues are bound to be unpopular—for example unbending strictness and a mind steeled against corruption.' There spoke a follower of Cato. He had need himself of these qualities in the following year, when the senators flocked out to congratulate Nero on the daughter Poppaea had given him. Extravagant honours were voted to all involved in the affair, including the Goddess of Fertility. Thrasea Paetus was expressly forbidden to attend the Palace—a warning of his imminent death. There was an abortive attempt at reconciliation, but from this time onwards the breach was never healed.

In 63 began the three-year period of abstention from the Senate and from all public business, which earned Thrasea notoriety throughout the empire and was a most effective criticism of the Emperor. At the end of this time his accusers can say: 'the official Gazette of the Roman people is carefully read, in every province and every army, to see what Thrasea has *not* done.'[20]

The final assault was launched in the year 66, in the atmosphere of terror after the exposure of the Pisonian conspiracy. It

was carefully timed to coincide with the visit to Rome of Tiridates, King of Armenia: Barea Soranus, friend of Thrasea and
fellow Stoic, just returned from the governorship of Asia, was
also involved in the attack. It seems very likely that the plan was
conceived by Tigellinus, Nero's latest favourite. At any rate it
was a friend and follower of his, Cossutianus Capito, who
stated the case against Thrasea at a private audience with the
Emperor. In his mouth (for there can surely have been no record
of the interview) Tacitus puts both the public and the private
arguments against Thrasea. The private ones must have been
especially effective with Nero. They are summed up in the
sentence 'he hates to see his Emperor happy!' This is the same
reason given by Suetonius, that Thrasea was condemned 'for
having the face of a schoolmaster.'[21] But Cossutianus also
invoked the ill-omened names of the republican Stoics, Quintus
Aelius Tubero and Marcus Favonius—'they attack the imperial
government in the name of liberty: once they have overthrown
it, they will attack liberty as well. It will avail you nothing to
have struck down a Cassius, if you let these rivals of Brutus
survive and flourish.' The historic memories which Thrasea had
done so much to keep alive were cleverly turned against him.

We are next[22] told of the charges against Barea Soranus. 'The
energy and fairness he had shown as governor of Asia had added
to his unpopularity with the Emperor. He had cleared the harbour at Ephesus, and refused to punish the city of Pergamum for
resisting with violence an attempt by Acratus, Nero's freedman,
to remove its pictures and statues.' (No doubt for the adornment
of the Golden House.) The actual charges, however, were friendship with Rubellius Plautus and an attempt to incite the provinces to revolutionary moves. The friends of Thrasea Paetus
divide into two parties on the question whether he should
attend the Senate to defend himself. The young Rusticus
Arulenus, then tribune, offers to interpose his veto at the meeting. Thrasea regards his suggestion as futile—unlikely to help
his own defence, and fatal to its originator. 'I have lived my life,'
he said, 'and I shall not now abandon the path I have trod for so

long. You are just beginning your public career, and have not compromised your future. In times like these, you must consider very carefully what political course you intend to chart.' He then decided to make a personal decision as to whether it was right for him to attend the meeting of the Senate. The decision was negative and Thrasea's last public act was to stay away from his own trial.

The session of the Senate[23] took place under armed duress, with two battalions of the Guard in full equipment in the adjacent temple of Venus Genetrix. After a speech from Cossutianus, the attack was taken up by the great informer Eprius Marcellus. In his harsh, violent manner he set out the official case against Thrasea. 'I insist that an ex-consul should attend the Senate; a priest, the national vows; a citizen, the oath of allegiance! Or has Thrasea already declared himself a traitor and the avowed enemy of our ancestral rights and institutions? Let this man who protects the Emperor's critics truly play a senator's part and show himself: let him declare in this Senate what reforms and changes he wants. We shall find it much easier to endure his detailed criticisms than the general condemnation his silence implies! Are world-wide peace, or the bloodless victories of Roman armies, something he finds objectionable? He grieves over public triumphs, regards the fora, temples and the theatres of Rome as so many deserts, and threatens to send himself into exile—a strange ambition—do not gratify it! The decrees of the Senate, the holders of public office, the very city of Rome, mean nothing to him. Let him withdraw his existence from a country he has long ceased to love, and now no longer sees.' It was a case that did not lack force.

The brief against Barea Soranus was stated by Ostorius Sabinus. It is chiefly notable by the way in which his daughter Servilia was brought into the case. This young widow was accused of spending large sums of money on magical rites, which undoubtedly she had done. Few scenes in the *Annals* are more pathetic than her attempt to answer her accusers.[24] 'She clasped the altar and cried, "I have never invoked forbidden gods, nor used black magic! My prayers have been unlucky, but all they asked were that you, Caesar, and you, members of the Senate, should spare my beloved father. I gave my jewels and my dresses and the other things that a lady of rank has, and I would have given my blood and my life if they had asked for it! I never saw the magicians before . . . I never mentioned the Emperor, except as a god. And my poor father knew nothing about it; if a crime has been committed, it is my fault." ' The plea aroused the sympathy of the Senate, but availed her nothing.

Thrasea, Soranus and Servilia, were allowed to choose their own deaths. Helvidius Priscus was banished from Italy. The trial provided two further *exempla*, one good and one bad. Publius Egnatius Celer earned himself lasting ill-fame as appearing for the prosecution against his friend and patron. The wealthiest man in Bithynia, Cassius Asclepiodotus, who had revered Soranus in his prosperity, did not desert him in his fall. The account of this famous trial ends with a curt recital of the rewards gained by the prosecution. They were: Eprius and Cossutianus 5,000,000 *sesterces* each, Ostorius 1,200,000 and an honorary quaestorship. These figures, and of course the speeches of the prosecutors, would have been available in the official *acta senatus*.

There follows,[25] and as a set piece, the death scene of Thrasea Paetus, which is conceived deliberately on the pattern of the death of Socrates. 'Thrasea was in his gardens when the consul's messenger came to him, and evening was drawing on. A gathering of distinguished men and women was in attendance, and he was listening with great earnestness to the Cynic philosopher Demetrius. To judge from Thrasea's attentive expression and a few words of the conversation that could be overheard, they were discussing the immortality of the soul, and the distinction between the body and the spirit. Then Domitius Caecilianus, one of his intimate friends, came to tell him the Senate's decision.' Thrasea insisted that his friends should leave and that his wife Arria should not follow her own mother's example—

'he persuaded her to live and not deprive their daughter of her sole support. He then took Helvidius and Demetrius into his bedroom, together with the quaestor who delivered the message. He offered the veins of both his arms, and when the blood began to flow he sprinkled the ground. Calling on the quaestor, he said "let us pour a libation to Jupiter the Liberator. You had better watch, young man—for you have been born (may heaven avert the omen) into an age when you may need the support of an example of fortitude." Then in torment at his lingering death, he turned to Demetrius'. . . . At this point the manuscript of the *Annals* breaks off and ironically enough we do not have Thrasea Paetus' last words. Nor can we learn them from any other source, unless they are those recorded by Dio: 'Nero may kill me but he cannot hurt me.'[26] But a more grievous loss is that we do not know whether Tacitus gave a summing up of the career and character of this remarkable man, nor, if so, what line he took.

One thing remains to be said before we are done with these signal examples of virtue. However much Tacitus may have admired the Stoic intransigents, he had no use for the philosophers, Greek or Roman, who were their spiritual and moral guides. The Cynic Demetrius, referred to so often by Seneca, and whom he compares with Socrates, Diogenes and Cato, only appears in Tacitus as the intimate of Thrasea Paetus and not in his own right, except when he earns a rebuke by defending Celer. Musonius Rufus, one of the most influential philosophers of the time, is shown in an absurd light in the *Histories*, when he tries to lecture the army of Vitellius, as it enters Rome, on the blessings of peace.[27] It is, says Tacitus, a display of untimely wisdom (*intempestiva sapientia*), and as for Egnatius Celer (the arch traitor, in Juvenal's words 'the Stoic who killed Barea, the informer who betrayed his friend')—he moves Tacitus to a passionate comment. 'This man affected the gravity of the Stoic school, and in dress and countenance would have served as a model for that honourable company. Inwardly, however, he was treacherous and crafty, concealing both avarice and lust. The bribe unmasked him. He should serve as a warning that notorious evildoers and obvious deceivers are no worse than false philosophers and treacherous friends,'[28] One almost feels from Tacitus that a philosopher should only be consulted at a death-bed.

Three of the Civil War generals, the Vitellianists Aulus Caecina Alienus and Fabius Valens, and Vespasian's supporter Marcus Antonius Primus, form a noteworthy group. Able and unscrupulous adventurers, they cruise like large pike in the troubled waters of the Civil Wars, until chased from their prey by larger predators. In the *Histories* (1, 52) they are prominent among the energetic and evil men in Vitellius' German armies: 'the legionary commanders Alienus Caecina and Fabius Valens were men of unlimited greed and fantastic recklessness.' Caecina was probably in command of the Fourth Macedonica, Valens of First Galbiana. Both owed their promotion to Galba, had been involved in shady financial dealings, and transferred their allegiance to Vitellius. By selecting them to command the two columns in which his armies advanced on Italy, he launched them into a strange, criminal and treacherous partnership.

Their personalities were very different. Caecina[29] came from Vicetia (Vicenza) in northern Italy; he was one of those tall, handsome, soldierly men whom the troops admire (Domitius Corbulo was like him in that, though a much more honourable man). At the head of thirty thousand troops, Caecina led them to the passes over the Pennine Alps on a march which brought death and destruction to the allies of Rome, and especially to the Helvetii (see pp. 151 and 184). Crossing the St. Bernard as soon as the pass was open, his troops came down past Aosta and into the valley of the Po, where they made contact with the outposts of Otho and attacked the strong base of Placentia (Piacenza). The general himself seemed to have left his cruelty and licence on the other side of the Alps: but he contrived to give offence by his manners.[30] Dressed in a Gallic cloak and trousers, he addressed Roman citizens in their togas, a piece of gaucherie which was aggravated by his wife Salonina, who rode a splendid horse with purple trappings. It did no one any harm,

says Tacitus: but people do not look kindly on men who have
suddenly ridden to greatness, and they demand moderation
above all from those who only recently were their equals. So this
flamboyant pair offended the egalitarian feelings of the north
Italian colonies.

Meanwhile the army of Valens had arrived, travelling through
the Cottian Alps and down past Susa and Turin: there was
friction between generals and their armies before they composed
their differences to defeat Otho at First Bedriacum (April 14th,
69). After the death of Otho both Caecina and Valens attended
the victory review held by Vitellius at Lugdunum (Lyons),
where the Emperor spoke in praise of them both and placed
them beside himself on the tribunal. After this, the two rivals
advanced with their master to North Italy: Caecina gave gladiatorial shows at Cremona, Valens at Bononia (Bologna). Both
generals conducted Vitellius round the battlefields of Bedriacum,
where the dead lay rotting in heaps, and explained to him the
course of the fighting. Then they proceeded to Rome, where
Caecina and Valens were made consuls, performed all the duties
of the Emperor, and 'hated each other with a hatred that they
had scarcely troubled to conceal in war, . . . and which now
burned the more fiercely in the midst of degenerate friends and
the rivalries of civil life.'

Tacitus[31] has a vivid picture of the contempt and suspicion
they felt for Vitellius, and the greed with which they plundered the
houses and gardens of the Roman aristocracy. But the approach
of the Flavian armies under Antonius Primus cut short this
plunderer's idyll, and they went divergent ways. Caecina was the
first to go into action: but Rome had been deleterious to him as
well as his army (see pp. 154, 155). He had his old ambitions, but
a newly-gained indolence—and he was inclined to make a deal
with the Flavians. But his troops were loyal to Vitellius and he
had much ado to shake them: not until after indecisive fighting,
the enemy capture of his birthplace of Vicetia, and the rebellion
of Vitellius' fleet at Ravenna, was he able to gather together the
senior centurions and persuade them to declare for Vespasian.

Still the common soldiers were obstinate: they threw him into chains, and continued the fight under loyal generals. After the fall of Cremona he was handed over to Antonius, who sent him on to Vespasian. It was a risky thing to do, for Caecina had remarkable powers of survival: he was soon high in the favour of Vespasian, and Antonius was reviling him for his cowardly surrender. There he passes from Tacitus' narrative, and we have to learn from other sources[32] of the last stages of his life, which were thoroughly in keeping. His favour with Vespasian continued, but he was at odds with Titus, who suspected him of adultery with Berenice. (That princess, too, had a weakness for tall military men.) His death is told by Suetonius. Titus, who knew Caecina was plotting against him, got hold of a copy of a speech which Caecina was going to make to the Praetorian Guard. He invited Caecina to dinner: the speech was produced: Caecina was put to death there and then.

The career and personality of Fabius Valens[33] are only less picturesque. He was the son of an equestrian family from Anagnia in Latium, and had earned some notoriety at the Ludi Juveniles in Nero's time. In command of a legion in Lower Germany at the beginning of the Civil Wars, it was he more than anyone else who persuaded Vitellius to bid for the imperial power, and on January 2nd he led his cavalry into Cologne and saluted Vitellius as Emperor. His reward was to lead an army of forty thousand men through the Gallic provinces to the Mt. Genèvre pass, a disgraceful march which inflicted many injuries on the Gallic states (see pp. 151, 152), and in which his personal rôle is summed up in Tacitus' words, 'whenever money was not available, he was bought off by lusts and adulteries.'[34] The forced partnership with Caecina took them on to Rome, where Valens deteriorated even more rapidly than his rival. He was broken in health when he moved north to face the Flavians, 'with a vast train of prostitutes and eunuchs, and at a slower pace than a general should keep.'[35] In fact, he was never to see action again. After the news of the Flavian victory at Second Bedriacum, he could still form the bold plan of seizing some ships, sailing to Gallia Narbonensis, and thence to Germany to try again. Sailing from Pisa, he got as far as Monaco, but soon afterwards was wrecked on the Ile d'Hyères. Then he was taken prisoner by the Flavians, imprisoned at Urbino, and finally put to death. His head was cut off and shown to the Vitellian troops, to rob them of the last hope of reinforcement from Germany. Tacitus gives him an obituary: 'he was a man of depraved morals, but did not lack ability: unfortunately, he sought a reputation for urbanity by playing the fool. At the Festival of Youth, under Nero . . . he acted with more talent than is respectable . . . He was a traitor to Galba, but faithful to Vitellius . . . the treachery of others gave him [Caecina] a reputation.'[36]

Marcus Antonius Primus[37] had perhaps the most remarkable career of the three. He was born at Tolosa (Toulouse). All we hear of his earlier career is that under Nero he was expelled from the Senate for his part in forging the will of a childless millionaire. Galba brought him back, and Tacitus calls his recovery of senatorial rank one of the horrors of war. At its outbreak he was in Pannonia, in command of the Seventh Galbiana: he tried to switch allegiance to Otho, but after First Bedriacum declared for Vespasian. This was a great asset to the Flavian cause, for he was, says Tacitus, 'vigorous in action, quick of speech, good at setting his enemies by the ears, accomplished in arousing strife and discord, always prepared to rob or bribe— to sum up, the worst of mankind in peace, but not to be despised in war.'[38] (*strenuus manu, sermone promptissimus, serendae in alios invidiae artifex, discordiis et seditionibus potens, raptor, largitor, pace pessimus, bello haud spernendus.*) This is one of the most pungent character-sketches in Tacitus.

His vigour showed to great advantage in his astonishing march at the head of the Danube troops across the Julian Alps, capturing Aquileia, and then making Verona his main base. With inferior forces, he engaged the Vitellians at Second Bedriacum, where his personal qualities were largely to thank for the victory. There followed the shameful sack of Cremona, the odium of which fell on him (see pp. 152, 153). Now he showed his talent for intrigue, writing secretly to Julius Civilis on the Rhine, to the Vitellians in Rome, and himself receiving ambiguous letters from Mucianus, urging delay. This was unfortunate, for when Antonius reached Rome the Capitol had already gone up in flames (see p. 167). After the murder of Vitellius, Antonius was for a short time in control of Rome. But soon Mucianus appeared—a more powerful man and even better at intrigue. Antonius was loaded with empty honours, offered a province, deprived of his troops, and edged from power. He went off to Vespasian, but was received with less favour than he expected. Vespasian owed him a real gratitude, for he had virtually won the war—but not according to plan, and the spoils were meant for the eastern armies. Here Tacitus breaks off, but from other sources we learn that Antonius got back to Toulouse and lived to a ripe old age, receiving congratulations and epigrams from the poet Martial.[39] He will not have lacked material for reminiscence.

The *Dialogus de Oratore*[40] offers proof that Tacitus does not only depend on action and events for the vivid portrayal of character. In that discussion, which is set in the reign of Vespasian, he uses four historical characters in the discussion of two major themes—the claims of oratory as against those of literature, and the reasons for the decline of Roman eloquence. It is the characters, not the themes, which are our concern. They are, the two great ornaments of the Roman bar, Marcus Aper and Julius Secundus, the poet and dramatist Curiatius Maternus, and the historian, poet, and aristocrat Vipstanus Messalla, whose part in the Civil War Tacitus so admired (see p. 20).[41]

Julius Secundus is somewhat lightly sketched, and it may be that his main contribution to the dialogue came in a part of the manuscript now lost: the other three are in high relief, sharply contrasting in outlook and style. Marcus Aper is the most striking: a self-made man, from an unfashionable part of the Gallic provinces, who has risen by his own talents, and is very well satisfied with what he has achieved. 'It was not so much that he was ignorant of literature—he despised it,' we are told: Aper himself is quick to remark, 'I hold nothing against poetry, *but* . . .' 'It is all very well to honour poetry, *but* . . .' *But*, the nub of the matter, why waste time on literature when oratory will open a real career to talent, a career that leads to wealth, honours, gratitude, troops of friends—and personal satisfaction besides? Aper has a professionalism of a kind very familiar in our own times, when in so many fields advances in technique are thought to justify scorn for one's predecessors. So Aper's line on the ancient *versus* modern orators debate—there are no ancients really, for Cicero and the rest were not so long ago, but judged by modern standards they do not impress.

Curiatius Maternus is set against this Gallic thruster. A poet and an idealist, he places the delights of poetry and the company of the Muses above worldly values—as to fame, is Homer esteemed lower than Demosthenes, or Virgil than Cicero? It was a view to which Tacitus himself subscribed, and Maternus has been taken as a mouthpiece of Tacitus. Certainly his political insight seems concordant—public oratory has declined with political liberty, 'the Emperor has disciplined eloquence, along with everything else.' Vipstanus Messalla brings to the discussion the ease and tolerance of a man of culture and social standing, rebuking, but in the most urbane way, the impetuosity of Aper and the utopianism of Maternus. Indeed, the whole tone of the discussion is genial and courteous, in a way which might be thought surprising both in Tacitus and his times. And there must be few other dialogues in either Greek or Latin literature where at least three major interlocutors are kept in such ordered balance. Plato, who excelled in the delineation of character, usually chose to subordinate his other *personae* to Socrates: perhaps only in the *Symposium* does he present a range of characters to compare with those of the *Dialogues*.

It must not be forgotten that the major figures in Tacitus play their parts with a full supporting cast of minor characters— slaves, freedmen, soldiers, barbarians, Roman citizens, all at some significant moment of speech or action. Such, for example, is the soldier Calusidius, whose cynical comment so effectually deflated a speech of Germanicus (see p. 141). He is no less memorable than the cream-faced loon who brings to Macbeth the news of the approach of the English army.[42]

Again, there is the fantastic episode of Caesellius Bassus,[43] who deceived Nero with the *ignis fatuus* of Dido's Treasure. 'This man was a Carthaginian and of unsound mind. Putting his trust in a dream, he sailed to Rome, bribed his way into the Emperor's presence, and told his story. This was that a huge cave had been discovered on his estates, containing a great quantity of gold—not minted coins, but ancient, unshaped bullion. Huge ingots lay about, in some places standing up like columns: hidden from remote antiquity, this reserve had now come to increase the felicity of the present age. His own theory, which he explained, was that these riches had been hidden by Dido when she founded Carthage. . . . ' Nero took no steps whatever to check the credibility of the author or his story. It became the talk of the day, encouraging the wildest hopes, and justifying the most lavish expenditure. At the Feast of the Juvenilia the orators proclaimed: 'the earth teems with a new fertility! We have only to stretch our hands to the wealth the gods provide!' Warships with picked crews were sent out to bring the treasure home with greater speed. It had yet to be found. Bassus made excavations on his own and his neighbour's estate, declaring now this place, now that, to be the site of the promised cave. Not merely soldiers, but farm labourers, were conscripted to help. The dénouement was ridiculous. Bassus came to his senses (it happens even to excavators). 'Protesting that his dreams had always turned out to be true before, and that this was the first time he had ever been wrong, he escaped from his disgrace and fear by suicide. (Other accounts say that he was arrested and released, after his property had been confiscated to compensate for Dido's Treasure.)' Bassus' plaintive cry, and Tacitus' dry comment, make an admirable postscript to this story of buried treasure.

At the conspiracy of Piso in the reign of Nero, two freedmen make striking appearances, one presented for good, the other for bad. An active part in the conspiracy was played by the freed-woman Epicharis,[44] who had wormed out the secret of the conspirators, 'how is uncertain, for she had never shown any previous interest in virtuous actions.' She began to chaff at their inaction, to tamper with the loyalty of the fleet at Misenum, and to try to recruit Volusius Proculus, a ship's captain. He denounced her to Nero. His evidence was unsupported, but Epicharis was arrested and kept in custody, for 'though Nero suspected the information was not false, it could not be proved to be true.' Eventually it proved to be true indeed, and Nero ordered Epicharis to be put to the torture, thinking no woman's body could bear the pain. 'But neither the lash nor the branding-iron, nor the anger of the torturers as they increased her agony to prevent a woman defying them—none of this caused her to weaken in her denial.' The first day of investigation revealed nothing. 'On the next day she was dragged out to face the same ordeals. Being carried on a litter (for her limbs had been dislocated and she could not stand), she tore off her breastband and looped it round the canopy of the litter. Then she slipped her neck into it, bore forward with all her weight, and choked out what little life she had left. A freedwoman, and brought to the extremes of agony, she had tried to protect men who were of no kin to her, and almost strangers. How much nobler this example than that of freeborn men, Roman knights and senators, who did not even wait for the torture to betray their nearest and dearest!'

In contrast to her heroic conduct was that of Milichus,[45] freedman of Scaevinus, who played the crucial part in revealing the conspiracy. Milichus had been ordered to sharpen the dagger with which Scaevinus was to assassinate Nero, then to get ready bandages for wounds and styptics. At this point his suspicions were aroused. 'His slave's mind now began to think of the rewards of treachery, and to conjure up fantasies of unlimited wealth and power. Considerations of duty, of his patron's safety, and of the freedom he himself had been given, flew out of the window.' His wife contributed 'a typically feminine and sordid argument'—the alarm had already been given, the rewards would go to the first to turn informer. Milichus determined to earn them. He denounced Scaevinus, who was arrested. There was a confrontation: such was Scaevinus' self-control that he almost carried the day against his accusers, but Milichus' wife named two of the conspirators, who broke down at the threat of torture. The secret was out, and the rest of the conspirators were smoked out and hunted down. Milichus was richly rewarded, 'and from that day took to himself the sobriquet of "Saviour" (*Conservatoris*) in Greek.' He had earned his reward —as also the *infamia* with which he has been immortalised by Tacitus.

CHAPTER FIVE
Emperors and Court

IT IS EASY TO SEE the problem presented to the historian by the
venerable figure of the founder of the Principate. In his lifetime
Augustus had possessed that mysterious combination of personal and political glamour to which the name of charisma is
applied. His memory was revered above that of any other
Roman. He had been accorded divine honours after death, and
his cult, closely identified with that of the goddess Roma herself, flourished in the major cities of the Empire. He was the
great model held up to successive Emperors, as, for example,
during the early, good, period of Nero. No succeeding Emperor
commanded such reverence until Trajan appeared to make a
second. *Melior Trajano, felicior Augusto*; such was the dual ideal
held out before Emperors of the second century.

But how was a historian to write of Augustus in the years
immediately after Trajan's reign? Tacitus' point of attack in the
Annals is chosen carefully.[1] The last years of Augustus' reign
were unhappy. His death allows a verdict from the historian. In
the first chapter of the *Annals*, we see Augustus as the last and
most successful of those who held extraordinary powers in
Rome. 'The world, exhausted by Civil War, passed into his
control under the name of the Principate.' A little later[2] on we
are told how the Principate was secured. First, the crushing of
all Augustus' enemies in arms. Then, 'when he had seduced the

army by gifts, the common people by the provision of cheap food, and everyone by the blandishments of peace, then little by little he began to enlarge his powers, to encroach upon the proper functions of the Senate, the magistrates and the laws. No one opposed him. Men of spirit had died on the battlefield, or in the proscriptions. The remainder of the aristocracy were rewarded by wealth and position in proportion to their readiness to accept servitude. Having done well out of the revolution, they naturally preferred the existing security to the dangers and uncertainties of the old régime. The provinces showed no hostility to the new system. . . .'

There is nothing here of the famous constitutional settlement of 27 B.C., which is described in Augustus' own words in the *Res Gestae*: 'In my sixth and seventh consulships, after I had brought to an end the Civil Wars . . . having attained supreme power by the consent of all, I transferred the state from my own power to that of the Roman Senate and People . . . after that time I excelled all in authority (*auctoritas*) but of power (*potentia*) I possessed no more than those who were my colleagues in each magistracy.' This is the basic formula for the Principate. Tacitus ignores it. There does, however, seem to be an ironic gloss on the last sentence in his remark 'The names of the magistracies remained the same.'[3] There is another ironic echo of the edict mentioned by Suetonius: 'May I be privileged to build firm and lasting foundations for the Government of Rome. May I also achieve the reward for which I hope; that of being known as the author of the best possible constitution [*ut optimi status auctor dicar*], and of carrying with me, when I die, the hope that these foundations will abide secure.'[4] And indeed, says Suetonius, he achieved this success, having taken great trouble to prevent his political system from causing distress to any individual.

Picking up the word *status*, Tacitus comes to a very different conclusion: 'So the state had been transformed, and the old free Roman character no longer existed. Equality among citizens had gone by the board; all awaited the Emperor's commands.'[5]

After his funeral, men of experience assessed the career of the dead Emperor (Chapters 9 and 10). The discussion is weighted on the adverse side. Not only is the case for the prosecution given at rather more than twice the length, but they are allowed to refute all the arguments of his supporters, and then to introduce new attacks which are left unanswered. Even the famous *pax Augusta* is not immune from attack. 'Peace there was indeed, but it was a bloody one': so Augustus' accusers. Tacitus represents it as debilitating, fatal alike to political freedom, to eloquence and to the other liberal arts. Other criticisms are advanced by Tacitus himself. There had been a great growth of flattery in the reign of Augustus, putting an end to the line of distinguished historians who had written about the Republic and about Augustus' earlier years.[6] His moral reforms, embodied in the legislation of 17 B.C., led to espionage and the invasion of privacy.[7] More surprising still, Augustus had deliberately chosen Tiberius as his successor because he had taken careful note of his vices, and decided that Tiberius would furnish the worst possible comparisons with himself.[8] Not all of Tacitus' references to Augustus are hostile, but it is the darker colours that prevail. We are left in no doubt that it was not from a pious founder that the Principate took its being. It is interesting that Tacitus felt he had yet more to say on Augustus, but doubtful whether the picture would have been modified had the projected work ever been carried out.

Tiberius is Tacitus' masterpiece.[9] Malignant, implacable and larger than life, he dominates the first six books of the *Annals* and indeed the whole account of the Principate. In a sense, this was bound to be so. The reign of Tiberius lasted for twenty-three years, as against fifteen for Domitian, the next longest of any Tacitean Emperor. Moreover, it was filled with great events —the mutinies of the northern armies, the death of Germanicus, the risings in Gaul, the career of Sejanus, his fall, and the resultant terror. Yet all this does not explain the intensity which Tacitus has concentrated in this classic of denigration. Tacitus himself adduces the treason trials caused by the *Lex maiestatis*, which form a recurrent theme throughout the reign. The first outbreak is noted[10] in the year 14, and its future course foretold. 'It is worthwhile to record the first tentative proceedings against Falanius and Rubrius, knights of modest means. They illustrate very well how this iniquitous procedure began, and how cleverly it was handled by Tiberius. For it began stealthily. Then it was suppressed: finally it burst into flames and destroyed everything.'

Soon after appears the first of the notorious informers (*delatores*), a certain Caepio Crispinus. 'Moody, obscure, and ambitious, he wormed his way into the Emperor's confidence by anonymous denunciations. Soon everyone of standing was imperilled. . . . Following his precedent, others rose from beggary to wealth, and brought catastrophe on their fellow citizens and finally on themselves.' We have been conditioned for the 'continuous bloodshed' of Tiberius' last years, culminating in the 'huge heap of dead' (*immensa strages*) of 33.[11] As we shall see, research[12] has shown that the *maiestas* trials and their victims under Tiberius were not on the scale that Tacitus would have us suppose. But *maiestas* trials, *delatores*, and their victims, were indeed the most terrifying aspects of Domitian's tyranny, and this leads to another link. Suetonius has recorded that Domitian admired Tiberius, constantly read his speeches and his memoirs, and took him for a model.[13] Tacitus has underlined the resemblance: part of his revenge on Domitian is to present his exemplar in the worst possible light.

How this was achieved has been analysed by modern scholars, in detail which it is unnecessary to repeat.[14] But it may be useful to note the pattern of the Tacitean indictment of Tiberius, which could well derive from that followed by prosecutors in the courts. In the first phase, prejudice is created against the accused: next, in apparent candour, some things are allowed in his favour—just enough to suggest fair-mindedness in the prosecution: then a final attack is launched to carry the day. We have already seen Tacitus using this device in the portrayal of

Augustus. Against Tiberius it is employed on a grand scale,
extending through six books, and involving *suppressio veri* as
well as *suggestio falsi*. It might be supposed, for example, that
Tacitus would at the outset have given an account of Tiberius'
life and career before he came to the throne in 14. He had shown
himself a great servant of the state, one of the finest generals in
Roman history, a skilled diplomat, and a splendid administrator. None the less, he had been treated abominably by
Augustus. Slighted and humiliated, he had repeatedly been
passed over in favour of younger rivals, and only recognised as
Augustus' successor in the last resort. If, in the process, he had
grown wary, suspicious, and hypocritical, it was not without
good cause.

None of this is allowed to appear. First comes the seizure of
power by Tiberius, aided by Livia, on (or perhaps before?) the
death of Augustus. Then the murder of his only rival, Agrippa
Postumus—'the first crime of the new reign.'[15] Next, the farce
of the 'debate' in the Senate, in which Tiberius' character
emerges in all its hypocrisy and dissimulation (see pp. 116, 117).
In only fifteen chapters, prejudice against Tiberius has been
established so firmly that his many good deeds can be recorded
without much risk of its being shaken.

The case for Tiberius is set out, at some length, in the account
of the year 23, when Drusus was poisoned and the reign of
Tiberius, in Tacitus' view, changed sharply for the worse (*mutati
in deterius principatus initium ille annus attulit*). He acknowledges
the scope allowed the Senate for free discussion and the handling
of public business, the careful choice of candidates for high
office, the sound administration of the laws—apart from the law
of treason. Taxation was fairly administered, the provinces
were not burdened by new imposts: the Emperor had few
estates in Italy: only a few freedmen were employed on his staff:
disputes between the imperial treasury and private persons were
decided in the public courts. But—and it is a large 'but'—'all
this was done, not in any gracious fashion, but after Tiberius'
grim and even terrifying manner.' (Here is something we can

understand, for the modern world abounds in these efficient, impersonal administrators, who do not behave *comi via*. They may be rewarded by a grateful government, but their colleagues accord them neither love nor even loyalty. So with Tiberius even in his best years.) Tiberius' admirably firm speech to the Senate on the death of Drusus follows.[16] Tacitus then moves on to more subtle disingenuousness. There was a rumour, still extant in Tacitus' time, that Tiberius had poisoned Drusus himself. It is given in full, and then refuted, with a stern warning to the reader against all idle rumours. 'I do beg all my readers not to prefer mere hearsay—however popular and sensational—to the plain truth, without embroidery.'[17]

Gullibility rebuked, we are ready to follow our unsensational guide to the plain truth of Tiberius' later years. It is a stark tale of horror, unredeemed by any lighter shades. First a long series of *maiestas* trials, then the intrigues of Sejanus, and the liquidation of most of the surviving members of Germanicus' family. Meanwhile, the Emperor has returned to Capri, to the enjoyment of who knows what vices; Sejanus governs Rome in his place as a tyrant. Then the Fall of Sejanus (lost in Tacitus) and the reign of terror. Finally, the appalling loneliness of Tiberius' last few years: the cynical choice of Gaius as his successor: the grisly scenes at Tiberius' deathbed at Misenum.[18] 'On the sixteenth of March the Emperor's breathing stopped: it was thought that he had reached the end of his mortal span. Gaius Caesar issued forth for the official beginning of his reign, surrounded by a huge crowd of well-wishers. But suddenly came the news that Tiberius had recovered his voice and sight: he was asking for food to strengthen himself after a fainting fit! Panic and general confusion. Gaius stood in a silent catalepsy: his high hopes in ruins, the worst to fear. But Macro (the Praetorian Prefect) kept his nerve. He ordered them to smother the old man in a pile of bedclothes, and to leave the room. So Tiberius came to his end, being then in his seventy-eighth year.' We are reminded of an equally grisly scene at the death of Stalin. As the members of the Supreme Praesidium—a much more sinister

crew than Macro and Gaius—stood round his bed, the dying
Stalin raised his left arm and pointed. At whom or what they
did not know, nor did they stay to find out.

As a coda, Tiberius is accorded[19] the most malicious of all
Tacitus' obituary notices. His character is peeled, layer by layer,
like an artichoke or an onion. 'As a private citizen, or holding
military command under Augustus, his conduct and reputation
were excellent. While Drusus and Germanicus lived, craft and
equivocation provided a screen of virtues. While his mother was
alive, Tiberius still showed good and bad qualities: while he had
Sejanus to love (or to fear), his cruelty was appalling but his
perversions remained hidden. In his last phase, there was a great
eruption of crime and vice: set free from shame and fear, he
stood out at long last in no other character but his own. . . .' At
this point the manuscript of Book VI broke off, and we do not
know whether this was Tacitus' last word on Tiberius. But, as it
stands, it is as deadly as Macro's bedclothes.

But we know that Tacitus' Tiberius, also, is composed of
layers. At the core is the Tiberius of history, and the narrative is
frequently in contact with him. Then there is the Tiberius of the
(hostile) senatorial tradition, also found in Suetonius and Dio.
This composite has itself been endowed by Tacitus with some of
the features and colouring of Domitian. As a further refinement,
it has been modelled on those archetypal tyrants to be found in
the philosophers and tragic poets—a Thyestes, an Agamemnon,
a Creon. We see this process in a famous passage (*Annals* VI, 6,
1), where Tacitus quotes a pathetic letter to the Senate from
Tiberius. 'What I am to write to you, members of the Senate, or
how—or what not to write at this time—if I know that, may the
gods destroy me with worse than the death I feel overtaking me
every day!'[20] On this Tacitus says: 'So surely had his crimes and
wickedness returned to torment him. Well did the wisest of
philosophers [Plato, but Tacitus disdains to name him] proclaim
that, if we could look into the minds of tyrants, we should find
therein bruises and lacerations, seared into the mind, like blows
on the body, by cruelty, lust, and evil designs. Neither Tiberius'

imperial rank nor his secure retreat could protect him from revealing his tortured heart and the penalties he had brought upon himself.'

It is precisely because the Tacitean Tiberius is raised above the level of mere history to that of tragedy and philosophy that it has a strange vitality that renders it impervious to historical criticism. In recent times, eminent scholars of many countries have set their hands to the rehabilitation of the historic Tiberius.[21] In a large measure, they have been successful. We now regard him as an able and conscientious ruler, under whom the Roman world, as a whole, was peaceful and prosperous. It is altogether proper that an historical injustice should have been righted. Yet the Tiberius of Tacitus retains its ability to provide a touchstone by which we may judge the minds and actions of the tyrants of our own times.

Of Gaius we have only forebodings. There is Tiberius' grim comment: 'He has Sulla's vices, without his virtues.'[22] And, indeed, it is hard to see how Little Boots, the soldiers' darling, could possibly have turned out well. Not surprisingly, Lucius Arruntius thought the prospect of his accession a further and compelling reason for suicide. 'If Tiberius, with all his experience, has succumbed so completely to the corruption of absolute power, what about Gaius? He is barely out of his childhood, he knows nothing, he has been brought up on the worst possible examples. Will he change for the better under Macro's tutelage? Macro was chosen, as the greater villain, to suppress Sejanus: he has committed more crimes and done even more harm to the State. I foresee a yet more grievous slavery ahead. I am resolved to liberate myself—from the horrors of the past and the horrors yet to come.'[23] These words he uttered with all the fervour of an oracle. Then he opened his veins. The result was to show that Arruntius had been wise to die.' We may lack Tacitus' account of the reign of Gaius, but of its tenor there can be no doubt.

Neither Nature nor Tacitus conceived Claudius on an ample scale. He is shown as something of a puppet, buffeted about between stronger elemental forces, such as the ambitions of his wives and the greed of his freedmen. Few men in history have borne such heavy matrimonial burdens as Claudius—his third and fourth wives being Messalina followed by Agrippina, with the lusts of one as insatiable as the ambitions of the other. In Tacitus, he lacks the grotesque qualities to be found in the *Life* by Suetonius, and, still more, in the ill-mannered *Apocolocyntosis* or *Skit on the Death of Claudius* by Seneca. But he is capable of liberal views on the rights of provincials (see p. 121), and is enlightened on Rome's relations with Parthia and with the free people of Germany (see pp. 207f, 231). Here again, modern scholarship[24] has favoured a rehabilitation of Claudius, for which Tacitus gives little support, and he has been called the best Emperor between Augustus and Vespasian.

The portrait of Nero is a study in degeneration—a proof (if one is needed) that absolute power corrupts absolutely. He begins with gifts of intelligence and taste, and has had a good education in the charge of Seneca. If he has leanings towards roistering, lechery and the arts, so do many other young men. Nor does he lack for good counsel. At first, with Seneca and Burrus as his advisers, his government is good. But he has the misfortune to be Emperor, and to have Agrippina as his mother and rival. And the murder of Claudius has taught the lesson that rivals can be removed. Unable to bear restraint of any kind, he passes from the murder of Britannicus in 55 to that of Agrippina in 59. After that fearful crime his reign is shown as a protracted orgy of lust, cruelty and extravagance. He causes the death of both his wives—the virtuous Octavia by design, the wicked Poppaea by accident. From 64 Rome is in the grip of a lurid horror—the Great Fire, the persecution of the Christians, the Conspiracy of Piso, and the terror which ensued (fatal to Seneca, Lucan, Petronius, Thrasea Paetus and many others) follow in unbroken succession. The only relief is provided by Nero's appearance on the stage—to us faintly comic, but to Tacitus degrading.

We lack Tacitus' account of his death. In fact, the last of the Julio-Claudians died, abandoned by all but three of his freedmen—a bungled suicide—'his eyes glazed and bulging from their sockets, a sight which horrified everyone present.'[25] Nor was he buried in the Mausoleum of Augustus, but his old nurse and his faithful mistress, Acte, carried his remains to the family tomb of the Domitii on the Pincian Hill. So much is to be gathered from Suetonius. If Nero has come to be thought of as the archetypal wicked Emperor, and indeed has supplied features of the Beast of the Apocalypse, it is clear much of the evidence comes from Tacitus. But modern scholarship, again, has wished to see what can be said on the other side. If Nero's personal character is beyond redemption, we must take into account the successes won in war and diplomacy, in Parthia and the East (see pp. 211ff). His philhellenism may have been genuine, and his artistic gifts more substantial than Tacitus will allow. And it is also true that—for whatever reason—his memory was honoured in the eastern provinces and by the common people of Rome.

The crowded action of the Civil Wars allowed no time for the leisurely exposition of character. Yet the three Emperors, whose reigns all fell within the year 69, are by no means passing shades, like the ephemeral Emperors of the mid third century. They were men of strongly contrasting characters, and their individuality is more strongly brought out in the narrative of Tacitus than in the more detailed biographies of Suetonius. Servius Galba was an anachronism—'damaged by his old-fashioned strictness and undue rigidity—qualities to which we are unequal in these modern times.'[26] Suetonius records a wider range of vices: Tacitus picks out these, with cruelty, as the cause of his downfall. In the *Life* by Suetonius he is shown as a strict disciplinarian as commander of the Rhine legions under Claudius, putting the troops through the toughest of field training, with himself at their head. Now, dealing in Rome with soldiers who had known Nero, his methods would not work, *capax imperii, nisi imperasset:* the verdict fits other old soldiers and marshals who have been dragged out and pitchforked into an emergency.

In Otho the troops would find an Emperor more to their taste
—Nero's crony, Poppaea's first husband, the kind of dashing
and brilliant rakehell produced by the times. But there was
another side to Otho. We have seen (p. 56) how he had shown
himself an energetic and capable governor of Lusitania; as
Emperor, he might well have achieved the rare distinction (confined, Tacitus says, to Vespasian) of improving with time.
Certainly there was a nobility about his end: defeated by the
Vitellianists at the first Battle of Bedriacum, he determined to
commit suicide rather than cause more bloodshed. Tacitus, who
had friends in the Othonian army, gives him an elaborate death-
scene.[27] Otho speaks kindly to all, rejects the plea of his men
that he should try again, and dies with firmness and courage.

Vitellius was a much worse man, but he met Otho in a contest
where the worse cause was sure to win. For him Tacitus has
little but contempt: but he was a man who could only win the
loyalty of those who did not know him, and he had to buy his
friends. He showed a morbid pleasure in inspecting the rotting
corpses on the field of Bedriacum. Gluttony and sloth were his
main characteristics: at the crises of his fortunes, when the
Flavians were marching on Rome, he was paralysed in mind
and body 'like those sluggish animals who, if you put food by
them, lie there sunk in torpor.'[28] Otho's readiness to die had
saved lives, to the advantage of the state.

Once again, one has to regret that we do not possess Tacitus'
full-length picture of Vespasian. Like Gaius, we have a foretaste
of his rule, but here what is forecast is good. Vespasian is the
man of destiny, confirmed by divine prophecies at Carmel and
at Alexandria. On the human level, he is contrasted with
Mucianus. Vespasian had fine military qualities, but for his
meanness, he could stand besides the great generals of the
Republic. Mucianus had the high civilian virtues, wealth,
munificence, sagacity in the conduct of affairs. Subtract their
vices, is Tacitus' comment, and blend their virtues in one person,
and the result would be an outstandingly good emperor![29] It is
an interesting formula, and perhaps we are intended to divine

Trajan in this recipe. For Vespasian himself, the tribute is paid that he alone improved while on the throne. We can scarcely know how Tacitus portrayed an *exemplum virtutis* who was also Emperor.

It would be perverse to claim that the change from Republic to Empire was a step in the emancipation of women. But the pre-eminence and wealth of the imperial court brought to its women opportunities of a kind never known in Rome before, though they had existed in the Hellenistic world, and notably at the court of Egypt. This was true not only for empresses and princesses, but also for mistresses (Acte, Poppaea), and even for poisoners (Locusta). No Roman woman ever wielded such power and influence as Livia, wife of Augustus and mother of Tiberius. The elder Agrippina, at her husband's headquarters on the Rhine, came dangerously close to playing the part of commander-in-chief. When Caecina's army was in retreat there were those fainthearts at headquarters who wanted to cut down the bridge over the Rhine. Agrippina prevented them. As the troops straggled in, says Tacitus, 'this noble-hearted lady played a general's part throughout these days, dispensing food and dressings to the needy and wounded with her own hands.'[30] He quotes Pliny's account of how she stood at the bridgehead, to praise and thank the legions as they came into camp. This alarmed Tiberius, who felt that something must be behind it. 'All this attention to the army was not for a foreign foe. What was left for the generals, when a woman inspects the camps, takes the salute by the standards, and even plans to distribute awards! . . . Agrippina counted for more with the army than the general or the commander.' These suspicions were played on by Sejanus, and led to the decision to recall Germanicus from his command.

The political ambitions of her daughter, Agrippina the younger, were yet more far-reaching, and for them Tacitus had no sympathy. He comments with disfavour on the position she occupied at the ceremony of Caratacus' surrender, which was made to her as well as to Claudius. 'It was a new thing, quite alien to the custom of our ancestors, that a woman should thus sit before Roman standards, but she was displaying herself as full partner in the empire her ancestors had won.'[31] And under Nero she thought to play more than a partner's rôle.

The women of the Julio-Claudians make up a remarkable gallery. To find their peers, one has to go to the women of Renaissance Italy, Lucrezia Borgia, Isabella Gonzaga, Caterina Sforza, or else to empresses of Byzantium, such as Theodora, Irene, or Zoë. Tacitus describes them with zest—the more keenly, perhaps, because in his lifetime the imperial ladies were either dull or virtuous or both, with the single exception of Berenice, visiting Rome during her brief liaison with Titus.

He is malicious towards Livia, lending his weight to the rumours (now discredited) that she plotted the deaths of successive heirs of Augustus to clear the way for her own son, Tiberius. More than that, he suggests that she may have caused the death of Augustus himself, when there seemed a risk that at the last moment he would prefer Agrippa Postumus.[32] It would seem that here Tacitus has foisted on to Livia the rôle actually played by Agrippina at the death of Claudius, hoping that the parallel will make plausible what he knows to be mere rumour. Already we have heard of the dismay Livia aroused as prospective dowager-Empress. 'There was Tiberius' mother,' men complained, 'with all her feminine excesses. We shall be the slaves of a woman. . . .' And on the judgement of the dead Augustus by the *prudentes*, she counts on the debit side. 'Livia had been a national disaster as a mother, a calamity to the house of the Caesars as a stepmother' (and a stepmother's hatreds were proverbial in the classical world).[33] In fact, she survived Augustus by fifteen years, dying in A.D. 29 at the age of eighty-six. She presented Tiberius with a problem which, on the whole, he handled with tact and dignity. It cannot have been easy for him to have her in Rome during so many years—Julia Augusta, with her wealth, her friends, her memories—and her alarming longevity. In his obituary notice of Livia, Tacitus finds some good to say. 'She preserved the chastity of her home with the strictness of an earlier age—though the ladies of that day would not have approved of her affability. A demanding mother, she was a compliant wife'—(compliant, that is, to Augustus' extra-marital affairs: 'I never take any notice of them,' she is said to have remarked). Tacitus' final judgement on her was that in her the craft of Augustus and the dissimulation of Tiberius met their match.[34] Perhaps it is really more of a compliment than he intended.

But Agrippina[35] is the most fully portrayed of the women of Tiberius' reign. We have already seen her in Germany, wife of the Commander-in-Chief, where her proud spirit and ambition marked her out. In Syria little is heard of her: it is not until after Germanicus' death, under suspicion of poisoning by Piso, that the limelight is again turned on his young widow (she was thirty-three), mother of his six (living) children, who had the blood of Augustus in her veins. On his death-bed, Germanicus had begged her to curb her ambitions, and to bow to cruel fortune. 'When she got back to Rome . . . let her not provoke the jealousy of those with more power than herself. This was said openly: in private, he is said to have revealed to her the grounds for distrusting Tiberius.'[36]

The warning about Tiberius she heeded: but she was not good at self-control. After Germanicus' death she was prostrate with grief and illness: but, although it was winter, she took ship with two of her children to carry Germanicus' ashes to Rome. 'Universal sympathy went out to this great lady, whose high marriage had once won her the respect and admiration of multitudes. Now she bore her husband's ashes in her bosom: she had no certainty of being able to avenge him . . . her very fecundity was now untimely, because it exposed her to fortune's blows.'[37] There followed the long, sad voyage. Agrippina's grief was such that she had to pause for a brief rest at Corcyra: at Brundisium the ship drew in to a harbour crowded with mourners—uncertain how to receive her, in silence, or with some phrase of greeting. 'Then, with her two children, holding the funeral urn, her eyes cast down, Agrippina left the ship. A loud groan went up from all.' The appropriate greeting had come, spontaneously. (So was it with those who saw Mrs. Kennedy, with her two children, in the terrible scenes that followed the President's death.) The funeral cortège, escorted by two companies of the Praetorian Guards, carried Germanicus' ashes to Rome, with unrestrained grief at every town on its route. Finally, they were taken to the Mausoleum of Augustus, through a crowded Rome: 'Soldiers under arms, magistrates without their badge of office, the people mustered in their tribes—all proclaimed that Rome had fallen, that hope had gone. So ready and so open was their talk that they seemed to have forgotten their rulers. But what struck Tiberius most forcibly was the universal popularity of Agrippina. "The glory of the country," they called her, "the one true descendant of Augustus, the only genuine pattern of old-fashioned virtue" '[38] (so much for Livia!).

It was Agrippina's high point of glory: in that emotional atmosphere the condemnation of Piso was inevitable, and he anticipated it by suicide. Agrippina's *pietas* was rewarded by this vengeance for her husband's death. But ahead of her lay thirteen bitter years, exposed to the suspicion of Tiberius and the open hatred of Sejanus. In 23, after the death of Drusus, Sejanus fostered rumours that Agrippina was aiming at the throne: her ambitions lent some colouring to the talk of treason. But the real attack on her did not begin until 26, and then it was by the prosecution of her friends and cousin Claudia Pulcra. There followed a painful scene between Emperor and princess. Headstrong as ever, Agrippina rushed to the Palace in full mourning, to find Tiberius sacrificing before a statue of Augustus. 'It is scarcely consistent,' she cried, 'to sacrifice to Augustus and persecute his descendants! His spirit has not passed into these dumb statues: I am its living embodiment, I spring from his divine blood!' A rash, and unnecessary reminder, which drew from Tiberius an apt quotation and no more. 'It is no injustice if you do not reign.'[39] Soon after there was another scene. Agrippina was unwell, and when Tiberius visited her she had a long fit of silent weeping. At last she came out with an

embittered *cri de cœur*. 'I am so lonely! Help me to find a husband! I am still young, and marriage is the only solace for a
virtuous woman! There are plenty of men in Rome who would
be willing to take into their home the wife and children of
Germanicus.'[40] (And any one of them, be it said, would at once
be a menace to Tiberius.) No wonder that the Emperor made
no reply.

It was at this point, with superb timing, that Sejanus struck
her down. His agents warned her that Tiberius was about to
poison her: she must never accept his hospitality. Agrippina
could not dissemble. Placed at dinner next to Tiberius, she sat
speechless, her food untouched. Tiberius passed a dish of fruit
to her: she said nothing, and handed it to her slaves. Turning to
Livia, Tiberius said: 'No wonder I have something unpleasant
in mind for a woman who makes me out to be a poisoner!'[41]
This was the breach between them, for soon after Tiberius
retired to Capri. The unpleasantness did not mature until
immediately after Livia's death in 29: then came one of those
menacing letters to the Senate, accusing Agrippina of presump-
tuous language and contumacy. The Senate hesitated. Tiberius'
real intentions were uncertain. Cotta Messalinus was ready with
a savage proposal—perhaps the death penalty. Then came a
queer twist. Junius Rusticus, whom Tiberius had appointed to
write up the Senate minutes, and was thus supposed to be in the
Emperor's confidence, advised the consuls not to put the motion.
'Sometime,' he said, 'the old gentleman might regret the destruction of the house of Germanicus!' Meanwhile the people
gathered, bearing effigies of Agrippina and Nero. Pamphlets
were circulated against Sejanus. A second letter came from
Tiberius, renewing the complaints, and demanding the matter
be considered *de novo*.

At this point the manuscript of Book V breaks off, but it was
now that Agrippina was banished to Pandateria. She survived
in exile another four years, and at least had the satisfaction of
seeing Sejanus into his grave. Then she starved herself to death
—or perhaps had been starved to look like suicide—two years

to the day after Sejanus had been killed. Tiberius did not hesitate to slander her memory, accusing her of adultery with Asinius Gallus. This, as Tacitus rightly says, was absurdly out of character. 'She was avid for power: but she had a man's vices, not a woman's frailties.'[42] ('*dominandi avida virilibus curis feminarum vitia exuerat.*') Such is his final verdict on this great lady. It also foreshadows her daughter, the younger Agrippina. But she had even more greed for power, and no scruples about using sex as a weapon to obtain it.

Valeria Messalina[43] did not want power. Her tastes were for luxury, debauchery and triumph over her rivals. The great-granddaughter of Augustus, through both sides of her family, she was married at the age of fourteen to the pedantic and elderly Claudius (elderly in Roman terms; he was forty-eight). She did her dynastic duty and produced two children, Octavia and Britannicus; after which she embarked on that career of high scandal in high places which has earned her a secure place in any list of the notorious women of history. So fine a flower of sensuality did not grow in isolation. Messalina was the product of a brilliant, wealthy and dissolute society, which began in the reign of Gaius, as a reaction against the gloom of Tiberius' last years, and persisted under Claudius. It was distinguished by its fashionable ladies, such as Julia Livilla, sister of Gaius, Lollia Paulina, whose enormous wealth and flamboyant jewels are recorded by Pliny, and Poppaea Sabina, 'the most charming woman of her time,' and mother of the even more charming Poppaea Sabina of Nero's reign. United by ties of the deadliest hatred, these ladies quarrelled and intrigued over estates, jewels, husbands and lovers. In this war of the larger cats, Messalina had more lethal fangs than her rivals. The enormous wealth of the imperial house was hers to command. Claudius was complacent. The imperial freedmen were ready to connive if there were pickings for them: the Emperor's favourites, such as Publius Suillius and Lucius Vitellius, were ready to help with intrigue or prosecution. So long as she kept her footing with Claudius, no one could stand in Messalina's way.

Tacitus' account of the early years of her marriage is lost, but
when the manuscript begins again somewhere in Book XI we
have an account of her greatest triumph.[44] She wanted to humili-
ate Poppaea Sabina, who had ousted her in the favours of the
ballet-dancer Mnester; she wanted to get for herself the finest
gardens in Rome—the Gardens of Lucullus, on the Pincian Hill.
Now these gardens were then owned by Valerius Asiaticus, the
wealthy and powerful senator from Gaul, who had so splendidly
embellished his native Vienne. By a brilliant right and left, the
young Empress brought them both down. First Valerius
Asiaticus was accused of plotting against Claudius, with his
wealth and his powerful following in Gaul. He was fetched in
chains from the pleasure resort of Baiae, denied a hearing in the
Senate, and cross-examined in Claudius' bedchamber.

The morals of a whole society are distilled in Tacitus' account
of this secret trial—or rather, its tone, for morals it had none.
Suillius first accused Asiaticus of corrupting the troops, both by
bribery and sexual licence: then the intrigue with Poppaea
Sabina was brought up: the last charge was one of effeminacy.
This stung, and Asiaticus spoke for the first time: 'Ask your
sons, Suillius,' he said; 'they will confess that I am a man!'
Then he began his defence, with all the eloquence of Gallic
oratory. Claudius was deeply moved. Even Messalina was in
tears, and slipped from the room to dry her eyes. As she did so,
she whispered to Vitellius, 'Don't let the defendant get away!'
Then she hurried off to complete the ruin of Poppaea Sabina,
sending agents who drove her to suicide. (This was concealed
from Claudius, and when Poppaea's husband dined in the Palace
a few days later, he was asked 'Why didn't you bring your wife?'
'She died,' was the short reply.)[45] Meanwhile, there was Valerius
Asiaticus. After a further burst of tears, Lucius Vitellius urged
the claims of his past services, and proposed that he should be
allowed to choose his own death. Claudius agreed. Valerius
Asiaticus, as might have been expected, died with style. 'After
his usual exercise in the gymnasium, he took a bath, and dined
in good spirits. Then, remarking that it would have been better

to die from Tiberius' plotting or Gaius' brutality than from a woman's treachery and Vitellius' filthy tongue, he opened his veins.' Before this, he had inspected his own funeral pyre, and ordered it to be moved to another part of the gardens, lest the flames should damage the foliage of the trees. So the Gardens of Lucullus passed unimpaired to their new owner.

The fantastic affair of Messalina's marriage with Gaius Silius, which led to her downfall and death only a few months later, has already been mentioned. It is to be noted that the more spectacular tales of her debauchery find no warrant in Tacitus. Such are found, for example, in the Sixth Satire of Juvenal, where she is shown slipping away from the Palace to play her nightly part as a common prostitute in a public brothel, picking up her fee, and leaving still unsatisfied.[46] They are almost certainly fictitious—attempts, prurient or malicious, to fill in the details of that secret memorandum which Narcissus handed to Claudius (See p. 47). The historic Messalina does not need embroidery.

Agrippina[47] the younger is much the most important of the Julio-Claudian women in the pages of Tacitus. Daughter of Germanicus, sister of Gaius, fourth wife (and niece) of Claudius, mother of Nero—she stood at the centre of all the intrigues of the palace for most of thirty years, linking the reign of Tiberius with that of Nero. Tacitus studied her memoirs with care and has given her a fully rounded portrayal, in which one divines something of that love-hate attitude he felt for Tiberius. The parallels—and the contrasts—between her life and that of her mother are always to the fore. We meet her first, in Tacitus, as a young princess, bestowed by Tiberius on Domitius Ahenobarbus. Suetonius[48] describes him as detestable in every way, and gives several unpleasant examples of his sadism. Their marriage lasted nine years, and produced the future Emperor Nero. She does not reappear in Tacitus until the year 48, when she is put forward as one of the three possible choices in place of the defunct Messalina.

Much had happened, in the interval, to Agrippina: some of it has a bearing on the woman she became in her days of power. She followed Gaius to Germany in 39: by now she was the lover of his possible successor, Aemilius Lepidus, and when he plotted against Gaius and was executed at Mainz, she was involved in his fall. Gaius' revenge on his sister showed his highly individual sense of humour. Their mother Agrippina had made her famous and pious winter voyage from Syria to Rome, carrying her husband's ashes. So the daughter was given her lover's ashes, in parody, and made to carry them across the Alps to Rome. Meanwhile, her brother sold her furniture and effects at auction at Lyons. So Dio Cassius[49] avers, and it accords with what we know of Gaius. Once this pious mission had been discharged, she was banished to an island, to be recalled in 41 by Claudius. Somehow, she avoided a clash with Messalina: only after her death did she use her charms to lure Claudius into marriage. There was the problem of incest: an obstacle, but it could be removed by legislation. And there was Lucius Vitellius again, so useful at these junctures. On his proposal, the Senate legalised marriage with a brother's daughter. It cannot be said to have opened the floodgates. Apart from the Emperor, only one other person took advantage of it.[50]

Married to Claudius, this Clytemnestra of a woman pursued three objectives with relentless vigour—to gather political power in her own hands, to strike down her enemies and to advance her own son Nero at the expense of Britannicus, Claudius' son by Messalina. She was remarkably successful in all three. 'From that time,' says Tacitus, 'Roman society was transformed. Everything was done at a woman's orders—and that woman no Messalina, who made public affairs serve only her appetite. Agrippina's was almost a masculine despotism . . . she had an unbounded desire for money, but only as a support for authority.'[51] She was granted the title of Augusta, the first Empress to hold it since Livia. She presided with Claudius on major occasions of state, as at the surrender of Caratacus, or the draining of the Fucine Lake. A long list of her personal enemies —Lollia Paulina, Statilius Taurus, Domitia Lepida—were driven to death or exile. Usually their estates went to Agrippina, or were shared with her supporters. Nero was married to Octavia, and Britannicus had clearly been pushed to the rear.

But, in the year 54, things began to go wrong. There were ominous portents: among them, the unprecedented deaths of Roman magistrates of every rank—a quaestor, an aedile, a tribune, a praetor, and a consul, within a few months. It only needed an Emperor—or an Empress? And Claudius was making alarming remarks. 'My fate,' he said on one occasion, 'is to endure the wickedness of my wives: but I punish them in the end.'[52] Two things played into Agrippina's hands. Narcissus had to go to Sinuessa to recover from an illness, and a new poison was invented by the famous Locusta. So Claudius ate the famous mushroom—the food of the gods, as Nero aptly called it—and Nero was on the throne his mother had won for him.

At the outset of Nero's reign, Agrippina's mastery seemed secure. The Emperor was a boy of seventeen. Seneca and Burrus, his advisers, owed their position to her. But, in fact, her influence declined—slowly at first, then rapidly, until Nero determined on her murder and Seneca and Burrus felt bound to connive at it. Agrippina fought a rearguard action with the greatest skill. She actually espoused the cause of Britannicus for a while. Nero poisoned him. Then she tried to influence Nero through his mistress Acte, whom she had opposed at first. Incest had paid in entrapping her uncle: she did not fail to use it on her son. But Nero had in the meantime found younger attractions in Poppaea, and it was through Poppaea, in the end, that he was brought to plan his mother's death. Through that, and through her own insupportable temper, of which Tacitus gives examples. On one occasion, Nero inspected the magnificent gowns and jewels that had been worn by the imperial ladies. 'He selected a dress and some jewels, and sent them—generously and spontaneously—as a gift to his mother. There was nothing niggardly about his gift, for he sent her the finest of all. But Agrippina complained that he was not adding to her wardrobe, but keeping her out of the rest: he was giving her a small dole only, though he owed everything to her.[53] This was just before the murder of Britannicus, which she brought on by suddenly taking him up. She threatened to take him to the barracks of the Praetorian Guard: that would be the place for a hearing between Germanicus' daughter on the one side, and the cripple Burrus, with his deformed hand, and the refugee Seneca, with his professor's voice, who claimed to rule the world. 'Gesticulating, screaming abuse, she would call to witness the deified Claudius, the ghosts of the Silani, and all the other crimes she had committed in vain.'[54] Britannicus' death soon followed. Then she took up Octavia. At this point Nero removed her from the Palace, and took away her personal guard.

'Nothing in human affairs,' says Tacitus, 'is so transitory and precarious as the reputation for power without the means to support it. Agrippina's threshold was at once deserted: no one comforted her, no one came to call, except for a few women, who could have done so from hatred as much as from love.'[55] The psychology is shrewd. Among these unloving visitors was a former friend, now a bitter enemy, Junia Silana, distinguished by her birth, beauty and lasciviousness. She saw a chance to destroy Agrippina by persuading Nero that she intended to marry Rubellius Plautus, one of Augustus' descendants, and control the Empire once more. Nero was panic-stricken, and was calmed with difficulty. Agrippina's spirit was not broken: she cleared herself of the charge and spoke with contempt of Silana: her objects were—as ever—vengeance on her enemies and rewards for her friends.

This was in 55. It was four years later that Nero took the decision to kill his mother, on Poppaea's prompting and his own feeling that 'wherever she was, she was intolerable.' Book XIV launches at once into the narrative of the matricide, in thirteen chapters which are perhaps the most highly-wrought passage in the *Annals*.[56] It has been criticised for showing a wilful neglect of historic proportion. Perhaps. But matricide is an appalling crime; when the victim is an Empress it has historic importance, the more, as Tacitus represents it as the turning point in Nero's

DT

reign, after which evil would always prevail. Given the Tacitean formula of depicting history as the clash of personalities— nowhere more evident than in his account of Nero's reign— this was bound to be a cardinal episode, and it should be read as a whole. Nowhere else does history come closer to poetry— tragedy, perhaps, rather than epic. The characters are shown in thought and action. Nero is at first, the smiling villain, later to pass a night of terror when the deed was bungled, and conscious of its full enormity only when it was done. His indecision is in contrast with the steadfast villainy of Anicetus, commander of the fleet at Misenum, ingenious in inventing the collapsible cabin which so nearly smothered its victim, resolute in super- vising the final butchery by conventional means. A good First Murderer, he overshadows Seneca and Burrus, who perhaps were not privy to the plot and only came into it when it was Agrippina's life or Nero's.

Agrippina, in this last tragedy of her life, moves on the heroic scale. She swims away from the wrecked ship, though wounded, and is picked up by men in skiffs and taken ashore. Safe, for the moment, in her Lucrine villa, she realises that the only way to escape the plot is to feign ignorance. She sends a messenger to Nero, announcing her escape from a terrible accident. He does not return. Instead, Anicetus and his assassins burst into the room. She is struck on the head by a club; as the centurion drew his sword for the death blow, she thrust out her stomach and cried, 'Strike my womb!' Then she died of many wounds. All these fearful events are enacted on a bright, starry night, amid the calm beauties of the Bay of Naples.

A short but wonderfully evocative passage—no obituary— and we are done with Agrippina. 'She was cremated that very night, with the briefest of rites, and on a couch taken from a dining-room. So long as Nero lived, her grave was not covered by a mound, nor enclosed in a stone tomb. Later, her household staff saw to it that she had a small mound: it stood on the road to Misenum, where the villa of Caesar the Dictator commands from on high a wide view over the bay (*quae subiectos sinus editissima prospectat*).' Kenneth Quinn has rightly commented on the dying fall of these last words. 'The effect of the two words *editissima prospectat* (to which sound and rhythm contribute much), is indescribable. We are left with a scene of peace and seclusion, uncontaminated now by any contact with the Julio-Claudian line, of whose mad exploits Tacitus made himself the historian.'[57]

But indeed, the associations of Misenum run further back in time than Julius Caesar. When Aeneas went to seek the Golden Bough at the bidding of the Sibyl of Cumae, he left an unburied comrade on the shore, '*indigna morte peremptum*.' This was Misenus, the trumpeter, who had followed Aeneas from Troy.[58] He was given a funeral, with archaic Latin rites, lovingly described by Virgil. Afterwards, 'dutiful Aeneas built him a huge sepulchre, and placed on it the hero's weapons, his arms, and his trumpet—all this on that high mountain, now called Misenus after him, and it will keep his name immortal through the ages.'[59]

Such were the simple pieties when the founder of the Julian house came to Misenum. But Tacitus has to do with its last descendant, Nero—Orestes. Flattery, on the grand scale, may nerve him to blacken his mother's memory, and to take up again his career of folly and wickedness. The people of Campania serve as a fickle chorus in this mini-tragedy. First they gather anxiously for news of Agrippina's safety, then they congratulate Nero at escaping her plot to murder him. 'But the face of nature does not change like the face of man: here before his gaze was the grim spectacle of that sea and shore, now re-echoing (as some thought) with trumpet blasts from the high hills, and with keenings from his mother's grave. So Nero left for Neapolis.'[60]

Poppaea we have already seen. Poor little Octavia was no match for her: divorced by Nero on the grounds of barrenness, she was then accused of adultery (by Anicetus!) and abortion. Her tragic life moved Tacitus to sympathy. 'For Octavia, the very day of her marriage had been the beginning of her death. She had come to a house where she had known nothing but sorrow: her father had been poisoned, to be soon followed by her

brother: her maid had been preferred to herself: then Poppaea
could only achieve marriage by ruining the legitimate wife. . . .
So this young wife, in her twenties, passed into exile among
centurions and soldiers . . . after a few days came the order for
death. . . . She was bound in chains, and arteries opened in every
limb, but she was so frightened that the blood would not flow.
The steam from a hot bath put an end to her. Then—a refinement of cruelty—her head was cut off, taken to Rome, and
shown to Poppaea.'[61] The whole picture is one of helpless
innocence. But there must have been a more positive side to
Octavia—she won the love of the Roman people, and the lasting
loyalties of her slaves. Yet one wonders by what influences, of
heredity or environment, the children of Messalina could have
been so noble as Octavia and her brother?

The dark figure of Tiberius is contrasted at the beginning of
his reign with the heroic and radiant Germanicus. But not for
long. At his triumph in 17, forebodings filled the minds of the
spectators. 'Brief and unlucky,' they reflected, 'are the darlings
of the Roman people!'[62] Two years later, Germanicus lay dead
at Antioch, amid universal grief. He was only thirty-four, and
men compared him with Alexander, who had died at much the
same age. Germanicus is indeed the one truly virtuous figure in
the pages of Tacitus—the only one, that is to say, who is both
good and great. Nor is Tacitus alone in this. A very similar
picture is to be found in Suetonius, and it is echoed in Dio.[63] It
is a compound of many ingredients, some due to historical
tradition, but some deriving from the character of the young
prince. In the first place, he was the heir to the popularity of his
father Drusus, whose military successes in Germany had been
outstanding, and who was credited—rightly or not—with the
design of restoring the Republic. And it is clear that Germanicus
himself possessed a charming personality. He was gracious and
kindly, and he did not lose these qualities in the two great
offices he held, first in Germany and then in the East.

The contrast with the stiffness and the haughtiness of Tiberius was painful. Men of the senatorial order could work with a man like Germanicus, without feeling that they had lost *aequalitas*. He was modest and gracious in his behaviour towards allies, and is credited with being merciful towards his enemies, though a German scholar has remarked that this quality is not conspicuous in his behaviour towards the Germans. He was the kind of general who says 'Come on!' and that is a man the troops will follow. In the battle in the forest of 16, he charges the most difficult enemy position at the head of a cohort of the Praetorian Guard. One thinks of Shakespeare's Henry V, and the resemblance is enhanced because Germanicus, too, wandered unknown at night through the camp, and heard his soldiers speak of him in terms only of praise.[64] His diplomatic mission in the East seems to have been carried out successfully (see p. 205), and Tacitus shows how highly he was regarded by the King of Parthia. But his qualities as a general are another matter, and the comparison with Alexander the Great has always been boggled at by modern scholars.

It was first made at the time of his funeral in Syria. Memories of Alexander were still fresh in that former Seleucid kingdom, and it may well be that the comparison began its life on the lips of Greek orators, expressing official condolences on the death of the great Roman. How sincerely they may have been meant it is impossible to say. But at least they will have been gratefully received, for as will be shown below (see p. 203), the Alexander myth exercised a potent influence on Roman commanders in the East. Note also, that Tacitus does not endorse it directly, though he does so implicitly and, as has been pointed out, in terms that could hint at Trajan.

It is hard to make sense of Tacitus' account of Germanicus' campaigns in western Germany, or to see the strategic and political ends they were meant to serve. Indeed the historian himself seems in doubt on these points. In A.D. 14, for example, we are told 'This was a period with no wars on hand except that against the Germans—a war undertaken not so much to extend the Imperial frontiers, nor for any worthwhile advantage, as to

wipe out the disgrace of the Army lost under Quintilius Varus.'[65]
Two years later, Germanicus sets up a trophy commemorating
the conquest of all the tribes between the Rhine and the Elbe. In
the same year he asks the Emperor for another season's campaigning to bring the war to a conclusion. This is not granted, he
is recalled to Rome for a triumph celebrated on May 26th,
A.D. 17, over all the peoples as far as the Elbe. Tacitus' comment
is: 'The war he had been prevented from finishing was, for this
purpose, regarded as finished.'

But if the citation for the triumph was fraudulent, so was the
inscription on the trophy. It may be accepted that there was a
need for a prestige triumph against Arminius, but was this not
achieved at Idistaviso? Again, the Rhine Army no doubt
needed action against the enemy to purge its mutinies. But why
were the campaigns on such a scale, and continued for so long?
It is of course possible that the solution is to be sought in
Tiberius himself. The Rhine armies had tempted Germanicus
with the offer of the throne; Tiberius may have come to the
conclusion that this general and this army would be better
occupied chasing Arminius in the Teutoberger Wald than
marching on Rome. After all, something might have happened
to the general in those forests, as it had done to Drusus years
before. But in fact, Germanicus did better than anticipated, and
then he could not be allowed to push his victories too far. Such
an innuendo would have been wholly congenial to Tacitus, but
he does not mention it. The victorious general recalled by a
jealous Emperor was a pattern he could recognise. Perhaps he
saw Agricola and Domitian prefigured in Germanicus and
Tiberius.

Tacitus, who had such insight into evil, bestows as a kind of
accolade a primacy in wickedness on Tiberius' great minister,
Lucius Aelius Sejanus. He sees it as something more than
human: 'it was the anger of heaven against the Roman state, to
which Sejanus' career and his fall, were equally calamitous.'[66]
None of his characters is more cleverly stage-managed. Sejanus
first appears in the *Annals* in 14, when Tiberius sends him on a

mission to the mutinous armies in Pannonia.[67] He is already Praetorian Prefect, and possesses great influence with Tiberius. His special task is to act as advisor (*rector juveni*) to the young Drusus, who is in command of the rebellious army. Nine years later he will poison that prince, and seduce his wife. The tragic irony of the phrase *rector juveni* would not be lost on Tacitus' audience. We hear little of him for the next few years, apart from glimpses of a grey eminence. In 16, at the height of the German campaigns, he warns Tiberius against the inordinate ambitions of Germanicus and Agrippina, knowing that Tiberius will store it up in his retentive mind.[68] At his trial in 20, Piso is tricked by Sejanus out of producing in the Senate a secret document which was thought to contain incriminating evidence against Tiberius.[69] But Sejanus is being reserved for a dramatic entry to the stage, and this comes at the beginning of Book IV.

Here, in the year 23, is the turning point of the reign of Tiberius, when that Emperor became cruel or entrusted power to cruel men. The root and cause of the change sprang from Aelius Sejanus, commander of the Guard. It is on the eve of his great crime, the poisoning of Drusus, that Tacitus will give us an account of his character and earlier career. His character is described in terms, which—as has been shown—convey unmistakable echoes of Catiline in Sallust.[70] 'He combined physical energy and audacity of mind; keeping his own secrets, he was prone to traduce others. In him were blended servility and arrogance: behind a mask of modesty there was an unrivalled appetite for power. Hence his extravagance and luxury, hence too—even more in evidence—his untiring activity. Aimed at the throne, this is as dangerous as excess.' His family origins are stated in simple and deprecating terms. He was born at Volsinii, and his father Seius Sejanus was a Roman knight. Nothing is said about his mother, but in fact from Velleius and other sources we learn a good deal. Her name was Cosconia Gallita, and she was of the highest Roman aristocracy, being connected with the Cornelii Lentuli and the Junii. Moreover, three of his brothers held the consulship.

Tacitus is building up a picture of a humble adventurer, but this is far from the truth. Sejanus might be a *novus homo*, but he was a very respectable one, socially at least on a par with the great minister of Augustus, Marcus Agrippa. But Tacitus' purpose becomes apparent in the scornful tones with which he speaks of Drusus' wife Livia condescending to commit adultery with Sejanus. 'So this princess, the grand-niece of Augustus, the daughter-in-law of Tiberius, the mother of Drusus' children, disgraced herself, her ancestors, and her posterity in an intrigue with a provincial adulterer. For risk and infamy, she sacrificed honour and position.'[71] Was ever princess so berated? Morally, Livia may have been wrong: socially, the fault was venial.

There is little doubt that Tacitus is right in stressing the peculiar powers exercised by Sejanus as sole commander of the Praetorian Guard. He was the first who had concentrated these troops and stationed them in a permanent camp in Rome, the Castra Praetoria. This must have been done somewhere about the year 20. He was at pains to see that his own nominees held commands, and cultivated individual centurions and even soldiers. Sejanus next set himself, according to Tacitus, to remove all possible competitors for influence with Tiberius. This brought him into conflict with the young princes of the imperial house, and with the widowed Agrippina. The murder of Drusus was achieved in an atrocious way. Having first made Livia his mistress, Sejanus then procured the assassination of Drusus by poison. We are asked to believe that this crime, committed in 23, was kept from Tiberius' knowledge for eight years. But Tiberius was more cunning than Sejanus, and never gave him any extraordinary command, let alone the promise of the succession. Above all, Tiberius employed the method in which he excelled—procrastination. In 26 Sejanus was bold enough to write to the Emperor, asking to be allowed to marry Livia. He received a temporising reply and a vague promise. 'I have schemes of my own, additional ties to link you with me more closely. I say nothing of them now. All I shall say is this: your qualities, your devotion to me, render nothing beyond your reach. In due course, I shall disclose them either to the Senate or to the people.'[72] The wording, of course, is that of Tacitus. But the recipient of such a letter must often have wondered how it was to be construed. And in the end, an ambiguous Tiberian letter was to be the downfall of Sejanus. Meanwhile, he had five more years of almost supreme power.

It was in this same year, 26, that Tiberius took his decision to retire to Campania, leaving Sejanus in charge at Rome. Accompanying the Emperor, Sejanus had the chance of rendering him a singular service. Tiberius possessed a villa at a place called Spelunca, where a natural cave was fitted out as a dining-room. Suddenly the rocks at the entrance of the cave collapsed, and several of the attendants were buried. This caused a general panic, and the guests at the dinner rushed out. 'Sejanus, on hands and knees, covered the Emperor against falling rocks, and was found in that position when soldiers came to the rescue. This increased his power: though he urged to disastrous courses his advice did carry the weight of one who was personally disinterested.' Modern archaeology has produced what could well be confirmation of this incident.[73] At the place now called Sperlunga, the Italian archaeologist, Jacobi, discovered in 1957 a very large number of ancient statues, most of them broken and shattered by the fall of rocks. It is not certain that the statues belong to the age of Tiberius. But if this is not the cave mentioned by Tacitus, the coincidence would be remarkable. Perhaps too, it would be remarkable if the rock-fall which brought Sejanus such good luck was wholly natural.

After 26, we hear of the continuing intrigues of Sejanus against Agrippina and her son Nero, and the ruthless use he made of criminal charges to bring down his enemies. We also hear how he got his own nominees into important posts in the provinces, particularly those which carried an army command.[74] All is leading up to the grand climax—the fall of Sejanus—which we do not have in Tacitus.[75] It was on October 18th, 31, that there occurred the famous sitting of the Senate at which the long ambiguous letter of Tiberius was produced. As it was read out, it became gradually clear to the Senate that the great favourite was to be overthrown. He was put to death, his statues were destroyed, his body lay three days by the banks of the Tiber to be insulted by the Roman people. Finally it was thrown into the river, and there began the persecution of the adherents of Sejanus which was so calamitous to the state.

It will be clear how the dice had been loaded against Sejanus. If Tiberius' administration prior to the year 23 was generally good, and if Sejanus was highly influential with him—'the partner of my labours'—then Sejanus deserves a share of the credit for those years. To admit this is not to agree with those apologists who maintain that Sejanus' ambitions just before his fall were really due to his care for the future of the state, knowing that after Tiberius' death it could scarcely be entrusted to Gaius or to Claudius.[76] That is to go too far. But we need to understand the extraordinary malignancy of the Tacitean account, in which are to be found combined the senatorial tradition, hostile to a *novus homo* who had risen so high, and who had brought ruin on their own families, and also the understandable vindictiveness found in the memoirs of the younger Agrippina against the man who had been the great enemy of the house of Germanicus.

Whether Macro, who succeeded Sejanus as Commander of the Guard, was really a worse man is something we do not know from Tacitus. At least his ambitions did not have so much scope: he was forced to commit suicide in 38, only one year after the accession of Gaius. It appears from Philo Judaeus that he tried to restrain the irresponsible young Emperor, and to lecture him on the art of government—both necessary but hazardous tasks.[77] After his death Gaius reverted to the former system of appointing two praetorian prefects at a time, and they do not play a leading part in Claudius' early years.

But in 51, thanks to the influence of Agrippina, a notable appointment was made, that of Sextus Afranius Burrus, who held sole command until his death in 62, and of whom Tacitus

gives a favourable impression. Burrus[78] came from Gallia Narbonensis, very probably from that attractive and prosperous
city of Vocontio, the modern Vaison. If he helped Agrippina's
intrigues in Claudius' last years, he withstood her when Nero
succeeded; there would have been a reign of terror then but for
Burrus and Seneca. Tacitus praises their mutual sympathy,
uncommon in those who held power. They established by different means an equal influence over Nero—Burrus by his soldierly
qualities and his austere character: Seneca by his lessons in
oratory and his dignified courtesy. They helped each other to
control Nero's dangerous years of adolescence, and joined
forces to oppose the savagery of Agrippina. In the end the double
burden proved too much, but at least they gave the Roman world
the five years of good government which became proverbial as
the *quinquennium Neronis*. We have seen how they were driven
to condone, and even to assist, the murder of Agrippina. From
condoning matricide it was a short step to indulging Nero's
artistic ambitions. Having failed to restrict them to chariot-
driving, Burrus was forced to witness Nero's début as a lyre-
player at the Festival of Youth[79]—a very disorderly occasion in
all respects. The audience was swollen by a troop of soldiers,
with officers and centurions, and also the Commander of the
Guard—grieving and applauding ('*maerens Burrus ac laudans*').
Three years later Burrus lay dying of what seems to have been
cancer of the throat, though there was a strong suspicion that
Nero had accelerated the process by ordering his throat to be
painted with poison. When the Emperor came to visit him and
asked how he was, he simply turned his face to the wall and said,
'*I* am doing well enough.' His death caused general sorrow.
Men remembered his virtues, and of his two successors, one was
a hardened criminal.[80]

Tacitus finds no good to say of Ofonius Tigellinus,[81] Nero's
aider and abetter in every kind of debauchery. His death—by
popular demand—in 69 elicits one of Tacitus' most savage
obituary notices. 'Ofonius Tigellinus was distinguished by
humble birth, the boyhood of a pervert, and the old age of a

debauchee. The command of the Watch, and that of the Praetorian Guard, and other such rewards of virtue, he had gained by vice—and attractive short cuts. Then he went in for sadism and avarice, the characteristic vices of maturity. Nero he corrupted to every kind of infamy (though he practised some Nero never knew), and ended by deceiving and betraying him. The clamour for his punishment was more insistent than for that of any other man. . . . Tigellinus was taking the waters at Sinuessa when the message reached him that his end was near. Surrounded by his mistresses, amid fornications, caresses, and other unseemly delays, he cut his throat with a razor. A belated dishonourable death brought discredit even on his infamous life.'[82]

A feature of the Principate was the opportunities it gave to the ablest of the imperial freedmen to rise to unprecedented influence and wealth—notoriously so, under Claudius and Nero.[83] This is a class of men—mostly Greeks and Orientals— of whom Tacitus writes usually with loathing and invariably with contempt. He does not explain the reasons which led Claudius to set up an elaborately organised Civil Service, with its great offices each under the charge of a freedman. The *ab epistulis* was a secretariat handling all official correspondence, the *a rationibus* dealt with finance, *a libellis* with petitions, *a cognitionibus* was the legal department, and so on. All this gave the Emperor an efficient Civil Service—which was long overdue. But it also gave to the men in charge almost unlimited powers of patronage, intrigue and self-advancement, and it is this that Tacitus seizes on.

The personalities of Claudius' powerful freedmen are vividly portrayed, especially those of Pallas and Narcissus, whose bitter rivalry was a leading factor of court intrigues. Pallas, in charge *a rationibus*, was the reigning favourite in 48, but he lost ground to Narcissus through failure of nerve over the Messalina affair (see pp. 44ff). This he recovered the next year by his successful backing of Agrippina as the new wife for Claudius: henceforward as supporter, confidential agent and lover, his fate was closely bound up with hers. In 50 he was able to persuade Claudius to adopt her son Domitius, the future Emperor Nero—fatal, in the event, for Claudius' own son Britannicus. Perhaps his influence was at its height in 52, when the Senate decreed a vote of thanks, a grant of 15,000,000 *sesterces*, and an honorary inscription to Pallas who, 'though descended from ancient Arcadian kings, had rather thought of the public good than of his noble lineage, and allowed himself to be numbered among the Emperor's servants.'[84] Tacitus has a sardonic comment for such flattery (see p. 121). When Nero succeeded, prospects for Pallas must have seemed even more brilliant, but it turned out otherwise. Nero did not relish haughtiness 'so inappropriate to his station,' and when he turned violently against Agrippina's supporters, Pallas was dismissed from office, from which, Tacitus says, he virtually ruled the Empire. Watching him leave the Palatine with his huge train of attendants Nero remarked 'There goes Pallas to swear his hands are clean!'—for Pallas had very wisely stipulated that there should be no going back over his past actions, and that his accounts with the state should be taken as balanced.[85] Balanced, that is, with a substantial sum to Pallas' credit, and, in Nero's view, it was his duty to die as soon as possible and leave it to his Emperor. This Pallas failed to appreciate, and, since he was thoughtless enough to survive into extreme old age, Nero poisoned him off in 62.

Narcissus[86] was private secretary (*ab epistulis*) to Claudius, and in 43 had discharged an important mission by persuading a reluctant army to embark for the invasion of Britain: it was through his influence that the future emperor Vespasian had been put in command of the Second Legion for that expedition. Narcissus' rôle at the fall of Messalina has already been described. The triumph it brought him was short-lived, and he came to repent of it, for the hostility of Agrippina bore hard on him in his later years. His loyalty to Claudius was such that he was willing to risk his life in that Emperor's service, and towards the end of the reign he pinned all his hopes on Britannicus, bidding him grow up fast, scatter his father's enemies, and take vengeance on his mother's murderers. He was also harassed by illness, and it was while he was taking a cure at Sinuessa that the murder of Claudius was carried through. Narcissus—not unnaturally—was one of the first victims of the new reign; he was hurried off to prison, harshly treated there, and committed suicide. Oddly enough, Nero opposed his death, since Narcissus' qualities of greed and prodigality were nicely attuned to his vices. This was in 54.

Callistus is a more shadowy figure, for the book is lost in which Tacitus describes the part he played in the assassination of Gaius Caesar in 41—not the first time, according to Dio Cassius,[87] in which he had taken part in plots against that Emperor. His experience in that reign had taught him to move cautiously, and in 48 he refused to take part in any drastic move against Messalina. At the auction of brides for Claudius his candidate was Lollia Paulina, and it seems that his influence did not survive her rejection. No doubt Agrippina saw to that.

Nero's freedmen form a less striking group. Polycleitus amassed a huge fortune, and was sent to Britain to inquire into the origins and aftermath of the rebellion of Boudicca. His stately passage through the provinces draws a ferocious comment from Tacitus (see p. 43).[88] It should be said that his recommendations seem to have been liberal and salutary. Helius, who was in charge of the imperial estates in Asia, was responsible with the *procurator*, Publius Egnatius Celer, for the first crime of Nero's reign—the poisoning of Junius Silanus, governor of the province, 'a man of mature age, blameless life, and a descendant of the Caesars.' Later, Helius[89] was brought to Rome, and gained Nero's confidence to such an extent that he was left in Rome as the Emperor's personal representative during Nero's tour of Greece (67). After Nero's death he transferred his allegiance to Galba. Of Nero's other freedmen, we find Antonius Felix behaving with cruelty and licentiousness as *procurator* in Judaea, and of Acratus plundering the art treasures of Greece for the Golden House.[90] The appointment of Balbillus as Prefect of Egypt is noted without comment. Never do we hear any good of a freedman.

In the year 69 there were plenty of pickings for the freedmen of successive Emperors, but they had to be gathered quickly. The challenge was not declined.[91] Icelus, freedman of Galba, plundered more extensively in the seven months after Nero's death than Polycleitus had done throughout his reign. His record was surpassed, in four months, by Vitellius' freedman Asiaticus, whom Tacitus calls 'a filthy slave.' His former status as a slave determined his punishment when the Flavians won power—he was crucified. These men had to work in trying times. The first two Flavian Emperors kept their freedmen under tight control, although later Domitian made some use of them. But they never again held such power as under Claudius and Nero, and under Trajan the posts they had once held were filled by equestrians.

An especial object of fear and loathing to the entire senatorial class was the operation of the law of treason (*maiestas*) and the opening it gave to the detested class of informers or *delatores*. This evil was most pronounced in the reigns of Tiberius, Nero and Domitian. Its calamitous powers derived from a very curious feature of Roman law—the absence of any form of state prosecutor or attorney-general.[92] Prosecutions, whether in a private or a public suit, were initiated by individuals. They laid information; if they so wished they also acted as prosecutors, and were rewarded by a fixed portion of the property of the defendant if convicted. Informers of this kind flourished under the Principate, and did not confine themselves by any means to cases of treason. In particular, the social legislation passed by Augustus gave opportunity for a great deal of prying into the affairs of citizens, until, as Tacitus said, the remedy was worse than the disease. But it was the law of *maiestas* that gave the informers their chance on a really large scale.

Provided with a permanent court under Sulla, the law of treason had been confined to major cases of assault on the dignity of the state. But now the dignity of the state was embodied in the person of the Emperor. It was natural that attempts on his life should be punished with the greatest severity; understandable that certain over-sensitive Emperors should also concern themselves with matters of criminal libel on themselves or on other members of the imperial family. This last development took place in the reign of Augustus.

Tiberius, asked early in his reign whether charges of treason should be brought before the court, replied with the ominous words, 'the laws must be enforced.'[93] The informers took this as a signal to go ahead, and brought a number of more or less trivial charges, which at first Tiberius tried to restrain. But it soon got out of hand. By 18 we are told that the charge of treason was the usual makeweight to every accusation. It was an opportunity for the unscrupulous orator, promising rich rewards for what Tacitus called 'a dangerous and bloody form of eloquence.'[94] The great *delatores* built up their own staff of private detectives, and indeed, it is not to be doubted, of *agents provocateurs* as well. We know from the history of Nazi Germany how such a system could poison social life. Acquaintances would say to each other, on parting, *Sie haben auch etwas gesagt* ('you too said something incriminating'). The great *delatores*, armed with the information they had gathered, would attack their private enemies, or sometimes simply people of wealth and prominence, hoping to secure reward on their conviction.

It was an odious system, destructive of the very fabric of society. Why then was it allowed to continue? One reason is that assassination was in a very real sense the occupational risk of the first-century Emperors. Suetonius, in his lives of the twelve Caesars regularly records the attempts made on them. And, as Domitian himself complained, assassination plots are never believed until they are successful. He was to provide a dead example of this truth. But, granted this, why did Emperors not provide themselves with a system of secret police and trusted prosecutors of their own? Probably because this would have been so highly invidious; it was better to allow the odium to rest on the *delatores* themselves, who could always be brought down when they were no longer of use. In the first century then, good Emperors might afford to dispense with encouraging the *delatores*, as was the case with Vespasian and Titus. Bad Emperors could hardly afford to do so, if they wished to survive. In the late empire recourse was had to a system of secret police, the dreaded *agentes in rebus*. But in the first century, those Emperors who wished to do so were content to foster a system which had its origins in republican practice. It was left to Trajan to say that he did not wish his dignity to rest on terrorising or endangering the citizens.

The men who exploited this hateful system of delation are high on Tacitus' list of villains. Under Tiberius there is Fulcinius Trio,[95] 'eager to win himself a bad reputation,' who played a part in the two most notorious trials of the period, those of Libo and Piso, but who eventually (35) fell foul of Tiberius, whom he described in his will as a man in his dotage, almost an exile because of long absence from Rome. Trio committed suicide before he could be brought to trial. Then there are Bruttedius Niger and Junius Otho, both protégés of Sejanus, and involved in his fall. In 22 they attacked Junius Silanus on charges of sacrilege against Augustus and treason against Tiberius. They are sharply differentiated by Tacitus. Junius Otho[96] was a former elementary schoolmaster, raised to the Senate by Sejanus: 'even these obscure origins were dishonoured by his shameful activities.' But Bruttedius[97] was a man of culture and attainments, who might have won the highest office. But he was a man in a hurry, who wanted to outstrip most of his equals, then his superiors, then his own expectations. 'Impatience was his downfall, as it has been of many good men who have spurned the slow, safe course of promotion for honours gained before their time.' Tacitus' comment would win approval in the corridors of Whitehall.

The great *delatores* under Nero are more formidable—notably Clodius Eprius Marcellus.[98] If we could recover the full details of this man's career, it would be a social document of the highest interest. He came from a humble origin in Capua, and made his way to a huge fortune, the Senate, and the friendship of Emperors, by his gifts as an orator and administrator. How he earned infamy—and 5,000,000 *sesterces*—by his attack on Thrasea Paetus, and how Helvidius Priscus clashed with him in the Senate in 69, is told above (see p. 64). Tacitus calls him grim and theatening, always ready to take a part in crime. Hated as he was in the Senate, he won the friendship of Vespasian, who gave him a three-year governorship of Asia (70–73) and a second consulship in 74. For reasons we do not know he later became involved in a conspiracy against Vespasian, and committed suicide in 79. His career is a vivid illustration of the opportunities of gaining wealth and power opened up to a new class of men under the Principate. His friend and contemporary, Vibius Crispus,[99] was a man of smoother manners, who was thus able to survive into Domitian's reign. Tacitus shows him walking out of the Senate House with Eprius Marcellus— Marcellus with furious gaze, Crispus all smiles. And in Juvenal's Fourth Satire, he is all smiles at Domitian's Privy Council, 'a man who never swam against the stream, not a citizen who could freely speak his thoughts and stake his life on behalf of truth. So he reached his eightieth year: these weapons kept him safe even in Domitian's court.' He is credited with the pungent reply to the question whether anyone was in Domitian's presence—*ne musca quidem*—'not even a fly.'[100] (The imperial fly-swatter had killed them all.)

At that same imaginary meeting of the Council were the other notorious informers of Domitian's reign—the blind Catullus Messallinus, 'bringer of death,' 'who slits throats with a whisper,' Fabricius Veiento, and the rest. These are the agents of Domitian's reign of terror, and there can be no doubt that they figured large in the later books of the *Histories*. All we have in Tacitus is an indignant naming of three of them in the *Agricola*. 'At that time (93) Carus Mettius had only won one victory: the raucous voice of Messalinus was confined to Domitian's Alban fortress. Massa Baebius was himself standing trial.'[101] These men will have been the *pessima exempla* of the *Histories*, and it is on their model that he portrays the informers of Tiberius' day, earlier by seventy years. There can be no doubt that he overcoloured the picture for Tiberius, as the researches of modern scholars have amply shown. But by now the pendulum has swung too far. We must not forget Seneca's[102] remark about the 'frenzy of prosecutions' under Tiberius. He had no memories of Domitian's terror to embitter him still further.

CHAPTER SIX

The Senate

THE SENATE UNDER TIBERIUS is made to cut a poor, and, ultimately, a contemptible figure. For this it had been pre-conditioned under Augustus. In that reign all the best men had died in battle or in the proscriptions. Those of the aristocracy who survived were rewarded by wealth and position in propor-tion to their readiness to accept servitude. 'Having done well out of the revolution they naturally preferred the existing security to the dangers and uncertainties of the old régime.' Moreover, after Augustus' forty-five years of power 'how many were left who could have ever seen the Republic'[1]—either in the Senate or in the state at large? And so the Senate, combining speed with hypocrisy (*falsi ac festinantes*) joined the headlong rush to slavery. As the reign of Tiberius is made to begin with a crime (*primum facinus novi imperii*), so the mark of the Senate is, from the first, that of flattery (*adulatio*). Indeed, they have already plumbed its depths: the one form of flattery still left open is to profess not to mind causing offence in using one's own judge-ment—the claim put forward by Messalla Valerius in the debate on the funeral of Augustus. But in fact this is what the senators fear most, and what they cannot avoid.

The debate[2] on the succession of Tiberius is presented as a conscious farce, on both sides. The one object of Tiberius was completely to disguise his feelings, the one fear of the Senate, to show any sign of understanding him. In the event no one spoke that day without giving offence: the Senate were reduced collectively to tears, entreaties, and the most humiliating forms of supplication. At last Tiberius grudgingly agreed to do what he had intended all along—and to accept powers he had already assumed. Suetonius,[3] it is to be noted, while he regards Tiberius' rôle as an impudent farce, shows the Senate as less sycophantic— there were voices heard saying 'oh, let him take it or leave it!' But neither will allow that there might have been sincerity in Tiberius' reluctance to shoulder alone the terrible burden whose thankless nature he knew so well—or justification in the Senate's fears of divided command, in view of what had happened in both the First and Second Triumvirate.

Again, it is from Suetonius,[4] not from Tacitus, that we learn of Tiberius' early wish to show himself 'a citizen on equal terms' (*aequalis civis*), and that on one occasion he found himself in a Senate lobby in a minority of one. Tacitus[5] would rather have us think of the remark of Gnaeus Piso at the trial of Marcellus (A.D. 15). 'I would ask you, Sire: when are you going to vote? If first, you set me an example to follow: if last I am afraid that I may, unintentionally, disagree with you.' Tiberius, we are told, was really shaken. But the comment was just. The '*aequalis civis*' had at his command the tribunician veto and the authority of the princeps: he had, too, a nature that loved power but hated flattery. Some are, indeed, more equal than others.

But, at times, the Senate was granted freedom to debate matters within its own competence, as with the questions of flood-control in Italy, or the rights of sanctuary for the temples of Asia. On the first, a plan was submitted for the diversion of streams and lakes feeding the Tiber. This was opposed by several of the municipalities. Among them the people of Florence, who showed foresight in claiming that 'if the Chiana should be diverted from its natural channel into the Arno, the result would be disastrous to them.' In the event religious scruples, or possibly engineering difficulties, caused the Senate to adopt the resolution 'that no action be taken.'[6] Religious scruples, as advanced by the delegates sent from the Asian cities on the question of rights of asylum,[7] proved to have their *longueurs*. The problem was remitted by Tiberius to the Senate in the most gratifying way—'a fine sight it was, on that day, to see the Senate engaged on the investigation of privileges granted by our ancestors, treaties made with allies, charters conferred by monarchs who lived before the days of Roman power, and indeed the very cults of the gods themselves: moreover, the Senate was at liberty, as in former times, to confirm or revoke.' So a hearing was given, first, to the people of Ephesus, then to Magnesia, then to successively Aphrodisias Stratoniceia, Hierocaesaria and the Cypriots (who advanced three shrines). All delved into Greek mythology and Roman history, with the eloquence of their race. And there were others. 'The Senate began to weary of the matter. They instructed the consuls to investigate the charters . . . and, in cases where a flaw appeared, to report back.' One can sympathise. But a legislative body needs stamina if it is to be effective. And Tiberius might have found one of his grim smiles for the wilting of the Senate before so small a fraction of the burdens he was expected to carry. Indeed, it was shortly after this that Tiberius did let fall his famous comment on the Senate (in Greek)—'Men ready to be slaves!'[8] Henceforth, says Tacitus, he will only record such motions as are particularly honourable or scandalous to an unusual degree. And it is, of course, the latter that predominate, for we are now at the start of the infamous trials for *maiestas*. 'It was a corrupt period, deeply tainted with servility (*tempora illa adeo infecta et adulatione sordida fuere*). And it was about to exchange sycophancy for persecution (*paulatim dehinc ab indecoris ad infesta transgrediebantur*).' Moreover, with the death of Drusus, the administration of Tiberius took a decisive turn for the worse.[9]

The treason trials are dealt with elsewhere. We lack Tacitus' account of the most dramatic sitting of the Senate when the *grandis et verbosa epistula* sent from Capri was read aloud to precipitate the fall of Sejanus. What honourable behaviour, then, is there to recall? Almost exclusively, it would seem, on the part of individuals in whom the spark of *libertas* was not wholly dead. Such was the distinguished jurist, Antistius Labeo, who died in 22, *incorrupta libertate*. But he kept his independence at the cost of his career: he never rose above the rank of praetor.[10] In 25 the historian Cremutius Cordus was attacked for having published an historical work in which Brutus was praised and Cassius called 'the last of the Romans.' He defended himself before the Senate in a dignified speech: but his case was hopeless, for Tiberius listened to the defence with a scowl on his face. Cremutius retired to starve himself to death: the Senate disgraced itself by ordering that his books should be burned by the aediles, 'but they were hidden, and published later, and they survive.'

'How fatuous,' adds Tacitus, 'to suppose that a little brief authority can be used to quench the memory of generations yet to come. To attack genius is to fan the light of its authority to a brighter glow!'[11] Here, again, events of the reign of Tiberius foreshadow those of Domitian. So they did in the case of Cocceius Nerva, grandfather of the Emperor Nerva. He had accompanied Tiberius in his retirement to Capri: in 33, he resolved to die, 'though he was in perfect health and there was no threat to his position.' Tiberius hastened to his side to implore him to desist: Nerva refused to speak to him or to take food. 'Those privy to his thoughts,' says Tacitus, evidently repeating a family tradition, 'aver that knowing from the inside the evils of the state, he was so horrified and so indignant that he determined to make an honourable end.'[12] Almost twenty years earlier, Lucius Piso had alarmed Tiberius by his threat to withdraw from Rome and retire to some distant place in the country: Tiberius urged his relatives (successfully, it would seem) to use their influence to stop him going.[13] By such indictments virtue could still rebuke vice. And even the Senate, filled with zeal for the liquidation of all the supporters of Sejanus after the fall of the favourite, could be swayed by the display of courage. For when Marcus Terentius, a Roman knight, was accused before the Senate, he boldly declared, 'I was a friend of Sejanus, and I sought to become so, and I was delighted when I succeeded.' And so, he went on to imply, had they all acted. The Senate was in no position to disagree, 'for the speech gave expression to what everyone was thinking. Its effect, together with their own criminal records, was to bring exile or death upon all who accused Terentius.'[14]

Those books of the *Annals* are lost which dealt with the reign of Gaius, as with that of Claudius before 47. They will have contained much of interest on the topic of the Senate—the brief honeymoon period with Gaius, followed by a new and more lurid terror, his assassination, and the debate in the Senate when consuls Sentius Saturninus and Pomponius Secundus proposed the restoration of the Republic. In that debate[15] the Senate enjoyed freedom of discussion but not of action: action was being taken in the Praetorian barracks with the oath of loyalty to Claudius. It would be worth much to have Tacitus' account of the scene in the Senate which ratified the decision already taken by the soldiers, and to compare it as an exercise in hypocrisy with that on the accession of Tiberius. As it is, the surviving books of the *Annals* give a rather colourless picture of the Claudian Senate. There are no great trials for *maiestas* with which it was concerned, for Claudius took as much legal business as possible in the imperial courts. No notable senators emerge in opposition to the *princeps*, like Thrasea Paetus under Nero. True, the Claudian Senate had to extend the scope of *adulatio*. Under Tiberius it had been paid to the Emperor, to the dowager Empress Livia, and to the Praetorian Prefect Sejanus in his days of power. For Claudius, the Senate speaks in terms of extravagant admiration on the capture of Caratacus—*multa ac magnifica patres disserere*.[16] When, in 49, Vitellius proposed the marriage with Agrippina—with an unctuousness that seems all his own—the Senate and others were ready with a fine show of spontaneity, 'At this, several senators rushed out of the Senate House, proclaiming that they would force the Emperor, if he delayed any longer. A crowd collected spontaneously, pro-

claiming that this was the will of the Roman people.'[17] Claudius
yielded under this duress.

The next year flattery was evoked by his adoption of Nero.
But what could be conceded when addressed to the Princeps irked
with his womenfolk and his freedmen. The political ambitions of
Agrippina were worse than the caprice of Messalina. But the
depths were really plumbed when in 52 the hated freedman
Pallas was voted a senatorial decree of thanks because, 'though
descended from ancient Arcadian Kings, he had rather thought
of the public good than of his noble lineage, and allowed himself to be numbered among the Emperor's servants.' 'Thus,' is
Tacitus' comment, 'an ex-slave worth 300,000,000 *sesterces* was
thanked for showing old-world frugality.'[18] In one context,
indeed, the reactionary views of senators are placed in a telling
contrast to liberality of the Emperor. This is in the discussion on
the admission to the Senate of nobles from Tres Galliae.[19] Envy,
xenophobia, and obscurantism are the mark of the views put
into the mouths of senators at a meeting of the Emperors' privy
council. The speech delivered in refutation by Claudius to the
Senate is enlightened, progressive, and informed by a true sense
of Rome's historical mission—and, stylistically, much superior
to the authentic text as preserved on the Tablet of Lyon.[20]

Under Nero the picture is more complex. The reign began well
for the Senate, for his advisers had held up the Principate of
Augustus as a model for the young ruler. Unpopular features of
the previous reign would be discarded: Nero would not take all
judicial business on himself; there would be control over the
imperial freedmen, and a strict division between public and
private business: the Senate should exercise its ancient functions.
These admirable sentiments, according to Dio,[21] were recorded
by the Senate on a silver plate and recited each year when the
consuls took up office. Nor was this new policy confined to a
declaration of intent. *Clementia*, the watchword of Seneca and
the youthful Nero, brought concessions to the aristocracy. On
more than one occasion, Senate and Emperor combined to
check the intervention of Agrippina in public affairs. The

appointment of Corbulo to command in the East was taken to indicate that great posts were once more open to merit. Relations between Senate and *princeps* in the early years of the reign are well seen in the question of revoking the rights of freedmen in cases of bad behaviour, which arose in 56.[22] There was strong support for this proposal in the Senate: but the consuls did not venture to put it to the vote without the knowledge of the Emperor. They therefore wrote to him, and he brought it before the *concilium principis* to find that opinion there was against any general ruling, though willing to see individual cases of complaint investigated by the Senate. It was a rebuff for the Senate, but Tacitus remarks that 'there was still some semblance of a free country.' For shortly afterwards the Senate was able to curb undesirable powers of the tribunes and the aediles. And when in 57 Nero—or his advisers—came up with a proposal for the abolition of customs-dues as a first step to tax reform, it was the Senate who put a stop to such ill-conceived tampering with the revenue of the state.[23]

But, in fact, the Augustan parallel could not last, depending as it did on the diminishing ability of Seneca and Burrus to control Nero's tendency to absolutism. And after the murder of Agrippina, by which they were so deeply compromised, *adulatio* became once more the condition of survival. Tacitus notes with grim disapproval the competition for favour among the eminent. The Senate voted thanksgivings at every shrine, the feast of Minerva (when the 'plot' against Nero was discovered) was to be commemorated by annual games, and a golden statue of the goddess set up in the Senate House. Agrippina's birthday became a black day in the calendar, like the disasters at the Allia or at Cannae.[24] Thrasea Paetus walked out of the Senate. 'This,' says Tacitus, 'endangered his own life, but did nothing to advance the cause of public freedom.'

From then on, the decline was swift. In 62 Burrus died and Seneca fell from favour: Nero was now unrestrained. After the death of Rubellius Plautus the farcical decrees of thanks from the Senate caused greater offence than the crimes themselves.

Worse followed the murder of Octavia, and Tacitus will no longer recount them. 'All readers of the history of these terrible times in my pages or another's, may fairly take it for granted that the gods were thanked for each instance of banishment or murder ordered by the Emperor. Indeed, such occasions, once the sign of public rejoicings, now marked only public disasters. But I shall still record senatorial decrees that plumbed new depths of sycophancy, or established new records of servility.'[25] Such were the failure to abandon the order for a triumphal arch on the Capitol after the news of the disaster to Paetus in Parthia —'regard for appearances triumphed over the knowledge of facts.' Knowledge of the facts did not deter the Senate's syco- phancy in the matter of Poppaea's daughter. They asked divine protection for Poppaea's pregnancy, dedicated a temple to Fertility after the infant's birth; and declared it a goddess when it died at the age of four months. On the eve of the Great Fire of Rome the Senate's only doubt about Nero was 'whether he was more abominable absent or present. Later, as happens in all fright- ful experiences, they came to believe that the worst was what had actually taken place.'[26] Such was the prelude to the 'vague, ill- directed conspiracy of Piso,' and to the terror that followed.

Yet, even when the Senate was its most abject, there were still men who made a stand for freedom. We have spoken elsewhere of Thrasea Paetus, and the 'stoic opposition' which he led, not always wisely (see pp. 58–67). Tacitus clearly prefers the line followed by Gaius Cassius, a man to be reckoned with as a good jurist and as the descendant of the Tyrannicide. In him lived the *severitas* of the old Republic—for he was a strict disciplinarian in the field, harsh to slaves and freedmen, overbearing to the allies. Against this he was unwilling to join in flattery to the Emperor, loyal to his family tradition, and prepared if need be to die for his beliefs. This he was not directly required to do, for when Nero's anger finally overtook him, he was exiled to Sardinia and old age left to do the rest.[27] But his pupil, Lucius Silanus, whom he had carefully educated, was executed as a possible source of sedition. Another independent was Memmius

Regulus, a man of fame—so far as fame could be won under the shadow of the Emperors—derived from influence, determination, and good name. Nero paid him the dangerous compliment of calling him 'the reserve of the Commonwealth.' Yet, says Tacitus, Memmius lived on even after this: his quiet life, elevation in rank, and moderate fortune were his safeguards.[28]

The *Annals* as we have them break off after the trial and death of Thrasea Paetus. That trial saw the Neronian Senate at its lowest, forced to condemn to death, in his absence, its most respected member. Yet senatorial opposition to Nero was not impotent, though it had to take the form of conspiracy. In the end the Senate had the satisfaction of proclaiming Nero a public enemy, and Galba his successor. And if suicide was the occupational hazard of the Roman aristocracy at that time, it was not evaded by the last Julio-Claudian Emperor.

The tragic events of the year 69 brought the Senate new experiences, mostly degrading. At times they were the sole representatives of constitutional authority, but never for long. Power always lay with men who could command the loyalty of the armies. And the strains of having to climb on to four successive band-wagons must have taxed all but the most athletic conscience. They were soon disillusioned by Galba. The adoption of Piso, presented as better than the hereditary principle, proved ineffective. A *princeps* there had to be, for Galba is made to discount the possibility of inaugurating another republic in a state where men 'could bear neither absolute power nor absolute freedom.'[29] The moment Galba and Piso fell, the Senate transferred its allegiance to Otho. Soon, it was recognised, another choice would be impending—between Otho and Vitellius. A real choice of evils, neither of them worth hoping or praying for, with the only certainty 'that the more evil of the two would be the winner.'[30]

Meanwhile there was an uneasy alliance, based on proximity, between Otho and the Senate. When the Praetorians threatened to get out of hand—and even to massacre the Senate—Otho treated them (according to Tacitus) to the most flattering estimate of that body's importance. 'Vitellius is the master of a few barbarian tribes, and has some sort of an army. We have the Senate. On our side, then, is the state, on theirs, the state's enemies. . . . The duration of Rome's empire, the peace of nations, your safety and mine, rest on the safety of the Senate. This order was instituted by Romulus, and has lasted without interruption or decay from the royal period to the Principate. As we have inherited it from our ancestors, so shall we transmit it to our descendants. You give the state its senators, the Senate gives it its Emperors.'[31] High praise: but the speaker was trying to forestall a massacre, not to expound the constitution. In fact, the arms of the troops who won the battle of Bedriacum gave the empire to Vitellius. Before that a part of the Senate had followed Otho to Modena, to endure the suspicions of Otho's troops, the ill-timed compliments of the local *ordo*, and the agonising scarcity of any reliable news about the outcome of the battle. It was not till they had reached Bologna that the fog of war lifted, and 'all hearts turned to Vitellius.'[32] A less secure refuge they could scarcely have found.

After the licence of Vitellius' passage from the Po Valley to Rome came the humiliations of his entry to the outskirts of the city. At the head of his uncouth northern armies, he came down like a foreign conqueror 'driving the Senate and people before him' as far as the Milvian Bridge.[33] The entry to the Capital was more seemly, and the army looked worthy of a better Emperor than Vitellius. Yet apart from gluttony, drunkenness, prodigality and sloth, Vitellius had some things in his favour. He entered the Senate. He allowed opposition. When Helvidius Priscus disagreed with him, he remarked, 'There is nothing strange if two senators disagree in a free Commonwealth: I used to disagree with Thrasea Paetus.'[34] Yet dealing with the Senate was not the most pressing of his cares. By the late summer the armies of the Danube had declared for Vespasian, and the fate of the Empire was again to be fought out in the cockpit of North Italy.

The Second Battle of Bedriacum and the fall of Cremona, in effect, decided the issue in favour of Vespasian. Tacitus is at

pains to insist that Vitellius' sloth threw away all chance of
opposing the Flavian army when it crossed the Apennines. The
large number of senators who followed Vitellius to Mevania,
'some in hopes, some in fear,' must have seen that the game was
lost long before the Vitellian troops surrendered at Narnia.
There were yet to follow the foolish attempt of Flavius Sabinus
to capture Rome ahead of the main Flavian army, and bloody
fighting in the streets and the headquarters of the Praetorian
Guard when at last the Flavians arrived. In all this there was
little part for the Senate to play.

But, in the closing weeks of 69, the Senate found itself
courted by Vespasian, his sons and his generals. What had been
won by the sword now needed to be made respectable. To the
Senate the immediate outlook must have seemed unfathomable
and menacing. True, the Flavians had won—but which Flavians? Three Flavian generals were now in Rome, all men of
ambition. A little behind them was Mucianus, whose action in
writing a personal letter to the Senate gave rise to anxious
debate.[35] Finally there was Vespasian. He was in Egypt, and
unable to reach Italy before navigation began again in the
spring. He had written an admirable letter: but was he really in
control? Such was the background to the historic debate of
December 22nd, 69.[36] The Senate had to satisfy many postulants.
It did so by approving a carefully graded set of rights and
privileges. First, the grant of *imperium* to Vespasian himself,
conferring on him all the powers granted to Augustus, Tiberius
or Claudius, and also the right to take whatsoever action he
pleased in the public interest. This is the famous *Lex de imperio
Vespasiani* whose seven surviving clauses constitute one of the
most notable of Latin inscriptions.[37] Vespasian and Titus were
given the consulship for the following year (70). Domitian was
granted praetorian powers. Triumphal honours went to Mucianus, and distinctions of various kinds to the generals.

The most important issues thus decided, 'they thought of the
Gods, and approved a motion to restore the Capitol.' Most
Senators simply raised their hands in assent, or spoke in careful

phrases, but Helvidius Priscus, then praetor-designate, managed
to deliver a speech which was 'complimentary to a good
Emperor . . . but which struck no false notes, and was received
with acclamation.'[38] 'This day,' says Tacitus, 'was for Priscus
the beginning of a grave offence and of high renown.' Both were
to be won by his boldness in following in the steps of his father-
in-law, Thrasea Paetus. At this point, and as a prelude to Priscus'
political career and ultimate martyrdom under Vespasian, a
character-sketch is given.[39] Helvidius Priscus had studied Stoicism 'to enable himself to take up a public career firmly braced
against all the chances of fate. He followed the teachings of that
sect of philosopher which holds that nothing is good but what is
honourable, nothing evil save what is base, and that power,
nobility, and all the rest that is external to the mind are neither
good nor evil. When still a quaestor, Thrasea Paetus chose him
for his son-in-law, and it was from him that he derived his deep
passion for liberty. As citizen and senator, as husband, son-in-
law and friend, and in all the other offices of life, he was invariably admirable.'

Such was the man, now praetor, who tried to inspire the
Senate into playing an honourable part. There was first the
question of the delegation to go to meet Vespasian. Helvidius
wanted it selected by the magistrates on oath, and made up of
'the best men.' Established practice was for a ballot. Established
practice prevailed. Then there was a financial crisis, and the
necessity for pruning public expenditure. It was proposed to
refer the matter to the Emperor: Helvidius maintained that the
Senate should be free to act. A tribune vetoed a vote on this
issue, in the Emperor's absence. On the restoration of the
Capitol, Helvidius proposed that this should be done from public
funds, with contributions from Vespasian. This was quietly
passed over. Next Helvidius took a leading part in an attempt to
hunt down the most notorious of the informers under Nero. On
this issue there was a genuine and heated debate.[40] The senators
were not dealing with public matters, but with their own affairs.
But in the end it was quashed by Mucianus and Domitian in the

interests of amnesty. For as soon as Mucianus reached Rome,
all hopes and fears centred on him. 'And on this issue too the
senators, as soon as they found themselves opposed, abandoned
the liberty they had just begun to practise.'

It is much to be deplored that the *Histories* do not survive to
take us further into the period of the Flavians. The treatment of
Vespasian would have been of particular interest. For, in that
reign, relations between Emperor and Senate were in general
more friendly than at any other time between Augustus and
Nerva. Moreover, it was in that reign that Tacitus himself
gained admission to the Senate and the chance of a distinguished
political career. And what of Titus, 'that darling of the human
race,' the Emperor who thought a day wasted when he had not
made a friend?[41] Even Nero was allowed to have made a good
beginning: could Tacitus have found a harsher side to Titus' two
years of power? And would the picture of a time-serving Senate,
its predominant characteristic from Tiberius to the accession of
Vespasian, have been modified by Tacitus' portrayal of its part
under the first two Flavians? We do not know. What we do
know is that Helvidius Priscus is being built up for martyrdom,
and Domitian for infamy. Domitian had played an ignominious
part in the fighting in Rome: early in 70 he was marked as
princeps 'only by extravagance and lust.'

> 'Flavia gens, quantum tibi tertius abstulit heres,
>   Paene fuit tanti, non habuisse duos!'[42]

Martial's verdict on the Flavians was most probably endorsed
in full detail by Tacitus—that the third of the line detracted so
much from the other two that it would almost have been worth
while not to have had his predecessors. Indeed, Tacitus may
well have boggled at 'almost.' For, while we do not have his
account of Domitian, two chapters of the *Agricola*[43] provide,
like the *argumentum* of a tragedy, the outline of what must have
been the main theme of his treatment of the Senate in that
reign. In the first we have a contrast—not perhaps wholly
sincere—between the Terror of Domitian and the felicity of

Nerva and Trajan. 'It stands on record that when Arulenus Rusticus wrote in praise of Thrasea Paetus, and Herennius Senecio of Helvidius Priscus, a capital charge was made against them. The sternest measures were taken, not merely against the authors, but against their books also. For the public executioners were charged with the duty of burning these books in the Comitium and the Forum. It was supposed that in those flames would be destroyed the voice of the Roman people, the freedom of the Senate, and the very conscience of mankind! Indeed, philosophers were expelled from the city, and every liberal profession driven into exile. No opportunity was to be left for the infection of honour. We have shown subservience to an astonishing degree: a former age knew the extremes of freedom, we have explored the depths of servility. Espionage deprived us of the power to speak, nay, even to listen—we should have lost our memories as well as our tongues, but it is not so easy to forget as to keep silent.

'But now at last our spirit revives. At the very dawn of that joyful day the Emperor Nerva united two things previously incompatible—the Principate and freedom. The Emperor Trajan daily augments the happiness of the times. Public security is no longer a matter of hope and prayers: it rests on a solid basis of hope fulfilled. But it is the essence of our human infirmity that a remedy should be slower in action than a disease. Slowly our bodies come to maturity, a single blow will snuff them out. . . . So with genius and learning, which are more readily suppressed than aroused. The delights of idleness take charge unnoticed: the indolence we once hated we grow to love. I must stress again that for fifteen long years so many died by accident or chance, that men of talent have been liquidated by the cruelty of the Emperor, and that we, this miserable remnant, have out-lived, if I may so put it, not only others but also ourselves. So many of the best years of our lives have been taken from us, that those of us who were young men have grown old, and those of riper years now stand on the edge of the grave. And all in silence. . . .'

There is a more specific indictment in chapter 45, prompted

ET

by Agricola's untimely death. 'He never knew the final phase of
Domitian's Reign of Terror, when he no longer allowed respite
or pause, but drained the state of its blood as if with a single
fearful blow.

'Agricola did not see the Senate House under siege, and the
senators beset with soldiers with arms—nor the massacre at one
and the same time of so many men of consular rank, the exile
and expulsion of so many noble ladies. . . . Ere long the hands of
the Senate dragged Helvidius to prison, tore away Mauricus and
Rusticus: on us Herennius Senecio shed his noble blood. Nero
at least turned his eyes away, and ordered the crimes he did not
witness. An especial feature of our agonies under Domitian was
to see and be seen. Our very sighs were noted down against us:
the Emperor's savage countenance, and that blush which was
his armour against shame, supported him well as he turned his
scrutiny on the pallor of so many men who had done no wrong.
Surely you were blessed, Agricola, not only in the fame you won
in life, but in the timely hour of your death. . . .'[44]

Other sources confirm what Tacitus says about the Senate
under Domitian, notably the letters of the younger Pliny. In
Book VIII, 14, Pliny speaks of the Senate as 'panic-stricken and
speechless' (*trepida et elinguis*): it was only summoned 'for the
most futile or the most evil ends' (*cum senatus aut ad otium
summum aut ad summum nefas vocaretur*). For six years senators
were forced to be the criminal accomplices (*participes malorum*)
of Domitian and the informers. And the loathing felt for Domitian is at its most intense in Pliny's story of Corellius Rufus, in
the agony of mortal illness, deciding against suicide in the hope
'that I can outlive that brigand if only by a single day (*ut
scilicet isti latrono vel uno die supersim*).'[45]

Such then, in outline, is Tacitus' picture of the Senate from
Tiberius to Domitian in the surviving books of the *Annals* and
the *Histories*. It is doubtful whether it would be much altered if
the lost books were restored. Vespasian and Titus, no doubt,
would add to the credit side, but the debit would be augmented
by Gaius and the later years of Nero. But its main features

would surely stand, deriving as they do from the position
assigned to the Senate in the Augustan principate. In retrospect,
it is clear that Augustus had designed machinery that only he
could work. The Senate still, in theory, exercised major political
powers: a Senator enjoyed high prestige: admission to the order
continued to be coveted. But, in fact, any of its powers could be
nullified or usurped by an Emperor who wished to do so. This
caused a standing conflict between the treatment actually
afforded to the Senate and what it felt to be its due, enhanced by
its view of itself as the heir of the Senate of republican times. A
tactful or a liberal Emperor might ease the tension, but this was
really no more than lengthening the tether by which the Senate
was bound. And when the *princeps* was a tyrant and a despot,
members of the Senate were his natural victims. Natural,
because it was from them that he himself had most to fear:
from their ranks, if at all, his supplanters would come. So when,
as under Nero and Domitian, 'Virtue itself was a cause for suspicion' (*suspecta virtus*), it was a logical development. Beyond this
there was something more. The Senate, as we have seen, acquired
judicial powers under the Empire, but none of its formal judicial
functions impress so much as its mandate to pronounce judgement on deceased Emperors. Roman feeling for their *memoria*
with posterity was high, even passionate: here the Senate
wielded real authority. Of the Twelve Caesars from Julius
Caesar to Domitian, five won the acclaim of being deified—
Julius, Augustus, Claudius, Vespasian and Titus. Nero was pronounced a public enemy, Domitian suffered *damnatio memoriae*:
the memories of Tiberius and Gaius were execrated in tradition.
In Book I of the *Annals* we see this work of assessment in process
of forming an estimate of Augustus. Judge of deceased Emperors, the Senate was a critic of living ones—informed, incessant,
and, generally, ill-disposed. Tension between Princeps and
Senate was thus inherent in the Augustan Principate. The hostile
senatorial tradition dominates the historical sources—at its
most trivial in the scabrous gossip of Suetonius, at its most
austere and sustained, in the pages of Tacitus.

CHAPTER SEVEN
The Army

THE ROMAN ARMY is by far the most conspicuous of the 'collective' characters in Tacitus. This accords with its historic importance in the early Empire. Placed by Augustus on the distant frontiers on guard against the barbarians, the armies of the Roman state became, in the last resort, the arbiter of its political destinies. It was not until 69 and the elevation of Galba to the throne that this 'high secret of Empire,' to use Tacitus' words, was divulged. The power, the appetites, and the venality shown by the armies in the Civil Wars of 69 were henceforward among the permanent factors of Roman politics. They might be bridled for a time by a Trajan or a Hadrian, but there was realism in Septimius Severus' political testament to his heirs, which was, roughly, 'Look after the troops, and to hell with the rest!'[1] That was almost a century after Tacitus wrote. But, even in the first century, he saw clearly that the Army had become one of the estates of the commonwealth. As Syme[2] has pointed out, he enlarged several times the traditional formula '*Senatus Populusque Romanus*' to include the soldiery: further, and, ominously, on two occasions the people drop out.

It is a defect of some modern studies of the Roman Army to show it as a monolithic organisation. Standardised in weapons, equipment, and tactics it certainly was, but it would be wrong to suppose that the troops were maintained at a uniformly high level of training and fitness for battle. Nor is this surprising. The armed forces of every one of the major combatants—Britain, America, France, Russia, Germany and Japan—experienced a wide range of triumphs and disasters in the six years' fighting of the Second World War. In the pages of Tacitus we meet the Roman Army over a period of some seventy years—almost five generations of serving soldiers. First to appear, chronologically, are the mutinous armies of the Rhine and the Danube at the accession of Tiberius: last, the loyal and battle-worthy troops whom Agricola led to war and exploration in the Highlands of Scotland. In between, we see troops in action on almost every frontier of the Empire, in every circumstance from victory to defeat, from heroic self-sacrifice to shameful mutiny. In the special circumstances of the Civil Wars, its virtues, and, especially its defects are larger than life. The valour shown in the Battle of Bedriacum is more than balanced by the bestial plunder of Cremona. *Quae mens exercituum?*[3]—what was the temper of the troops?—is with good reason the question which the historian sets out to answer at the beginning of his account of the Civil Wars.

The *Agricola* shows how Roman troops responded to the leadership of their commanders—or its absence. For the design of bringing into high relief Agricola's campaigns in Scotland, it was necessary to include at least an outline of fifty years' fighting in Britain. *Hunc Britanniae statum, has bellorum vices.* 'Such was the condition of Britain, and such the story of its wars.' Praise or blame went to earlier governors, according to whether they matched the temper of that warlike province. They included some of the ablest generals of the day. Excellence is attributed both to Aulus Plautius, who led the invasion of 43 (and under whose auspices the future Emperor Vespasian won his first victories), and to his successor Ostorius Scapula.[4] The latter, though he defeated Caratacus in Wales, was brought to his grave by the obstinate resistance of the Silures. Suetonius Paulinus, who suppressed the great rebellion of Boudicca, had *constantia*—the quality of resolution when things were at their worst. But other commanders failed to engage the enemy or to control their own men.[5] Such were the elderly Didius Gallus and, more strikingly, the two governors who had the essential but unspectacular task of pacification after the Boudicca rebellion—Petronius Turpilianus and Trebellius Maximus. No expedition could be undertaken in their time, and the troops got out of hand. When the Civil Wars broke out Trebellius was faced with a mutiny that finally drove him overseas; the province was ruled by the legionary commanders.

His successor, Vettius Bolanus, 'did not harass Britain by military efficiency.' Under Vespasian there were great generals and fine armies. Petilius Cerialis conquered the Brigantes of northern England in a series of hard-fought campaigns; Julius Frontinus subdued the powerful and warlike Silures, in their mountain redoubt in South Wales.[6] Agricola came as the third of this distinguished line. He began by taking the field in late summer—to the surprise of the enemy and his own army—for a campaign in North Wales.[7] He himself led the marching column into the Snowdon mountains; his resolution solved the problem of crossing the Menai Straits without boats. When his Batavian cavalry swam their troops across to Anglesey the enemy collapsed: nothing, they thought, could defeat an army that fought in that fashion!

Wales subdued, he turned north. Exploration, conquest, consolidation—three years' methodical work brought him to the Forth and the Clyde. From the coast of Galloway he looked across to Ireland, and made plans (rather inadequate!) for its conquest.[8] A fleet was sent to circumnavigate Britain.[9] It reconnoitred the Western Isles, discovered Orkney, and induced the natives to make some kind of submission; and sailed as far north as the half-legendary Thule, which may be the Faroes. Another voyage round Britain was of a less formal kind. A cohort of German tribesmen, the Usipi, newly levied and sent to Britain, mutinied against their Roman instructors, cut out three light galleys, and sailed them round the north of Scotland to be shipwrecked on the Dutch coast. Their adventure, which involved cannibalism and ended in slavery, provides a commentary on discontent among the auxiliary troops.[10] Apart from this, Agricola kept a sharp eye for the doings of officers and men, and a sharper eye for the lie of the land. Experts acknowledged his brilliant siting of forts: 'no fort sited by Agricola was ever captured by the enemy, surrendered, or abandoned.'[11]

Archaeology can substantiate for his Highland campaigns. The Ordnance Survey map of Roman Britain attests his shrewd choice of an advanced base at Inchtuthil[12] on the Tay, and the masterly way in which he blocked the Highland glens with the series of forts, camps and signal-stations which lead round the eastern fringe of the mountains and on towards Inverness. It was a disciplined, aggressive, and high-spirited army that followed Agricola to the crowning glory of victory at Mons Graupius in 84. A notable feature was the way in which naval forces were used in support. 'Cavalry, infantry, and marines often mixed in the same camps, sharing their rations and their pleasures. As soldiers do, they competed in boasting of their exploits and their dangers: one side told of the deep recesses of the forests and mountains, the other, of winds and waves: here was land, and the enemy, there, the conquest of Ocean.'[13] With this army, Agricola smashed the confederate forces of the Highland tribes, perhaps not far from the field of Culloden. The fruits of the great victory were never gathered—Britain had been completely conquered and was then immediately abandoned. *Perdomita Britannia et statim omissa.* Modern historians have tended to approve Domitian's assessment of the Highland problem, rather than that of Agricola and Tacitus. But at least the troops had done all that could be fairly asked of them.[14]

The first appearance, chronologically, of the Roman Army in the pages of Tacitus is less felicitous. The accession of Tiberius in 14 was followed by mutinies in the armies of Pannonia and Germany. These were grave events, especially the latter, for the German armies had in Germanicus a commander whom they might run—if he could be tempted—in a bid for the throne against Tiberius. Tacitus devotes no less than thirty-six

chapters to the two mutinies, and a further sixteen to the offensive in Germany which Germanicus ordered as the most salutary
sequel.[15] This adds up to more than half of the first book of the
Annals: the second phase of Germanicus' campaigns occupies
about a quarter of the second book. By the end of the second
book the reader of the *Annals* has come to understand a good
deal about the psychology of the Roman soldier, the conditions
in the great military bases along the Rhine and the Danube,
and the nature of warfare against the peoples of free Germany.

The Rhine armies at this time disposed of eight legions, four
in Lower and four in Upper Germany.[16] There were seven
along the Danube, although the mutiny was confined to the
three in Pannonia.[17] Both armies had been under the command
of Tiberius. The Rhine legions in 4 B.C. and A.D. 4 had fought
triumphant campaigns which took them as far as the Elbe, but
in A.D. 6 Tiberius was withdrawn to cope with the great rebellion
in Pannonia. This was not quelled until A.D. 9, after three years
of bitter fighting; then the disaster to the legions of Varus
brought Tiberius back to the Rhine to stand on the defensive.
Neither army had seen much action for five years: conditions of
pay and service had deteriorated: they had a list of grievances
which could more easily be aired in the disturbed atmosphere of
a change of rulers. In Pannonia there were local conditions to
fan the flames. Emona (Ljubljana) had been founded as a colony
for the discharged veterans of the Danube army, but bitter
resentment had been caused by reports that the lands distributed
were either barren limestone or deep morass.[18] And in the
summer of 14, the commander, Junius Blaesus, had committed
two serious mistakes. He had encamped three legions together
for the summer manœuvres: then, using the death of Augustus
as an excuse, had failed to provide a proper programme of field
training. The stage was set for agitation, and the agitators duly
appeared.

'There was in the camp a certain Percennius, who had
formerly led a clâque in the theatre, but was now a common
soldier. He had a ready tongue, knew the intrigues of the

theatre, and how to raise a following. The soldiers were in doubt as to the conditions of service after Augustus' death: he would work on their minds in long conversations by night, or as the day ended. All the better elements moved away, and he was soon surrounded by the scum of the army.'[19] Percennius' talent for demagogy did not lack material. 'All these years,' he told the mutineers, 'you have been patient to the point of vice. You have served in the army for thirty or forty years, you are old men, and your bodies hacked away by wounds. Even discharge brings no end to your service. You are kept with the colours, still under canvas, still doing the same fatigues, though they give it another name. . . . In any case, the soldier's life is hard and unprofitable: his body and soul are valued at 10 *asses* [about 3½*d*.] a day. From that you have to pay for uniforms, weapons, and lodgings, give bribes to avoid the harshness of the centurions, or to buy yourself off duty. It's an endless round of blows and wounds, harsh winters, summers in the field—bloody battles, or a barren peace! . . .' The crowd roared applause. 'Each had a grievance: one man the stripes of lashes: another his grey hairs, others old uniforms and ill-clad bodies.' But, angry as they were, they lacked something of the true militant revolutionary. . . . 'they even talked of joining the three legions into one, but rivalry put an end to that: each man wanted his own legion to be first!'

At this point Blaesus intervened, and was just able to persuade them to go no further, but to send a delegation to lay their grievances before the Emperor, and await the outcome. The troops took note that disobedience had brought results that good behaviour would never have done. Things soon took a turn for the worse, owing to the behaviour of a task force sent out to build the roads and bridges. Villages were plundered, a town was looted: and, for the first time,[20] Tacitus portrays one of those disciplinarians of the old school who drove the men beyond endurance. 'Their especial anger was directed against Aufidienus Rufus, the camp commandant. They took away his carriage, loaded him with equipment, and put him at the head of the column. With many jeers they asked him how he was liking the long marches and the heavy burdens. For Rufus had been a private, then centurion, and finally camp commandant. He had brought back the old tough methods: having known severe toil himself, he was all the more hard-bitten because of what he had endured.' The last few words, '*Eo immitior, quia toleraverat*,' describe a recurrent army type. So, too, is the centurion Lucilius,[21] whom the soldiers had nicknamed 'Give-us-another,' from his amiable habit of breaking his staff over a soldier's back, and then calling out in a loud voice for a second and a third. He was lynched. In modern armies such sergeants get shot in the back. More agitators appeared, among them a certain Vibulenus, with a gift for working on the lachrymose feelings of the troops and a wholly fictitious story of a murdered brother, who had been sent as a delegate from the German armies. 'If it had not been discovered that he never had a brother, they would almost have reached the point of killing their commander.'

Such were the conditions that confronted Drusus when he arrived as the Emperor's representative, at the head of two cohorts of the Praetorian Guard and other picked troops, and accompanied as advisers by several leading politicians. In the event, the mutiny was quelled, partly through the authority exercised by the Emperor's son, but even more through chance and the adroit exploitation of the troops' superstition. At a crucial point there was an eclipse of the moon. 'It was a night of menace, likely to end in violence. But chance brought a respite, for in a clear sky the moon was suddenly seen to grow dark. The soldiers, ignorant of science, saw an omen of their present troubles in the eclipse of the luminary. "Our plans will turn out well," they thought, "if light and brightness return to the goddess." So they clashed together bronze vessels and sounded the war-horns and trumpets'—as is still done in certain parts of the East during eclipses. 'As the moon grew brighter or dimmer, they rejoiced or despaired. The clouds came up and covered her from view, they thought she was lost in darkness. Minds that have once given way to superstition are highly susceptible, and they began to lament that it meant that their labours would be endless, that the gods themselves were turning from their crimes. Drusus thought that the opportunity should not be lost, but that what chance brought his way should be turned to wise use. . . .'[22] The wise use, in fact, was to employ the loyal centurions and men to discredit Percennius and Vibulenus with the soldiers, then to murder them and hunt down the rest of the ringleaders. By this the teeth of the rebellion were drawn.

But yet again Nature came to the support of authority. An exceptionally early winter added to the soldiers' troubles. Heavy and continuous rains made it impossible for them to leave their tents, to meet together, even to keep the standards upright, for these were blown away by gusts of wind or carried away by floods. And they still had hanging over them the fear of the wrath of Heaven. 'It was not for nothing that the stars had grown dim, the tempests had raged, in the face of their impiety. The only remedy for their disasters was to leave these unhallowed, polluted camps, to clear themselves by making atonement, and to return to their own winter quarters.'[23] And so they did—first the Eighth and the Fifteenth, finally the most obdurate, the Ninth. The mutiny in the Pannonian army was over.

The mutiny of the Rhine legions displays the same pathology, but now the scale is ampler and with more varied incident. Here Germanicus was in supreme command over two army groups— the first, in Lower Germany, consisting of four legions under Aulus Caecina, while in Upper Germany another four were under Gaius Silius.[24] Active rebellion was confined to the troops in Lower Germany, and was sparked off, as in Pannonia, by Caecina's negligence in bringing troops together for summer manœuvres (near Cologne), and then failing to keep them actively occupied. The grievances of the men were the same, but it was now not a matter of a few ring-leaders, but of a general widespread sullenness and resentment.[25] The German legions— and especially the Twenty-first and Twenty-second—had been replenished after the disaster to Varus with what Tacitus calls *vernacula multitudo*,[26] a mob of slaves, unused to work and prone to insolence. These played on the simple minds of the rest, and together with the grievances of the veterans, provoked an explosion for which Tacitus uses the language of morbid psychology—*vaecordia, rabies, lymphati*.

There were other complicating factors. The German armies were conscious of their strength and their fighting record under Augustus: 'they proclaimed that Rome's fate lay in their hands: their victories extended the Empire, whose Emperors took from them their titles.'[27] They even hoped—vainly, as it turned out—that Germanicus would place himself at their head and oust Tiberius from the throne. On the side of authority there was the popularity of Germanicus himself and of his wife Agrippina, not to speak of that *legionum alumnus*—the soldiers' playfellow, Caligula, 'Little Boots,' the future Emperor Gaius. These were cards that could be, and were, played at the right moment. Moreover, this was an army with an unfinished task—vengeance on the Germans for the massacre of Varus and his three legions. Action in the field was the panacea for Roman soldiers.

The outset of the rebellion was violent and terrifying. 'Rabid with anger, the troops fell upon the centurions—those time-honoured objects of a soldier's hatred, the first victims of any violence. They threw them down and flogged them, sixty strokes apiece, one for each centurion in the legion. Then the mutilated, bleeding, dying men were thrown out of the camp, or into the Rhine.'[28] Such were the scenes among the Russian armies in their last phases of disintegration in 1917.

Caecina lost his nerve: Germanicus was away supervising the census in Gaul. He hastened to the camps of the disaffected legions, and addressed them in a *contio* which is one of the most dramatic reported by Tacitus. Indeed, it has been called theatrical: even if Germanicus lacked the *histrionale studium* of the rebel Percennius, he knew the arts of oratory. In the course of his speech,[29] the fatal offer was made and rejected. 'As the men crowded round him, they said, "If you want the Empire, Sir, we're ready!" At this, he leaped down from the tribunal as though contaminated. Their weapons barred his way, and they threatened him if he did not return. "Death is better than disloyalty!" he cried, drew his sword, and pointed it at his own breast. The soldiers near him drew it away ... but, at the back of the crowd, and even, incredible though it sounds, some in the front ranks, urged him to strike. One man, Calusidius, drew his own sword and offered it, saying, "Take this, it's sharper!" ' Calusidius' cynical gesture miscarried. 'Angry as they were, the men found this a brutal gesture, a sign of a bad character.' In the pause Germanicus' friends hustled him away.

Germanicus now took counsel with his staff. The situation could not be met without concessions: these were published at once: discharge to men of twenty years' service, conditional release to men of sixteen years' service, who would be kept on the list for hostilities only, payment of legacies. It was a palliative, but it worked for a while. But the arrival of a delegation from the Senate, headed by Lucius Munatius Plancus, provoked a great outburst. The men thought he had come to nullify their gains and made Plancus the scapegoat for their fury. He was nearly lynched, and only by taking refuge with the standards did he save his life. The men did not much like the Senate and its delegates. But the unparalleled event of the murder of an envoy of the Roman people, in a Roman camp, and on the altar of the gods, did not take place. Plancus, now, was got away: the troops were cowed for a while.[30]

Criticism, by now, was mounting against Germanicus for his handling of the revolt. Why not go to Upper Germany, call in the loyal legions, and use them to put down the rebels? Why not at least send Agrippina and his little son out of danger? At last, after long argument, he was prevailed upon to follow the latter course. Psychologically, it was a shrewd move. 'So they set out, a pitiable group of women. The General's wife, a refugee, clasping her baby son to her bosom, weeping, the wives of his friends forced out with her, equally distraught.' Nothing, at that moment, could have had a more wholesome effect on the troops. 'What is this noise of weeping? What disaster does it mean?

These noble ladies—and no centurion to escort them . . . none of the escort due to the wife of the Commander-in-Chief! And they're going to the Treveri, going to trust themselves to foreigners!'[31] There was pity for Agrippina, when they thought of her noble descent. Pity, too, for 'Little Boots,' born in the camp, brought up with the soldiers as his playmates. 'But jealousy of the Treveri was what really swayed them'—an interesting comment on the feelings of a Roman army to provincials. Germanicus saw that the hour had come, and he did not lose it. Another and longer *contio*, no less artfully composed, brought the men to heel. Begging for mercy, they urged him to punish the guilty, forgive those who had forgotten their duty, and lead them into action against the enemy. 'Call back the lady, Sir,' they said, 'and our little playmate: don't let him be a hostage with the Gauls!'

The request for Agrippina he refused, since winter was near, and her time was coming upon her. But Caligula should return: the rest was up to them. They were changed men. They rushed off and dragged the ringleaders in chains before Gaius Caetronius, Commander of the First Legion. Judgement and execution were carried out in this way on each and everyone. The legions stood round, swords drawn: the condemned man was displayed on the rostrum. . . . If they shouted 'Guilty!' he was executed there and then. The soldiers rejoiced in the slaughter, as though it purged them of their guilt. Simple minds, indeed: but they needed understanding. The First and Twenty-second had now been brought to heel. Disaffected veterans were sent to Raetia to protect that province. The roll of centurions was revised: only those well-spoken of by tribunes and soldiers kept their commissions.

But with the Fifth and Twenty-first, encamped at Vetera (Xanten) sixty miles from Cologne, disaffection still raged. A task force was got ready, made up of the Rhine fleet and auxiliary regiments, to put it down if necessary. But so crude a move was unnecessary: it was possible to get the troops to be their own executioners. Germanicus sent a despatch to Caecina.

'I am coming with a strong force. Unless you punish the agitators as they deserve, I shall employ indiscriminate massacre.' Caecina, at this stage, did not fail. Rallying the loyal elements, he proceeded to exterminate every possible revolutionary and criminal. The loyalists burst unexpectedly into the soldiers' quarters, butchering them unawares. 'This was civil war of an unprecedented kind. There were no battles, no opposing armies. Messmates were splitting up into parties, taking up arms. Shrieks, weapons, bloodshed were obvious: the reasons for them mysterious: the outcome, uncertain . . . *carte blanche* was given to the mob, they could glut themselves with vengeance. It was later that Germanicus entered the camp. Bursting into tears, he exclaimed, 'This is no remedy—this is a massacre!'[32] Then he ordered the bodies to be burned. Theatrical, to the last. The dying Augustus was reported to have asked his friends, 'Have I acted well in the farce of life?' Germanicus had his share of the family talent.

The troops had now to atone for the spilling of brothers' blood. There was only one way. 'Only wounds won in battle, and displayed on their guilty breasts, could appease the shades of their slaughtered fellows.' It fell to the Marsi to provide the opposition. Scouts had reported a festal night of banquets and ceremonies impending: a Roman force made a march through the forests and fell on an unsuspecting and drunken foe. 'The Germans were in bed, or sprawled over their tables, no watch was kept. Carelessness and confusion reigned: they had no thought of war. Yet, if it was peace, it was the peace of crapulousness and exhaustion.'[33] The butchery of the unarmed warriors were followed by an indiscriminate massacre of the tribe, the ravaging of territory, and destruction of holy shrines. The Marsi had not played their part very well: they had provided victims, but few Roman breasts could yet display the wounds required. Fortunately their neighbours, the Bructeri, Tubantes and Usipetes, were more alert. They ambushed the returning Roman columns in the forest: Germanicus could urge his troops to turn shame to glory (*properarent culpam in decus vertere*). A furious charge was followed by the massacre of the Germans, confidence returned to the Roman troops. They had forgotten the past when they were led back to winter quarters.

Next year, morale restored, the troops were led by Germanicus against bigger game than the Marsi. The two long passages (I, 55–71 and II, 5–26) in which Tacitus recounts the German campaigns of 15 and 16 may be reckoned the finest military narratives in the *Annals*. Their historical importance is discussed elsewhere: here, we are concerned with their dramatic effects. Ostensibly, they present a picture of high achievement, and the re-establishment of Roman prestige.

In the first campaign the Chatti and Cherusci are attacked and defeated. Six years after the disaster to Varus, a Roman army comes to the battlefield, and buries the bones of the dead. Next year, on the plain of Idistaviso, a great Roman victory is won over German forces led by Arminius. A second battle, on ground chosen by Arminius, gave the same result. A trophy was set up with the proud inscription: THIS MONUMENT WAS DEDICATED TO MARS AND JUPITER BY THE ARMY OF TIBERIUS CAESAR AFTER THE CONQUEST OF ALL THE TRIBES BETWEEN THE RHINE AND THE DANUBE.[34] Another year, Germanicus thought, and the war could be wound up. Arminius would have been laid by the heels, the fighting power of the Germans broken, the long-delayed project of a German province realised. Tiberius did not think so. Germanicus was recalled. The decision will not surprise the attentive reader of Tacitus. For the impression he conveys is that the Roman Army was at the limit of its resources, physical and mental. The fate of Varus and the reputation of Arminius haunted the minds of officers and men. They were operating in a physical environment which they hated and feared—the dark forests and fens of western Germany, the marshes and quicksands of the North Sea coasts, the unfamiliar tides and storms of the Atlantic. It was like Agricola in Scotland, but on a larger scale, against a much more formidable enemy.

Again and again the tone is appropriate to the lurid, the fearful, the supernatural. As the army of Germanicus

approached the scene of the disaster to Varus, their minds
were filled with awe and foreboding. No man with him but was
overcome with pity when he thought of friends and relations, of
the chances of battle and of the lot of man. So they trod that
unhallowed ground of evil memory and hideous aspect.
There was the camp of Varus, its wide expanse and its headquarters testifying to the work of three legions. Next a half-
ruined earthwork and a shallow ditch showed where the
last survivors had gathered. In the middle of the battlefield
bones lay white, scattered where the men had fled, piled up
where they had made a stand. By them were broken weapons,
horses' limbs, skulls fixed to tree trunks. In the groves hard by
were the barbarians' altars, where the tribunes and senior
centurions had been sacrificed as victims. The survivors of the
disaster, who had escaped from the battle or from captivity,
showed where the generals had fallen, where the eagles had been
seized. 'Here was where Varus got his first wound: over there he
died by his own hand. That was the mound from which Arminius made his speech; here were the gibbets and pits for the
prisoners; thus in his insolence did he mock our eagles and
standards.'[35] How many in that army shared the feelings of those
who set up the famous tombstone to the soldier lost in the 'war
of Varus,' *confectum bello Variano. ossa conferre licebit*[36]—'we
shall gather his bones'? Now they could.

Later Caecina was sent ahead to reconnoitre the forests, and to
provide bridges and causeways over the deep marshes with their
treacherous expanse. (Here we come to the passage from which
excerpts have been given on p. 37.) As the army of Caecina
crossed the Long Bridges,[37] ceaselessly harassed by the enemy,
'the general had a fearful dream. He saw Quintilius Varus,
blood-boltered and rising up from the fen; the spectre called
and beckoned him, but he refused: it stretched out its hand to
touch him, but he thrust it away.' This apparition is surely one of
the most terrible in the portentous company of classical ghosts.

In the great North Sea[38] surge of the later summer of 16, the
horror comes from Nature rather than man. It was a calm sea at

first, broken only by the thousand ships as they proceeded, rowing or under sail. But soon came a burst of hail from a black bank of clouds, accompanied by sudden squalls from every direction, which cut off visibility and impeded steering. The soldiers became panic-stricken. Ignorant of the perils of the sea, they got in the way of the sailors, tried clumsily to help, and interfered with the routine of the skilled navigators. Then everything, wind and wave alike, gave place to a great southerly gale, drawing its strength from an endless belt of storm clouds, born in the waterlogged lands and deep rivers of Germany, and striking more chill because of the nearness of the frozen north. Ships were overwhelmed, driven far out to sea, or on to islands with sheer cliffs or hidden shoals. Scarcely had these dangers been avoided when the tide turned, to set in the same direction as the gale. Now the anchors would not hold: they could not bail out as the waves burst in: horses, mules, baggage, arms, were cast overboard to lighten the hulls as waves dashed over the side, or water seeped through the joints.

'The Atlantic is the stormiest of all seas, the climate of Germany the foulest in the world.' Here, then, was disaster on a new and unprecedented scale. On one side were the shores of enemy country, on the other, seas so wide and deep that this is thought to be the last, landless ocean. Some of the ships were sunk: more were cast away in far, uninhabited islands, where the troops either starved to death or ate the bodies of the horses washed up with them. Germanicus' warship was the only one to make a landfall in the territory of the Chauci. All those days and nights he spent on the cliffs and headlands, reproaching himself as responsible for this dreadful disaster. It was as much as his friends could do to stop him from throwing himself into the sea. At long last, the waters flowed back, the winds turned favourable, and the ships came limping in. Some were short of rowers, others used garments for sails, still others were being towed by ships in better case. These were hastily patched up and sent off to search the islands. In this way, most of the troops were rescued. Many, too, were returned by the Angrivarii, recently

surrendered, who ransomed them from the inland tribes. Some
had even been driven ashore in Britain, and were sent back by
the petty kings of that island. As they came in from their far
adventures they had marvels to tell: fearful hurricanes, strange
birds, sea monsters half human, half animal. All these they had
seen or imagined in their fears.[39] The birds and monsters sort
better with the fabulous voyage of Brendan among the islands of
the Atlantic west than the campaigns of a Roman army.

But even in this outlandish theatre of war the Roman
military virtues are seen. Caecina's nerve might fail him in the
mutiny, but it was not shaken on the retreat across the Long
Bridges. 'Caecina had spent forty years in the army, as soldier
and general: he had known triumph and disaster, and he kept
his nerve.' On the common soldier the retreat bore hard. 'The
soldiers had no tents: the wounded no dressings. As they
divided up the rations that were stained with mud and blood
the men spoke bitterly of the deadly darkness, of the single day
that was all that was left for so many thousands. But the night
passed, and on the next day the Romans won a victory that
neither they nor the enemy expected. . . . The brute mass of the
German infantry were slaughtered, so long as daylight and the
fury of our men lasted. At length, as night fell, the legions
re-entered their camp. They had more wounds than ever,
and no less hunger, and yet they had everything—strength,
health, abundance—in the possession of victory.[40]

In the *Annals* only one other Roman general matches
Germanicus—Domitius Corbulo. He, too, had to work with
unpromising material in his Armenian campaigns—an army
whose morale was impaired not by mutiny, but by soft living.
The policy of basing the main strength of the Euphrates army in
the cities and towns of Syria paid few dividends, but the
conditions[41] which greeted Corbulo when he took up his
command were alarming even by the low standards of the East.
'His legions had been brought up from Syria, where they had
grown idle in peace-time service. They could not tolerate the
duties of a camp. Veterans there certainly were who had never

manned an outpost nor stood a watch, who had never seen a ditch or a rampart, who had no issues of helmet or breastplate. Sleek racketeers, they had done their military service in towns.' Corbulo's remedial measures were drastic. 'Those unfit for service were discharged, and their places filled by troops levied in Galatia and Cappadocia, with the addition of a legion from Germany and auxiliary cavalry and infantry units.' These measures cost him two seasons of campaign. There followed one of the toughest training programmes ever recorded for a Roman army, through the terrible winter of 57–58 on the bleak plateau that surrounds Erzerum and Lake Van. 'The whole army was kept under canvas, although the winter was so severe that the frozen ground had to be dug out to allow tents to be pitched. There were many cases of limbs lost by frost-bite: men died on guard. One man was seen carrying a load of wood: his fingers were so frost-bitten that they stuck to the load and dropped off, leaving him with only the stumps. The General himself went about the camp lightly-clad, bare-headed. He was present on marches and fatigues, with a word of praise for the energetic, and of cheer for the sick—an example to the whole army. But the harsh climate and rough conditions led to many desertions and derelictions, and he had to adopt a policy of strictness. In other Roman armies first and even second offenders are forgiven: with Corbulo death followed immediately for desertion from the colours. This was shown by experience to be salutary, and better than a more sympathetic policy. Corbulo had fewer desertions than in armies where pity was shown.'[42]

It was this toughened army that Corbulo led to his brilliant success of 58 and 59, culminating in the capture of Artaxata and Tigranocerta. He had made it a force that was superior to any in that theatre of war, one that allowed neither enemy fortifications nor the difficulties of the terrain to stand in its path. The summer march[43] of Corbulo's army across the Taurus range in 59 may be set as a military feat beside that of the Rhine legions through the forests of Germany in 16. 'General and army were becoming worn out with fatigue, though they had suffered no

losses in battle. Meat was all they had to hold starvation at bay'
(and meat was not highly thought of by the Roman soldier).
'Water was scarce: the summer blazing hot. On the long
marches their general's stamina was their only asset; he endured
all the exertions of the common soldier, and more. At last they
reached cultivation, and were able to harvest the crops. . . .'
Fed on corn and its products, and given a general with *ratio* and
constantia, Corbulo's army would do anything he asked of it.

Other Roman forces in that theatre of war were less fortunate.
The Fourth and Twelfth legions were led to disaster in Armenia
under Caesennius Paetus, a commander who is shown in the
worst light from first to last. Sent out to turn Armenia into a
Roman province, he begins by a foolish and public disparage-
ment of what Corbulo had done.[44] He neglects bad omens at the
crossing of the Euphrates: worse, he neglects to provision his
army or to provide for the winter. His first summer's campaign
was ill-planned and largely ineffective: it was represented in
despatches as virtually winning the war. Then the troops were
scattered, and there were indiscriminate grants of leave. When
his follies drew down on him the assault of the main Parthian
army, he failed to observe their movements or to follow any
rational strategy of his own. There followed the unnecessary
disaster[45] at the Roman base at Randeia, where the Parthians
rose above their normal level of siegecraft, and the Roman
defence was so half-hearted that the position was surrendered
before it could be reached by a relief force under Corbulo. The
Roman troops withdrew in humiliation. 'The enemy entered the
fortifications before the Romans had left them. Lining the roads,
they would recognise some captured slave or draught animal
and seize it: clothing and weapons were snatched from the
terrified Romans, who did not dare to resist for fear of starting a
battle.' The beaten legions now had only their legs, which they
put to use in a disgraceful retreat. 'Paetus marched forty miles
in a single day, abandoning all the wounded, and the panic
on his retreat was as shameful as cowardice in battle.'

Corbulo and his army met him on the Euphrates. 'There was

no display of decorations and weapons, such as might seem to point the contrast between the fate of the two armies. Corbulo's men were downcast, and so dismayed at the plight of their fellows that they could not restrain their tears. The lamentations were such that they could barely carry out the ceremony of saluting the standards. Gone were the old rivalry in valour, the desire for glory. Such emotions belong to success; now there was room only for pity, and especially among the lower ranks.'[46] There were further humiliations in store for this army and its commander. When Corbulo took over supreme command of the Eastern forces, the Fourth and Twelfth Legions were sent back to Syria—'They had lost all their best men, and the rest were shaken: they no longer seemed battleworthy.' As for Paetus, he returned to Rome, fearing the worst. But Nero let him off with a sarcastic remark. 'I am going to grant you an immediate pardon: for you are a very timid man, and your nerves might not stand the strain of a long period of uncertainty!'[47] A few years later, in the rebellion of Civilis, another Roman army was to provide an even more dramatic case-study in demoralisation.

Armies and their doings crowd the pages of the *Histories*. Almost never do they appear in a good light. Small wonder. For the events were those of the calamitous year A.D. 69, and the armies were not the armies of the Roman People, fighting in their country's cause against her foes. They were hired mercenaries, following, for their own selfish ends, selfish and corrupt leaders. The outcome of struggles such as these could only be the victory of the worst elements—*deteriorem fore qui vicisset*—the survival of the unfittest.

A frightful gulf had opened up between the armies and the state. When Otho bribed his way to favour among the Praetorian Guard, he used two guardsmen, Barbius Proculus and Veturius, to bribe his way. 'These two common soldiers undertook to transfer the Empire of the Roman People—and transfer it they did.'[48] When the rights of the Roman People were so blatantly disregarded, the people of the provinces could only fear the worst. The Vitellian armies, advancing from the Rhine to Italy in two columns under the command of Valens and Caecina, behaved towards the provincials like ruthless conquerors. At Divodurum (Metz) in the territory of the Mediomatrici a sudden and inexplicable frenzy seized the troops of Valens, and they butchered four thousand of the populace. 'Such panic did this spread in Gaul that hence-forward entire communities, with their magistrates, would go out as suppliants to meet the army on the march. Women and children would lie down on the roads: everything was done as though to appease the fury of an enemy, and that not in wartime but to gain peace.'[49]

At Lugdunum, the citizens enlisted the troops as their allies to bring to a conclusion their old quarrel against their neighbours of the rich and famous city of Vienna.[50] 'Be our avengers,' they cried, 'destroy this nest of Gallic rebels! Everything there is alien and unfriendly: we are a Roman colony, a part of your army, faithful alike in triumph and disaster.' But the people of Vienna were ingenious and wealthy. They met the advancing Roman troops in the guise of suppliants: this carefully staged appeal to pathos was followed by the more tangible argument of handsome bribes to the soldiers—and their general. So the inhabitants of Vienna purchased their safety. Their fellow countrymen at Luc,[51] who could not afford what Fabius Valens demanded to avoid the destruction of their city by fire, were allowed payment in kind by rape and adultery. The Helvetii,[52] who stood in the path of Caecina, were even more unfortunate. Their territory was plundered, and the pleasant spa-town of Vicus Aquensis (Baden) was destroyed. When they were so rash as to use their own militia to protect themselves, that amateur force was cut to pieces—many thousands were killed, thousands of others sold as slaves. The destruction of their capital at Aventicum (Avenches) was now threatened: it was barely averted by the eloquence of their leading citizen, Claudius Cossus, who pleaded their cause before Vitellius in person.

After their victory at Bedriacum, these same Vitellianists behaved in an even more atrocious manner to the people of northern Italy. 'The troops of Vitellius, billeted through the towns and colonies, robbed, plundered, violated and polluted everything. They were for rapine and plunder, lawful or unlawful: they spared nothing sacred or profane. Some there were who put on uniform and murdered their private enemies. The soldiers who knew the countryside well, marked down big estates for plunder, together with their rich owners. Death was the result of resistance. Their commanders could not try to control them: indeed, they were in their power.'[53] '*in omne fas nefasque avidi*': such was the temper of the troops who fought in that—as in any other—Civil War. Bitter experience had taught the people of Rome to dread such wars above any other experience. Virgil had summed up these *impia bella* once and for all, in the words he wrote of the struggle between Octavian and Antony.

> fas versum atque nefas, tot bella per orbem,[54]
> tam multae scelerum facies.

(Good and evil turned upside down: so many wars ravaging the world: so many hideous aspects of crime.)

But never was there such a piling up of horrors as at the sack and destruction of the Roman colony of Cremona—the work of the Flavian army under Antonius. It followed a period of bitter fighting, culminating in a savage assault on the fortifications. A signal atrocity had occurred in this phase—the killing of a father by his son. 'I give the fact and the names,' says Tacitus, 'on the authority of Vipstanus Messalla. Julius Mansuetus, from Spain, enlisting in the Rapax Legion, left behind him a young son. When this boy grew up he was conscripted by Galba into the Seventh Legion. He met his father, felled him to the ground, and as he bent over his dying enemy, recognised him and was recognised: embracing his father as he bled to death, he prayed in the most pathetic tones that his spirit would be appeased, and that he would not reject him as a parricide.' 'This crime is the work of the state,' he cried, 'what responsibility does one soldier bear for a civil war?' This appalling incident became known to the whole army, and they cursed and complained of this bloody war. But their zeal to despoil and butcher kinsmen, relatives and brothers did not abate. ' "A crime has been done!" they cried— as they did it themselves.'[55] (It may be recalled that Shakespeare has a doublet of this incident in the scene at Towton Field at the climax of the senseless misery of the Wars of the Roses.[56])

Such was the army into whose hands fell the rich colony of Cremona, crowded with people from all parts of Italy who had come for its famous fair. Tacitus[57] is at pains to exculpate Antonius from having given the signal for its burning: rumour had seen a grim significance in the unknown voice that replied when he complained of the temperature of his bath-water, 'It will be hot enough presently!' In fact, the city was already in flames. Its destruction followed. 'Forty thousand armed men burst into the city, and an even greater number of slaves and camp-followers, whose taste for lust and cruelty was even more depraved. Neither rank nor age afforded any protection against indiscriminate rape and slaughter. Venerable old men, women in their last years, worthless as booty, were dragged around to make sport. If a marriageable girl or handsome young man fell into their way, they were torn to pieces by the savagery of their ravishers, whom they led to destroy each other in their turn. Men carrying off money or some rich temple-offering were cut down by others of greater strength. Some, scorning what lay before their eyes, tortured and beat the owners of property to make them dig up hidden treasure. . . . An army so diverse in language and custom, made up of Roman citizens, allies and foreigners, embraced every kind of lust, knew no common code, and would stop at nothing. Cremona lasted for four days. When everything, human and divine, had collapsed in flames, the only building to survive was the temple of Mefitis outside the walls, saved by its position—or by the divinity. Such was the destruction of Cremona, 285 years after its foundation.'[58]

Rome herself endured many atrocities from the troops of Otho, Vitellius and Vespasian indiscriminately. But the great city, with its dissipations and its unhealthy climate, had its own means of revenge, of which the Vitellian army in particular had a sharp experience. They had appeared as aliens, especially the German auxiliaries from the northern frontiers. 'The men were a fearsome spectacle, clad in furs and bearing huge spears. Unused to city life, they could not dodge the crowds in the streets: they would fall down on the slippery pavements, or in collision with passers-by: then there would be quarrels, blows—finally, the sword.'[59] But the formal entry of Vitellius' army into Rome in August 69 was impressive. 'The eagles of eight legions were displayed, and the standards of twelve cavalry and thirty-four infantry units of auxiliaries. Camp commandants, tribunes, senior centurions, wearing white cloaks, marched before the eagles: other officers, medals and equipment shining, marched beside their companies. The decorations and necklaces of the rankers shone brilliantly. It was a splendid show—worthy of a better Emperor than Vitellius.' But once in Rome, discipline was not maintained. 'The temptation of a big city and all its manifold vices enslaved their bodies, as lust enfeebled their spirits. Finally, disregarding even hygiene, they camped on the notoriously unhealthy ground of the Vatican, and this gave rise to heavy mortality. The Tiber was close at hand, and the Gauls and Germans, always liable to illness, were laid low by their passion for bathing and inability to stand the heat.'[60] The bacteria of the Tiber in late summer must have been indeed a formidable enemy.

When the Flavian threat grew sharper, it was a demoralised army that Caecina led north. 'As the German army left the city it presented a very different spectacle. Physical vigour and mental alertness were not to be seen: the ranks were thin, and the march sluggish. The soldiers could not endure the sun, the dust and the weather: unfit as they were for any physical stress, they were all the more ready for mutiny.'[61] The *Histories* have much to record of atrocity and disgrace. Nothing, it is fair to conjecture, would have more deeply moved the historian and his readers than the ignominy that fell on the Rhine legions in the last phases of the Civil War. Under an elderly and incompetent commander, their generals waiting for the right moment to sell out to Vespasian, surrounded by hostile Germans and treacherous Gauls, the troops could fairly plead confusion. But one man saw where the duty of a Roman soldier lay and did it to the end. This was the legionary commander, Dillius Vocula.[62] His military skill was not of the highest: Tacitus points out that he could win a victory, but was weak at exploiting it. But the old Roman *virtus* was nobly displayed in the last scene of his life, in the camp at Novaesium. The Gallic armies of Classicus and Tutor are only two miles away: Vocula knows that his own soldiers plan to murder him and swear allegiance to the Empire of the Gauls.

The splendid speech which Tacitus composes for him contains, as Syme has shown, unmistakable echoes of Livy: in such terms did the younger Scipio rally mutinous troops. Vocula's last appeal invokes the whole military tradition of Rome, and its presiding deities. 'Jupiter Optimus Maximus, whom we have honoured by so many triumphs through eight hundred and twenty years, and you, Quirinus, father of the city of Rome, I beseech you that, if it be not your will that this camp be preserved pure and undefiled under my command, guard it at least from pollution by Tutor and Classicus! Let these Roman soldiers either be innocent of crime, or let them feel a tardy but allowable remorse!'[63] The appeal failed. At this point, the men were beyond redemption. Vocula was murdered by a Roman deserter. In the same chapter Tacitus describes the sequel in taut and astringent words. 'Classicus, invested with the insignia of a Roman Emperor, then found words enough to recite the oath of allegiance. All present swore fidelity to the Empire of the Gauls. Promotion to senior rank was granted to Vocula's murderer, the others were rewarded to the extent their crimes deserved.'[64] In such tones of fastidious disgust had Virgil hastened over Aeneas' first fornication with Dido in the cave.[65]

At another Roman camp, Vetera, the troops at least bravely endured a siege until famine compelled them to sue Civilis for their lives. These submissions were not accepted until they had

sworn allegiance to the Empire of the Gauls. Even this did not
save them. Plundered and humiliated, they were escorted out of
camp and then German troops treacherously fell upon them. A
few survivors retreated to the camp, but in the end the Germans
captured it and completed the massacre. Their fate haunted the
minds of Vocula's troops—the Sixteenth Legion and its auxiliaries—when they were ordered to march from Novaesium to
Trier. 'The time of departure came upon them as a more bitter
hour than they had expected. Within the camp the shoddy
appearance they presented had not been especially remarkable,
but the open country and the light of day laid bare their shame.
The images of the Emperors had been torn down, and their
standards bore no honours, though on either side those of the
Gauls shone bright. The column was silent, like a long funeral
procession: it was led by Claudius Sanctus, who had lost one
eye, and was even feebler of intellect than ugly of expression.'⁶⁶
(Such officers always appear at times of disaster!) Their ignominy was doubled when another legion joined them, having
deserted the camp at Bonna. At the news of the capture of the
legions all who had dreaded the name of Rome but a little earlier
rushed from the fields and houses to enjoy in full measure the
unparalleled spectacle. 'The cavalry squadron of Picenum could
not bear the jeers of the crowd . . . they rode off to Moguntiacum. On the way they chanced to meet Longinus, the murderer
of Vocula; by killing him they took the first steps to exonerate
themselves from guilt with posterity. But the legions, their
course unaltered, encamped outside the walls of Trier.' Later,
they were withdrawn to the territory of the Mediomatrici,
around Metz.

The chances of war were yet to restore these men to the
Roman allegiance. When the ramshackle Empire of the Gauls
began to disintegrate under the hammer blows of Petilius
Cerialis, they took the oath to Vespasian. Eventually they came
to meet his victorious army at Trier, to find what perhaps they
least expected—magnanimity. 'They stood there in full knowledge of their guilt, their eyes fixed on the ground. No greetings

passed between the two armies: when men tried to console or show them they made no reply. They hid in their tents and avoided the light of day. Neither danger nor fear benumbed them so much as their shame and humiliation. The very conquerors were struck dumb, and could only plead for them with silent tears. Finally Cerialis brought them some comfort, asserting that it was all the work of destiny, accomplished through the discord between the troops and their generals, and the treachery of the enemy . . . Vespasian had forgotten their former misdeeds, as he had himself. Then they were received again into the camps, and an order of the day published through all companies forbidding any to get into a brawl or argument, or to reproach a fellow-soldier with mutiny or disaster.'[67]

CHAPTER EIGHT

Rome—City and People

THE ROME THAT TACITUS KNEW was the *Nova Urbs* or New City that had arisen after the Great Fire of 64, with its regular plan, its wide streets, its buildings of fire-proof material, further protected by spacious colonnades. This is the city described by Pliny[1] in 73; he mentions its thirteen miles of walls, seventy miles of streets within the built-up area, and concludes with the opinion that 'no city in the world can compare with Rome.' And indeed, only Antioch and Alexandria could claim rank as great cities. Its population, perhaps one million under Augustus, may have risen to $1\frac{1}{2}$ millions under Trajan.[2] It was by far the largest agglomeration of human beings which had yet appeared on the face of the earth. To supply its wants called for great feats of organisation and civil engineering. Since Italy could not feed it, the harvests of Egypt, Africa, Sicily, and Sardinia, contributed to the *annona* or annual corn supply for Rome. Its needs for water were met by a vast organisation, which we know of through the description of one of its most energetic supervisors, Frontinus, who wrote in the reign of Nerva. He describes the eight major aqueducts, which could deliver 220 million gallons of water each day; this he rightly hailed as a proof of the greatness of the Roman Empire.[3]

While Tacitus was writing the *Histories* and the *Annals* the Emperors Trajan and Hadrian were carrying Rome to its high point of urban magnificence. The city centre had been extended

beyond the historic Forum Romanum by the addition of no
fewer than five new fora, those of Julius Caesar, Augustus,
Vespasian, Nerva and, above all, the magnificent Forum of
Trajan, with its complex of buildings for political, legal, cultural
and economic use. The whole surface of the Palatine had been
converted into a palace quarter by the work of Emperors,
beginning with Tiberius and ending with Domitian. Here again,
the climax of magnificence was reached by the great buildings
constructed for Domitian by Rabirius. At last the Roman
Emperor was housed in a style suitable to the master of the
world. The Roman people were provided with amusements on
an equally lavish scale. There were two theatres, each of which
could seat about 15,000 people. Some 50,000 could glut their
deplorable tastes for gladiatorial shows and beast-baitings in the
Colosseum, built by Vespasian and Titus. The Circus Maximus,
devoted to the popular sport of chariot racing, reached its
greatest extent under Trajan, when it could certainly seat 250,000
people, and perhaps another 100,000. Athletics were never
popular in Rome, but the Stadium of Domitian provided
accommodation for 15,000 spectators of these events. There
were numerous public libraries, collections of art, and statues;
indeed there is an exaggerated story that the city's population
in stone and marble was equal to its human population.

But there was another facet to imperial Rome. This was the
private squalor described, especially, in the *Satires* of Juvenal.[4]
The city's poor were housed in vast apartment buildings, and
exposed to the jerry-builder and the racketeering landlord.
Noise was incessant, worse by night than by day. There was no
public transport. The rich had litters: others had to walk.
Medical services were rudimentary, and there were no public
hospitals. Epidemics were frequent—in that of 79, 10,000
deaths are reported in a single day. At a less spectacular level,
honest work was scarce, prices were high, and the general
pressure was to live beyond one's means. Here, Juvenal's phrase,
'*ambitiosa paupertas*,' is a telling one.[5]

The narrative of Tacitus notes, especially, public disasters in

Rome. There are serious Tiber floods in 15, leading to the setting up of a commission to report back on the problem of flood control in the Tiber Valley and beyond. It arouses vigorous protest from the municipalities who object to losing their natural waters. In particular the people of Florence do not wish to see the Chiana diverted from its natural channel into the Arno. In the end it is decided 'that no action be taken.'[6] Fires are more frequent and more disastrous than floods. There was one in 27 which ravaged the entire Caelian Hill: another in 36 on the Aventine: and of course the worst of all—the Great Fire under Nero. Notice is also taken of new buildings, often in perfunctory fashion. There are repairs to the Theatre of Pompey under Tiberius, and to sundry temples. A triumphal arch is built for Drusus and Germanicus in the same reign. Under Nero there is an amphitheatre in the Campus Martius, and a new gymnasium. A sinister event was the building of barracks for the Praetorian Guard in 23 by Sejanus. This brought an armed camp into the city. From it the troops would issue to massacre the citizens, as they did at the time of the murder of Galba in 69, and in it the empire itself would be bought and sold.

Occasionally Tacitus will allow himself an antiquarian excursus. Thus the Great Fire on the Caelian Hill leads to an account of the settlement there of the Etruscan Caeles Vibenna, and to remarks on other Roman place names of Etruscan origin.[7] The extension of the *pomoerium* under Claudius prompts an account of the line originally traced by Romulus. 'Beginning, then, from the Cattle Market (where now stands the bronze statue of a bull, the animal used in ploughing) the *pomoerium* furrow was drawn, for the purpose of marking out the city, so as to include the Great Altar of Hercules. Thence its course, marked by stones at set intervals, ran along the low slopes of the Palatine hill to the altar of Consus, then to the old Curia, then to the chapel of Lares, and from there to the Forum Romanum.'[8] This passage is the most important literary source for the course of the ancient *pomoerium* or boundary mark of the city of Rome.

A good deal of topographical detail is inserted into the account of events in the city. We can often follow the movements of the principal characters in Rome. For example, when Piso returned after the death of Germanicus 'he landed by the Mausoleum of Augustus, in broad daylight and when the banks were crowded with people, which gave great offence. A great train of clients followed Piso, and Plancina had her women friends; they all looked very cheerful as they passed on their way. His unpopularity was heightened because his house, which was gaily decorated, stood close to the Forum. There were banquets and dinner parties, and all so conspicuous that they could not be hidden.'[9]

For all these events, Rome and its topography were the background to the action. But at times they provide the action as well, and on a scale to call forth all Tacitus' powers of description. In the *Annals*, the most important of these is the Great Fire of 64, and its sequel;[10] in the *Histories*, the destruction of the Capitol in 69, and its rebuilding in the following year.[11]

As a picture of public disaster, Tacitus' account of the Great Fire, though much shorter, invites comparison with Thucydides[12] on the Plague of Athens. But they describe contrary processes. A little before the Plague passage Thucydides had given, in the Funeral Speech, a picture of Periclean Athens, the most advanced society of its day. Then he shows how it collapsed into moral anarchy under the stress of the Plague. In Tacitus' account of Nero's Rome, moral collapse has preceded physical disaster.

The public banquets that marked Nero's return from Naples reached their climax in the notorious party given by Tigellinus. 'I shall quote it,' says Tacitus, 'as a model of its kind, having no taste for the repeated description of orgies. A raft was built on the lake of Agrippa, and here the banquet was served while the raft was towed about by other vessels. These were fitted out in gold and ivory; their rowers were selected perverts, divided according to their age and the vices which were their specialities.

FT

Rare birds, wild animals, even marine monsters from the ocean, had been procured. On the quays of the lake were brothels, filled with women of rank, and opposite them naked prostitutes, with lewd posturings and obscene gestures. At nightfall, the nearby woods and houses re-echoed with songs, and were ablaze with lights. Nero tried every pleasure, licensed and unlicensed. It seemed that there were no further depths of degradation for him to plumb. But then, after a few days, he entered on an actual parody of marriage with one of the filthy crowd of homosexuals, called Pythagoras. The Emperor wore the bridal veil; witnesses were present, there was a dowry, wedding torches, and a nuptial couch. Everything was in public, even down to those items which are usually performed in darkness when the bride is a woman.' Disaster followed the Fire. How soon is not stated: only later does it emerge that Nero had left Rome and was staying at Antium. Tacitus describes a retribution that was as swift—though not so total—as that which fell on the biblical cities of the Plain.

To summarise the chapters on the Great Fire would be to do them an injustice: they should be read as a whole in a good translation.[13] This done, a short commentary may be found helpful. First, the origins of the Fire, in the Circus Maximus. A moral could have been drawn. Tacitus avoids it. He is factual and concise. The Fire began among inflammable material stored in the shops on the outer façade of the Circus on its north-east side. But indeed it is clear that the Circus Maximus as a whole was a major fire-risk, with its two upper storeys and much of the seating of wood, to say nothing of the accretions on its outer face. Once it was well alight, its sheer size—600 metres long, 150 metres wide—made it a gigantic firebomb in the heart of Rome. And on July 19th, 64, there was a high wind which spread the flames so quickly as to nullify all efforts to contain them. It looks as though a fire-storm was generated of the kind so dreadfully familiar in the bombed cities of the Second World War. On the sixth day the Fire was brought to a halt at the foot of the Esquiline by the most effective methods known to the fire-brigades of antiquity—an artificial fire-break made by the wide-spread destruction of buildings in its path.

The respite was short. A second fire broke out in suspicious circumstances, in the Campus Martius among slum property owned by Tigellinus. The well-known inscription from the Altar of the Fire of Nero[14] speaks of it as raging for nine days; this second outbreak, then, presumably burned for three. Once it was over, only four of the fourteen Augustan regions were intact: three were destroyed to ground level: in the other seven a few badly damaged houses survived. The three totally destroyed regions were III (Subura), X (Palatine) and XI (Circus Maximus). Undamaged were, in all probability XIV (Transtiberina), I (Porta Capena), V (Esquiline) and VI (Quirinal). To this list of destruction by areas Tacitus adds a second—a selection of the more famous monuments and antiquities lost. He does not—and in the nature of ancient statistics it is scarcely to be looked for—give even an estimate of the loss of life.

Such was the Fire on its physical side. But, as always, for Tacitus the main drama is played out in men's minds. After the helplessness, panic and despair of the city populace—vividly described—we hear of the rumours, widespread and irresistible as the Fire itself, that fastened the guilt on the Emperor. Here Tacitus' powers of innuendo are used to the full. Rumours are duly labelled as such. Alternatives are given. But so deftly are the rumours inserted, that the balance has been quietly tilted in their favour. At the outset we are told 'whether the Fire was started by accident, or contrived by the Emperor, is uncertain: historians give both accounts.'[15] So far the scales are even. But then, we hear that Nero did not return to Rome from Antium until the Fire had reached his own palace—the Domus Transitoria. The Fire could not be checked until it had destroyed the Palatine and all in its vicinity. Then Nero took measures, prompt and generous, to house and feed the refugees, and to reduce the price of necessities. 'But these earned him no gratitude' (though the point is, surely, were they effective?). Because a widespread rumour had it (*pervaserat rumor*) that as the city was burning,

Nero entered his private theatre and sang *The Fall of Troy*, comparing the modern with the ancient calamity. Again, before the vast area of destruction is noticed, it is said that Nero 'appeared' to be seeking the glory of founding a new city, and giving it his own name. The charge is not repeated in the description of the rebuilding of Rome, though it could well have been. Instead, stress is laid on the use Nero made of the opportunity afforded by the disaster to his country by embarking on a selfish piece of architectural prodigality—the building of the Domus Aurea or Golden House of Nero.[16]

The Golden House, Tacitus is at pains to point out, was remarkable for more than its gold and jewels—'these are the usual trappings of luxury, and have become commonplace.' Its novel features were rather 'its meadows, its lakes, its artificial wilderness, now of woods and now of open spaces, and its vistas. Severus and Celer were the architects and engineers.' The description is amplified by a passage of Suetonius. 'The entrance hall was designed for a colossal statue, 120 feet high, bearing Nero's head. So vast were the grounds, that triple colonnades ran for a mile. There was, too, an enormous lake, surrounded by buildings made to look like cities. The parklands contained fields, vineyards, pastures and woodlands; there were a great variety of animals, domestic and wild. Some parts of the palace were overlaid with gold, and studded with jewels and mother-of-pearl. The dining-rooms had ceilings of ivory, with sliding panels to allow flowers and perfumes to be showered down upon the guests. The main dining-room was a rotunda, which revolved slowly, day and night, like the vault of heaven itself. There were baths with a lavish supply of both sea-water and sulphur water. When the palace was completed on this sumptuous scale, Nero's approval as he dedicated it was confined to the remark "At last I can begin to live like a human being!"' The Golden House was, in fact, conceived as a luxury villa, in a splendid park on a scale of imperial magnificence, and set in the heart of Rome. A modern estimate of its extent is 125 acres. What Nero conceived as a lavish gift to himself was an even more generous present to the propaganda of his adversaries. The resentment of the people is summed up in the anonymous epigram

Roma domus fiet, Veiios migrate, Quirites,[17]
si non et Veiios occupat ista domus!

(Rome will become a palace: Roman citizens, migrate to Veii! Unless that hated palace has reached Veii too!)

In a few years time the Flavians were to gain easy popularity by converting the Emperor's private indulgences to the pleasures of the people. The lake was filled in to provide the foundations for the Flavian Amphitheatre or Colosseum, the Baths were converted to public use, under the name of the Thermae of Titus. After the still uncompleted palace was damaged by fire in 104, its remains were covered over to form the substructures of the Thermae of Trajan. So the hated palace was literally buried. Centuries later its frescoes and statues were rediscovered to evoke an excess of admiration among the artists of the Renaissance.[18] A more balanced appraisal is possible today. The Domus Aurea is rightly seen as a landmark in the history of Roman architecture and taste, no more and no less to the discredit of its begetter than is the Pavilion at Brighton.

The affair of the Domus Aurea is one of two pendants added by Tacitus to the main account of the Fire. There can be little doubt that, in its author's eyes, it was the more important. The other[19] tells how Nero, still looking for a scapegoat for the disaster, found one in an obscure set of religious fanatics, already hated by the people for their crimes, and visited them with exemplary and atrocious punishments. Thereby he overshot the mark and provoked an unlooked-for compassion towards them. Time and the course of history have combined to make this perhaps the best-known single passage in Tacitus. For here is authentic evidence, in a non-Christian source of the highest standing, of the early existence of a Christian community in Rome, and of the prejudice and hostility it aroused. It would be too long a task to unravel all the errors implicit in the passage. Suffice it to say that most of them arose from the belief that the Christians were an extremist sect of Jews.

'Their founder, one Christos, had been put to death by the procurator Pontius Pilate in the reign of Tiberius. This checked the abominable superstition (*exitiabilis superstitio*) for a while, but it broke out again and spread, not merely through Judaea, where it originated but even to Rome itself, the great reservoir and collecting-ground of every kind of depravity and filth.' The depravity and filth specifically associated with early Christianity were charges of cannibalism, infanticide, and incest brought against it by a misunderstanding of the nature of the Eucharist. Another charge it bore through association with the Jews—that of 'hatred of the human race.' Jewish monotheism with its hostility to other religions was alien to the easy-going tolerance of the Roman world. The Jews were marked by a savage and uncompromising fanaticism such as they displayed only a few years later in the defence of the fortress of Masada.[20] So the Christians of Rome, 'hating the human race,' were capable of starting the fire. To will such an enormity was to be guilty of it: they were *sontes* (guilty). They deserved the most severe punishment—but not the outrages inflicted on them. The tearing apart by wild beasts, the turning of a man into a living torch—such were the persecutions under Nero. Juvenal bears out Tacitus. They took place in the Gardens of Maecenas, and also, perhaps, in the Circus of Gaius and Nero, which stood on the Vatican. And close by the Circus (*in Vaticano ad Circum*) stood the cemetery in which, so tradition asserts, was buried Peter, Apostle of the Romans. In the last few years the excavations conducted in the Grotte Vaticane have come very close to confirming this tradition of the earliest Roman church.[21]

The re-building of the city is shown[22] for what it was—a piece of rational and enlightened town planning on a major scale. Arrangements were made at public expense for the clearance of the site and the disposal of rubble. There is a graduated scale of subsidies to those completing private buildings by a given date.

A master plan prescribes the alignment of roads, the width of streets, and the height of houses. To prevent future disaster by fire, the use of fire-proof stone is required, inspectors are appointed to secure a better service of water from the public supply, householders are required to keep fire-fighting apparatus on hand. A tribute is paid to the beauty (*decus*) of the *Nova Urbs*, though at the same time Tacitus quotes the wholly understandable view of those who thought that the old city with its tall buildings and narrow streets had been healthier, and that the wide open spaces of the new one reflected unduly the sun's heat.

No names are mentioned in connection with this splendid piece of urban renewal. Modern scholarship is inclined to see in it the work of Severus and Celer, who had earlier been saddled with the discredit of Nero's Golden House. Nor does Nero get any praise for his care of public amenities, apart from the mention of his name in connection with the cost of removing the rubble. As ever, in Tacitus, blame is distributed where due: praise is harder to obtain.

The burning of the Capitol was, for Tacitus,[23] the culminating atrocity of the year 69. It occurred during the furious and useless street-fighting between the supporters of Flavius Sabinus, who had occupied the Capitol, and those of Vitellius, whose cause was by now effectively lost. After describing the outbreak of the fire, Tacitus adds his reflections on the criminal folly of the deed, and the grandeur of the historic temple thus destroyed. 'This criminal act was the most grievous and shameful disaster to befall the Commonwealth of the Roman People since the foundation of the City. Assailed by no foreign foe, with the gods—had our morals allowed it—propitious to us, the seat of Jupiter Optimus Maximus, founded by our ancestors as the pledge of Rome's Empire, the temple inviolate when the city surrendered to Porsenna and when it was captured by the Gauls, this temple was burned in the frenzied strife between our own Emperors. It was publicly besieged and publicly set on fire, and what were the motives for conflict? What prize counterbalanced this enormous disaster? Were we fighting for our country?

'King Tarquinius Priscus vowed its erection in the war against the Sabines, and laid its foundations, on a scale more suited to a destiny of greatness than to the modest resources of the Roman people at that time. Later, Servius Tullius, with the support of our allies, and Tarquinius Superbus, with the spoils of wars after the capture of Suessa Pometia, advanced its building. But the true glory of the work belongs to the days of freedom. It was Horatius Pulvillus, in his second consulship, who dedicated a building so magnificent that all the vast wealth of the Roman People in a latter age has seemed to embellish rather than to enlarge it. It was rebuilt on the same site after the fire which, 415 years later, destroyed it—in the consulship of Lucius Scipio and Gaius Norbanus. After his victory was won, Sulla undertook its restoration: but this one thing eluded his usual good fortune. It bore the name of Lutatius Catulus, amid all the great buildings of the Caesars, to the time of Vitellius. This was the temple that was then burned down.'[24]

To the enemies of Rome throughout the world, this self-inflicted destruction seemed a portent. In Gaul, in particular, where the rebellion of Civilis was in progress, the Druids[25] took it as a sign that the supremacy of Rome was ended, and that the Empire of the world was now passing to the northern peoples. For obvious reasons, the rebuilding of the great Temple was the first task of the new government of Vespasian. The inaugural ceremony (June 21st, 70) is thus described.[26]

'The task of restoring the Capitol was entrusted to Lucius Vestinus, an equestrian, but commanding a power and reputation second to none. The *haruspices* he consulted advised that the remains of the old building should be carted off to the marshes, but the temple re-erected on the former site: the gods were averse to any change in its design. On June 21st, in fine weather, the whole area to be consecrated for the temple was surrounded with wreaths and garlands. Soldiers entered, men of lucky names, carrying branches from propitious trees. Then

Vestal Virgins, with boys and girls whose parents were both alive, purified the whole space with water drawn from sacred springs and rivers. Then Helvidius Priscus, the praetor, having hallowed the whole area by the sacrifice of a bull, a stallion, and a boar, and having placed the entrails on the altar, solemnly repeated after the Chief Pontiff, Plautius Aelianus, a prayer to Jupiter, Juno and Minerva, and the gods who protect the Empire, to enlist their support for the project, and to bring divine aid to prosper the plans for their temple which had been begun by the efforts of man. He then touched the wreaths, with which the foundation stone and the ropes around it were bound. At the same time the other magistrates, the priests, the senate, the knights and a large part of the common people, vied with each other in their zeal to drag along the huge stone. In every part of the foundations were placed ores of gold and silver, never melted down, but in their original state. The augurs had forbidden that any metal or stone intended for some other purpose should be allowed to profane their work. The height of the building was increased; this was the sole innovation that religion would allow, and the only respect in which the ancient temple seemed less than magnificent.'

It is to be noted that the part played by Helvidius Priscus and by the magistrates is strongly stressed. Suetonius is at pains to emphasise the cheerful way in which Vespasian played a part in the common task of restoring the Capitol after he had reached Rome. 'Vespasian in person inaugurated the restoration of the Capitol after the fire. He collected the first basketful of rubble and carried it away on his own shoulders. He also undertook to replace the three thousand bronze tablets which had been lost in the fire, and searched everywhere for copies of the inscriptions engraved on them. These venerable and suitably phrased records of Decrees of the Senate and Ordinances of the People dealt with the alliances, treaties and privileges granted to individuals, going back almost to the foundation of Rome.' This Temple, however, was to be the shortest lived of all the temples of Jupiter Optimus Maximus. It was again destroyed by fire in 80. It was the hated

Domitian who restored a newer and yet more magnificent temple—destined this time to a life of more than four centuries.

The huge cosmopolitan population of Rome also appears as a collective personality in the pages of Tacitus. Since the time of Augustus the people had had no political responsibility; the attempt by that Emperor to provide a limited measure of self-government in the wards and regions into which he divided the city was no sort of compensation for the political rights in the *res publica* of which he had deprived them.[27] They lived for mass amusements—*panem et circenses*, in Juvenal's oft quoted phrase.[28] When either was in short supply, they would riot and cause panic among the authorities. Many of them were of foreign origin—Tenney Frank has estimated this element as high as 90 per cent. In Juvenal's Third Satire it is revulsion from this mob of foreigners which reinforces the discomforts of a city life to persuade Umbricius to leave his native Rome.

Decent provincials, too, were disgusted by the degenerate tastes of the Roman mob, as, for example, when they hectically applauded Nero on the stage at the celebration of the Quinquatria in 65. 'The Roman mob . . . applauded in rhythmic cadence. They sounded pleased; perhaps, having no sense of public outrage, they really were. But there were some who came from remote country towns, from backward districts of Italy where perhaps something of an older morality still lingered on, or visitors from distant provinces, or embassies, on private business, who were unpractised in loose conduct and found the spectacle intolerable. Their hands lacked the stamina for continuous clapping, and they were unequal to the dishonourable task.'[29] In the *Agricola* Tacitus has the phrase '*hic aliud agens populus*'—'the people with their other preoccupations'; it is a good description of the irresponsibility of urban man in the mass.

To judge from Tacitus the character of the city populace had deteriorated between Tiberius and Nero. In Tiberius' time they could make their voice heard. In 29, at a crucial hour, they

rallied to the support of Agrippina and her son, and at any rate
caused the postponement of their deaths.[30] In 32 the exorbitant
price of grain all but led to a rebellion. 'For several days in the
theatre grievances were voiced in bolder terms than were usually
directed toward the Emperor. Tiberius was highly incensed. He
criticised the magistrates and the Senate for not using their
authority to control the people: he enumerated the provinces
from which he had collected grain, pointing out that this had
been got in much greater quantity than under Augustus. So a
Senate resolution was drafted in terms of archaic stringency to
rebuke the people, and the consuls lost no time in publishing it.
That the Emperor kept silence, was not, as he had hoped, taken
as a sign of restraint, but as a token of arrogance.'[31] At any rate
some kind of a dialogue was still possible between the Emperor
and the people. But in the *Histories* they appear as a fickle and
degenerate mob.

Such was their behaviour when on January 15th, 69, they
crowded as a man to the palace. 'Slaves were in among them,
and with a bedlam of cries, they clamoured for the death of
Otho and the conspirators, just as if they were demanding a
turn at the circus or at the theatre. Not that they showed any
judgement or sincerity (before the day was out they would
raise a different cry with no less enthusiasm), but simply because their tradition was to flatter any and every ruler with
uninhibited applause and empty demonstrations.'[32] They wanted
a victim, no matter whom. Before the day was out, they got
Galba.

Tacitus does spare them a little sympathy in their clash with
the troops of Vitellius.[33] These soldiers, rivals among themselves,
were of one mind in an assault on civilians. 'The worst massacre
occurred at the seventh milestone from Rome. Here Vitellius was
distributing food to the troops, prepared for each man on the
lavish scale of a gladiator's rations. The city population had
flocked out, and was present in every part of the camp. Catching
the soldiers off their guard, some robbed them, cutting their
belts, and saying, with their cockney impertinence, "Got your

swords?" The soldiers were unused to being laughed at, and took this insult very hard, using their swords to attack the unarmed civilians. Among others, the father of a soldier was murdered at his son's side; then he was recognised, and the massacre of innocent people came to a halt.'

The panic caused by these northern soldiers inside the city itself has already been described. The city mob appears at its worst during the ferocious street fighting between the forces of Vitellius and the Flavians. 'The city populace watched the fight like connoisseurs: cheering and encouraging now this side, and now that, as though at a mock battle. If one side or the other gave way, they cried out indignantly that those who had taken refuge in shops and private houses must be dragged out to have their throats cut: this way, they got more of the booty for themselves, for while the soldiers busied themselves with massacre and bloodshed, the spoils went to the mob. The whole city presented a bloody, unnatural spectacle. Here were battles and wounds, there baths and cafés. Here were pools of blood and piles of corpses, there prostitutes and their clients. All the lusts of a corrupt peace coincided with all the horrors of a sacked city: you would think the country was in the double grip of madness and debauchery.

'It is true that armed men had fought previously in Rome. They did so twice under Sulla, once under Cinna, nor was there less cruelty involved. But now there was an appalling callousness. Not for one minute did the frantic pursuit of pleasure halt. They rejoiced and exulted in the scene as an extra amenity for the holidays; caring nothing for the parties, they were delighted by the disasters to the state.'[34] The plebs of Rome has become a sadistic and degenerate mob. Vespasian judged their tastes very well when he built them the Colosseum as a present to mark the return of peace.

But although Tacitus describes the pathology of the mob, he does not enquire into its causes. Here, much more is to be gained from Juvenal.[35] The *Satires* give a very good idea of the conditions the poor of Rome had to endure—the unending assaults on privacy in their crowded tenements, the humiliations inseparable from the social system, the scarcity of honest employment, and the irresponsibility caused by the loss of political rights. Modern sociologists are familiar with the violence that is bred from overcrowded urban conditions. The Colosseum was a rough-and-ready attempt to provide an outlet. But Tacitus would have thought it beneath the dignity of history to enquire into such themes as these.

CHAPTER NINE

The Provinces

IN HIS TREATMENT OF THE PROVINCES Tacitus differs essentially from that of the modern historian. Ever since the days of Mommsen, the leading theme of Roman imperial history has been accepted as being all that is comprised in Pliny's phrase about 'the boundless majesty of the Roman peace.'[1] Under this rubric we expect to be told of the Romanisation of much of northern and western Europe, North Africa and the Danube lands—the building of roads, the founding of cities, the massive exploitation of resources, the complex interaction of local and metropolitan cultures. Strongest and most enduring in the broad lands between the Straits of Gibraltar and the Rhine, this great work of civilisation also went forward in Britain, in the Alpine lands, on the eastern shoreline of the Adriatic, and in the valleys of the Save and Drave. The Arab conquests have overlain a parallel work in Africa, which extended from Libya to Morocco. All these new lands were more or less integrated into a single world state with the older and more developed cultures of the eastern Mediterranean and of western Asia.

All this Tacitus understood very well. If he does not set himself to describe it, it is because it fits neither his concept of history nor his method of writing. The latter was episodic, little suited to the sustained treatment of broad themes. And, for Tacitus, history should eschew economies and culture for politics and war. A passage of the *Agricola*[2] shows that Tacitus knew, none better, what the Romanisation of the provinces entailed. He has this to say of one aspect of Agricola's work in Britain.

'The following winter (79–80) was devoted to beneficial schemes to induce people, whose scattered dwelling, and barbarous ways made them warlike, to become docile and accustomed, in public and private, to the building of temples, town-centres, and private houses.

'The energetic were praised and the laggards censured—as a result, competition for his good-will took the place of compulsion. Indeed, he began to educate the sons of British chiefs in liberal arts, praising the natural ability of the Britons as superior to the trained skills of the Gauls. As a result, a people who had formerly rejected the Latin language began to aspire to eloquence! Even our national dress became fashionable: the toga was often seen. Gradually a taste for the more corrupting luxuries became general—such as the use of colonnades, hot baths, elaborate dinner-parties.'[3]

But then at the end comes the extraordinary comment: 'This the poor Britons took to be "civilisation"; in reality it was part of their slavery.' Is this Tacitus' inability to resist an epigram, even though it deprives Agricola of the credit for a liberal and humane policy? Perhaps, but more probably it springs from his view that to the reader of history, war is more interesting than peace—Agricola the conqueror of Caledonia more attractive than Agricola the founder of the Forum at Verulamium. To be *ferox provincia*—a warlike province—is the way to win space in the pages of Tacitus.

Consider Spain.[4] In the period of which Tacitus was writing the Spanish provinces were perhaps the most flourishing part of the Roman world. The province of Baetica was virtually another Italy. Gades (Cadiz) had become the wealthiest port in the western Mediterranean. From the leading families of Roman Spain came emperors, writers and scholars—Trajan, Hadrian, Lucan,

Seneca, Quintilian, Martial to name no more. The mines of Sierra Morena and New Carthage had long been the most extensively worked in the ancient world. The conquests of Augustus had opened up a new source of mining wealth in Cantabria and the north-west, whose exploitation—a triumph of hydraulic engineering—is described in a lengthy passage of Pliny.[5] All we hear of Spanish mining in Tacitus is when the wealthiest mine-owner, Sextus Marius, was put to death in the reign of Tiberius on a charge of incest with his daughter. Here Tacitus does look to economics rather than morals—'it is clear that his wealth was the cause of his ruin, for although his gold and copper mines were taken over by the State, their revenue went into the Imperial Treasury.'[6]

We do not know what Tacitus had to say about the work of Vespasian in Spain, which included the granting of municipal rights to more than two hundred cities. But, in what survives, we hear of the atrocious murder of one governor of a Spanish province, the banishment of another and the nine years in office of a third.[7] The three legions holding Spain are duly recorded in the Army List under Tiberius. Spain vies with Gaul in making good the losses of Germanicus in 15. The Spanish provinces are thought to be wavering in their allegiance at the time of the rebellion of Julius and Sacrovir in 21.[8] As governor of Spain, Galba makes his bid for the throne in 68.[9] And that is all. In other words, nothing about Spain in her own right: only as she contributes to the affairs of Rome.

In Africa the case is similar and even more striking. It is true that the books are lost which have contained the account of Claudius' establishment of the two new provinces of Mauretania, and of the brilliant campaigns of Suetonius Paulinus beyond the Atlas Mountains.[10] They might have been preceded by an excursus on the extension of Roman power westwards from the old province of Africa into the lands formerly ruled by King Juba. But, as it is, Tacitus' chief concern with African affairs is the rebellion of Tacfarinas, a desultory affair chiefly notable as the graveyard of Roman military reputations.[11] As for the Danube provinces—apart from the army mutinies in 14 and the movement of troops in 69—they scarcely appear at all.

Britain, by contrast, figures large. *Ferox provincia*, and the scene of Agricola's greatest exploits, she had earned her passage. Even so we do not have Tacitus on the Claudian invasion, nor on the forward movements under Vespasian, when Petilius Cerialis overcame the Brigantes in the north, and his successor Sextus Julius Frontinus defeated the hitherto invincible Silures and secured military control of Wales. All these episodes Tacitus will have treated at length, but the surviving accounts of the struggle with Caratacus and the rebellion of Boudicca are among the best pieces of military narrative in the *Annals*.[12] Britain is also, of course, the setting for well over half of the *Agricola*. The excursus on the geography, resources and peoples of Britain (*Agricola*, 10–13) is comparable to that in the *Germania* (1–27), and indeed to the chapters in the *Histories* devoted to the land and the peoples of Palestine (V, 2–10).

In Britain, Tacitus is conscious of having something new to contribute—the additions to geographical knowledge resulting from Agricola's campaign in Scotland, then for the first time adequately explored. And so he has. Horizons expand. We hear of the Orkneys and of Ireland. There is speculation on the long days of the northern summer, and the sluggish waters of the northern ocean.[13] Much of this is naïve, but it is counterbalanced by a splendid description[14] of the sea lochs of the Western Highlands, a type of scenery unknown in the Mediterranean world. 'Nowhere does the sea exercise a wider domain: not merely does it carry a mass of currents in all directions, but its ebb and flow is not contained by the coastline: it penetrates far inland and works its way between the ridges of the mountains as though in its own domain.'

The struggle between Rome and the Britons over some forty years of intermittent campaigning is presented as one between the native freedom (*libertas*) and peace (*pax Romana*). It is as fair to the native cause as it can be, seeing that it is written wholly from a Roman standpoint. Caratacus fought bravely, and is made to speak boldly—even in captivity—for freedom. 'Because you wish to rule the world, does it follow that everyone will accept slavery?'[15] There is no palliation of the Roman brutality, injustice and incompetence that sparked off the rebellion of Boudicca. The most eloquent denunciation of Roman imperialism ever written is put into the mouth of Calgacus, the Highland chief who opposed Agricola at the battle of Mons Graupius.[16] And yet one comes away with the impression that the patriot chiefs of Britain are valued mainly because they provide the Romans with a worthy foe. Certainly the pacific governors of Britain get a very poor press in Tacitus. This is especially true of Petronius Turpilianus and Trebellius Maximus, the men who accomplished successfully—so it would seem—the gigantic task of pacification and reconstruction after the defeat of Boudicca. It is the fire-eaters among the governors who come off well—Ostorius Scapula, Suetonius Paulinus and above all Agricola.[17] Conqueror and pacifier in one, Agricola is the model of what a Roman governor should be, to whom all his predecessors provide a foil.

In recent years the trend has been to discount this picture of Agricola, and indeed to be severely critical of Tacitus on Britain. It is true that the *Agricola* contains only eleven place-names, that its British geography is often vague and imprecise, and that the narrative of British campaigns is hard, and sometimes impossible, to reconcile with the discoveries of modern archaeology. But the best measure of our debt to Tacitus is to ask what happens when we no longer have his narrative to guide us? From the withdrawal of Agricola to the building of Hadrian's Wall is about forty years (84–125). And what do we know of it even today, compared with the period between 43 and 84, for which Tacitus is the main authority?

There is a more complex picture in the provinces of Gaul, due to the wide differences in density of population and level of culture in the broad lands between the Pyrenees and the Rhine. Augustus had surveyed the whole problem, in person and at length, and his arrangements for Roman administration bore the characteristic spaciousness of the times.[18] The old province of Gallia Narbonensis, with its flourishing cities, was culturally an extension of Italy. It remained under the administration of the Senate and always looked to the Mediterranean world rather than to the interior of Gaul. Along the Rhine from Basle to the sea was created a vast military zone, divided between the two provinces of Upper and Lower Germany. Here was the biggest concentration of troops in the Roman Empire—eight legions in the time of Tiberius, seven in that of Nero. Strategically this formidable force looked in both directions—eastwards to guard against the free Germans and westwards to coerce any seditious movements in Gaul.[19]

Gallic nationalism, which had burnt so bright during the rebellion of Vercingetorix, was by no means extinct. The next move was to set up three new provinces in the old Gallia Comata, the lands conquered by Julius Caesar. Gallia Belgica, on the north-east, had some ethnic unity; it comprised the tribal areas of peoples of Belgic stock. In the middle was the huge sprawling province of Lugdunensis, which reached from the middle Rhône as far as Brittany. To the south-west lay the third province, Aquitania, reaching as far as the Pyrenees, and governed from Burdigala (Bordeaux). No important military forces were stationed in these three provinces, except that the governor of Lugdunensis had troops at his disposal. The separate Gallic states had their local militia, but these were of limited military value.

We hear little of Aquitania in Tacitus, except for the period (74–77) when it was governed by Agricola. His appointment was thought by many to be unsuitable, for this was a peaceful province, and he was a military man.[20] But here as elsewhere, Agricola proved himself to be flexible. He paid due attention to business in political affairs and in the courts; in private life he had the ease and affability so important for society in Gaul. He

did not compete with his colleagues among the other provincial
governors, nor did he quarrel with the imperial financial agents.
It is, for Tacitus, a rare and valuable picture of the government
of a peaceful province. We have no reason to suppose that
Agricola's governorship was unique, but it enables us to understand how Romanisation developed in this part of Gaul.
Burdigala and Tolosa both became flourishing cities, and, in
fact, during the later empire, the whole valley of the Garonne
was one of the most prosperous parts of the western provinces.[21]

There was a less happy story in Belgica and Lugdunensis.
There were many tensions between the Roman armies on the
Rhine, the Gallic allies, and the free Germans across the river.
Gallic nationalism was ready to spring to life in some of the
states, when Roman maladministration or disaster gave it an
opening. So it is that Tacitus has to record three rebellions[22]
between the reigns of Tiberius and 69. The first, that of Florus
and Sacrovir, was, in fact, on a modest scale. The rising of
Vindex was against Nero the Emperor rather than against Rome.
But in the year 69 the rising of Julius Civilis and its many
ramifications were a far-reaching and serious rebellion, which
brought many humiliations on Rome.

The ingredients of the rebellion in 21 are interesting. It arose
not long after the death of Germanicus and among two wealthy
Gallic states with a good record of loyalty to Rome—the Aedui
and the Treveri.[23] The leaders, Julius Sacrovir and Julius Florus,
were both men of the old royal stock among their people who
had served in the Roman auxiliary forces. Tacitus dismisses their
followers as 'a crowd of men in debt or bondsmen of their
chiefs.' Their grievances in all probability were the familiar ones
—the high cost of Romanisation and the rapacity of Roman
money-lenders. The first stages of the rebellion were quickly
nipped in the bud by the use of the Roman troops stationed at
Lugdunum. Nor did the movement among the Treveri in the
valley of the Moselle get very far. But among the Aedui the
story was rather different. Here Sacrovir captured valuable
hostages—the sons of Gallic chieftains who attended the famous

school in Augustodunum.[24] Moreover he disposed of nearly
40,000 troops, although only one-third of these were armed as
Roman legionaries. He had a special weapon of a curious kind—
the Gallic gladiators who were clad in armour from top to toe,
and were called 'The Iron Men.'[25] It required a regular expedition, led by the governor of Upper Germany, to subdue the
rebel forces. In the event, the Iron Men, intended as one-man
tanks, proved a fiasco. Sacrovir and his followers committed
suicide and the rebellion was over, although it had caused much
alarm in Rome, where its ramifications were thought to extend
over many of the other Gallic states and even into Spain.

We lack Tacitus' own narrative for the very different rebellion
of Vindex.[26] Here the rising was instigated by the governor of
Lugdunensis in person. Vindex, too, was of the old native royal
line, but it seems that his was not a nationalist movement. It was
rather the first phase of the rebellion against Nero which brought
Galba to supreme power. But Vindex failed to win much support
from the Gallic states, and he too was put down by the Roman
troops from the Rhine armies, headed by the famous Verginius
Rufus. This will have been an affair of high interest to Tacitus,
who almost thirty years later, pronounced the funeral oration
for Verginius Rufus. Senatorial tradition always portrayed
Rufus as a great patriot; had he been less self-effacing, the
miseries of the year 69 could well have been avoided.

The rebellion of Civilis[27] was altogether more complex, as it
was more serious. It could only have been broken out against
the background of the unprecedented demoralisation of the
Rhine armies after they had been defeated by the departure of
the best troops to win the throne for Vitellius. The great Batavian chief, Julius Civilis,[28] saw in this the opportunity to play his
hand; others had wished to use him as a tool. There is no doubt
that he was approached by the agents of Vespasian to create disturbances in Gaul. Tacitus mentions this, but understandably
does not stress it. Civilis himself had served in the Roman
auxiliary army. But he had been badly treated, and the

opportunity to pay off his old scores and to win freedom for his people was one that he could not resist. The former Roman auxiliary officer ends up as a full-scale nationalist rebel, his hair dyed red and left uncut until the Roman cause should be defeated, his little son encouraged to use Roman prisoners for target practice with his bow.[29]

And indeed if Civilis reverted to primitivism, he did not lack for company. There was a messiah called Mariccus who appeared among the Boii; eventually he was thrown to the wild beasts in the arena, but they would not touch him. Tacitus shares their repugnance—he is ashamed to speak of this humble fanatic.[30] Among the free Germans there was a priestess called Veleda, who lived in a high tower buried in the forest; she predicted triumph for the German cause, and was to receive the present of the captured flag-ship of the Roman squadron on the Rhine.[31]

More important were the political ambitions released as the rebellion grew and prospered. These came out at a conference of anti-Roman elements held at Cologne.[32] The free Germans wanted the end of Roman rule on the Rhine and loot in the provinces of Gaul. The dissident Gallic chieftains—Julius Classicus and Julius Tutor among the Treveri, Julius Sabinus from their neighbours the Lingones—wanted to substitute a Gallic for a Roman empire. Its boundaries were grandiloquently fixed at the line of the Alps; it was to have a Caesar of its own (but who would that be?), and would secure the allegiance of the Roman troops on the Rhine. Incredibly enough, this last ambition was, fleetingly, realised. Treachery, incompetence, and despondency led to the loss of all military bases in Lower Germany; indeed the only points Rome controlled on the whole Rhine frontier were now Moguntiacum and Vindonissa. So the ephemeral vision of an *Imperium Galliarum* appeared.

But the real decisions had been reached elsewhere with the victory of the Flavian armies. The recovery of Gaul must have been first on the list of Vespasian's military priorities. This was recognised in time by the Gallic states who had remained loyal or had stood aloof from the rebellion. A conference[33] was summoned to meet in the territory of the Remi, who had always been faithful allies of Rome. Here the issue was squarely posed —the *pax Romana*, or freedom according to Civilis and Classicus? This was a vital debate, of which Tacitus has preserved the main outlines. The chief representative of the war party was Valentinus, of the Treveri: he had that unrestrained eloquence so admired among the Celtic peoples. 'In a carefully prepared speech he brought out all the charges usually made against great empires, and hurled insults on the Roman people.' But the Roman cause had solid arguments on which to draw. They were put forward by Julius Auspex, a noble of the Remi, who stressed the blessings of peace, and the power of Rome. The latter could scarcely be denied; Petilius Cerialis had been appointed to lead an overwhelming force of nine legions to suppress the rebellion.

On the Gallic side all was confusion. They were quarrelling about where their capital was to be, says Tacitus, before they had even won the war. In the end the assembly praised the spirit of Valentinus, and followed the advice of Auspex. Letters were sent to the Lingones and Treveri, bidding them lay down their arms.[34] It was a notable triumph for the pro-Roman cause in Gaul, and a faithful service by the Remi. Yet Tacitus speaks of it with a marked lack of warmth. His enthusiasm is reserved for the self-confidence with which Cerialis dismissed the force which the loyal Gallic states had sent to his assistance. 'He caused it to be announced that the legions were sufficient for his command. The allies should resume the duties of peace, they could be confident that the war was as good as over once its conduct was in Roman hands.' Far from provoking resentment, the rebuff seems to have been taken in good spirit by the Gauls, for Tacitus adds the comment: 'They took up their duties all the more readily, because they had been rejected.'[35] The epigram does not lack point; the comment is odious. It is the counterpart, in a historian of relatively enlightened views, of the hatred which the Roman soldiers had come to feel towards the provincials.

Ever since the defeat of the native militia who served with Vindex, we are told that the Roman army had begun to look on the Gauls 'not as allies, but as strangers or even enemies.' This accounts for the brutal conduct which was too commonly displayed by Vitellius' troops on their march south—the massacre of four thousand people at Metz, a greater disaster only narrowly averted at Vienna, and the butchery and slavery which overtook the unhappy people of the Helvetii who stood in the path of Caecina. Not that the armies of Vitellius could be accused of discrimination; they were perfectly prepared to do the same thing in Italy.[36]

We lack Tacitus' account of the closing stages of the war against Civilis. Book V breaks off when he has been almost driven back to the Island of the Batavians, and is making an attempt to call Cerialis to a parley. No other historian narrates his end. But all these rebellions—even that of Civilis—are really no more than surface currents. The tide itself was setting, steadily and irresistibly, towards Romanisation in Gaul. It was marked by the policy of urbanisation, set in motion by Augustus in Narbonensis, and followed with hardly less vigour by Claudius in the Tres Galliae. Lugdunum[37] by A.D. 50 was the greatest city north of the Alps, and something of an imperial centre in its own right. Here was the seat of the imperial cult, and here the Gallic states met in an annual conference.

The cost of urbanisation could be met by the growing wealth brought about by security and a huge increase in trade. The burden of debt might bear heavily on some individuals such as Florus and Sacrovir. When Cerialis reminded the Treveri, in his famous speech, that they were at risk because they possessed gold and wealth, he was using the most powerful of all arguments for the Roman connection. Individuals profited as much as communities. There were several wealthy and powerful senators who derived from Narbonese Gaul. The famous debate, already quoted, on the extension of the rights to enter the Senate to the great chiefs of Tres Galliae, shows very clearly what was at stake.[38] If in the long run a solid majority of the states of Gaul chose the *pax Romana*, they did so with their eyes open.

Tacitus has a few valuable things to say about the personalities of some of the cities of Gaul. Massilia,[39] for example, was a place where Greek culture and provincial parsimony were nicely blended. Indeed, the chief temptation offered by this forerunner of Marseilles was apparently that of undue devotion to Greek philosophy. But Massilia lived in the past. Other cities lived in a rather hectic present, notably Lugdunum and Vienna. There was between them rivalry of long standing, which was brought to a head in the year 69.[40] Lugdunum was a Roman colony, and had developed as a large and cosmopolitan centre of perhaps 200,000 people. Vienna was smaller: the capital of the Allobroges, it still kept some memories of its Celtic past. But it was extremely wealthy, and as a centre of culture felt superior to the newer foundation northwards up the Rhône. Lugdunum's chance came when the troops of Vitellius appeared on their way south. They urged them to besiege and sack Vienna, so full of plunder. 'Go and avenge us,' they said, 'and wipe out this nest of Gallic rebellion. They're foreigners there, and enemies, we are Roman citizens, and part of the Roman Army,' But there was enough wealth in Vienna to bribe its way out of danger, with 300 *sesterces* and supply for every soldier and a huge *douceur* for the commander. The moment of danger had passed for Vienna.

To these sketches of cities in Gaul may be added two from the Germanic lands. Cologne[41] (Colonia Claudia Agrippinensis) was founded in 51 in the territory of the Ubii, a friendly German tribe, who had been settled in new lands on the west bank of the Rhine. A happy symbiosis quickly developed between the Roman colonists and the German tribesmen. It met with a testing time during the rebellion of Civilis. The free Germans across the Rhine despised the Ubii as renegades, and envied the swift growth and prosperity of their city. They would have been glad to destroy it, but Civilis had private ties with the colonists. Even so, the tribal council of the Ubii found themselves presented with harsh demands. They must destroy the walls of the colony, butcher all Romans, divide up their property and allow free crossing of the river. Finally they were told: 'resume the customs and *Kultur* of your fathers, throw off those pleasures which the Romans employ more skilfully than arms to enslave the subject peoples. As a racially pure and untainted people, forgetful of your servitude, you will meet other Germans on equal terms, or even rule over them.'

The Ubii could only make a temporising reply, conceding some demands. But on one point they were firm. 'All strangers whether from Italy or the provinces, who were on our territory, have either died in battle or fled to their own country. As regards those who settled here in former days and contracted marriages among us, and as for the children subsequently born to them, this is now their native land. We cannot suppose you so cruel as to wish us to kill our parents, brothers, and children.'[42] Here is a signal tribute to Romanisation; even in this hour of stress, the Ubii felt themselves a single *patria* with the Roman colonists. In the end, they gained time by an appeal to Civilis and Veleda, and returned, as soon as events allowed, to the Roman allegiance.

Another type of symbiosis was to be seen in Raetia, between the provincials and the Hermunduri, a pro-Roman tribe living beyond the Danube in what is now Franconia. 'The tribe of the Hermunduri,' says Tacitus,[43] 'is faithful to the Romans. For this reason our commerce with them, alone of all the Germans, is not conducted on the river bank, but far within the province in the noble colony of Raetia. (Augusta Vindelicorum—Augsburg.) They pass over freely and not under guard. To all other peoples we show only our arms and our military positions, but to the Hermunduri we open up our houses in town and country—and they do not envy them.'

The Danube provinces figure little in Tacitus, and almost invariably in a military context. Pannonia provides the setting for the great rebellion in the Roman Army in the first year of Tiberius. In 69 the intervention of the Danubian armies on the side of Vespasian is decisive. There is a good deal to say about affairs in the client kingdom of Thrace, until that turbulent area was made into a province by Claudius in 46. The most striking of these passages is the account of an assault on a Thracian hill-fort by the troops of Poppaeus Sabinus in 26.[44] Crowded with women and children, horses and cattle, and desperately defended, the fortress was invested by the Roman Army and ultimately starved out, just as was done on a more spectacular scale at Masada in the Jewish Wars. A Roman reader might have been reminded of the famous siege of Numantia by Scipio Aemilianus. Another good battle piece is the description[45] of the defeat inflicted on the Roxolani by the Third Legion. It gains in value because there is so little in literature about the deeds of the Roman Army on the Danube, as compared with that on the Rhine.

Even the great campaigns under Domitian and Trajan against the Dacians are but ill recorded. So, save for one battle, are those of Marcus Aurelius against Marcomanni. 'Attention was concentrated on the civil wars, and foreign affairs were neglected. This emboldened the Roxolani, a Sarmatian tribe, who had wiped out two auxiliary units in the previous winter, to invade Moesia with high hopes of success. They had nine thousand cavalry, and their savagery and sense of triumph led them to thoughts of plunder rather than of battle. They were dispersed and off their guard when the Third Legion, with auxiliaries in support, suddenly fell upon them. The Romans had made everything ready for battle: the Sarmatians were scattered, loaded down with booty, and deprived of their horses' speed by the slippery nature of the ground. They were butchered, as though bound hand and foot.

'It is remarkable how the courage of the Sarmatians seems something extraneous to themselves. In an infantry engagement they are the most cowardly of fighters: but scarcely any line of battle can withstand their cavalry charges. On this occasion it was a wet day, and the ice was melting: they could not use the long poles and swords, which they wield with either hand, because of the slipping of their horses and the weight of their coats of mail. These were worn by the chieftains and most important warriors: formed of plates of iron or very durable leather sewn together, they are a complete protection against blows, but make it hard for men who have been overthrown by an enemy charge to regain their feet: moreover, the Sarmatians became bogged down in the deep, soft snow. But the Roman soldier was unhampered by his breastplate: he could assail the foe with lance or javelin, and as the occasion required, come to close quarters with the stabbing sword against the lightly-armed Sarmatian, who lacked even the protection of a shield. At last the few survivors of the battle took refuge in the marshes, there to perish from their wounds or from the bitter winter. When the news of this victory reached Rome, M. Aponius, governor of Moesia, was awarded a triumphal statue, and the legionary commanders, Fulvius Aurelius, Julianus Tettius and Numisius Lupus, received the insignia of consular rank. Otho was delighted, and took personal credit for the success, as though his own warlike qualities, his armies, and his generals had thus glorified the state.'

Here is something to be set beside the account in Dio Cassius[46] of that battle in Moravia where the Rain God intervened so dramatically on the Roman side, as is depicted on the column of Marcus Aurelius.

In the eastern part of the Roman world two countries were of paramount importance—Egypt and Syria. The survey of the state of the empire in 69[47] contains a masterly summary of the salient features of Roman Egypt in the first century. 'Egypt and the forces needed to hold it down had from the time of the deified Augustus been ruled by Roman knights as viceroys. The most suitable arrangement had seemed to be that a province so difficult of approach, so important for the corn supply, so quarrelsome and unstable because of its superstition and licentiousness, and one which knew nothing of Roman law or Roman magistrates, should be kept as an imperial possession. It was then ruled by Tiberius Alexander,[48] a native of that country.'

The country continued to be administered, as it had been under the Pharaohs and the Ptolemies, as a royal estate; on to this were now engrafted some of the features of a Roman province. The prefects who exercised vice-regal powers were drawn from the equestrian order. Ever since the time of Cornelius Gallus it had been realised that it was dangerous to allow any senator to visit Egypt.[49] Many of these prefects were of eastern origin, and Tiberius Claudius Alexander himself was a Jew of Alexandria.

Egypt is certainly difficult of approach by land, protected as it is by the deserts of Sinai and of Libya. The experience of both Napoleon and of Rommel substantiates this. It was of vital importance for the *annona* or corn supply of Rome, the bulk of which was carried by the huge freighters that plied between Alexandria and Ostia. The holder of Egypt could hold Rome to ransom. Hence, in the year 69 Vespasian lays his hands on the '*claustra annonae*'—the key to the corn supply of Rome.[50] Hence the alarm of Tiberius at the visit of Germanicus to Egypt in 19, not diminished by his affable demeanour towards the Egyptians and his care to relieve their wants. Germanicus was far too important a person to be at large in that country, and his professed interest in its antiquities was regarded with suspicion.

Rebellious and unsettled Egypt certainly was, and all Roman Emperors dreaded the insolence of the mob of Alexandria.[51] The animal gods of Egypt were profoundly alien to Rome, and the combined effects of superstition and cruelty are vividly underlined by the Fifteenth Satire of Juvenal,[52] which might almost have been written as a gloss on this passage of Tacitus. Juvenal describes the terrible riot which broke out between the inhabitants of two neighbouring villages, devotees respectively of Set and of Hathor. Its worst atrocity was an instance of cannibalism, the victim being lynched and eaten, bones and all. There are several parallels to be cited from contemporary literature. Egypt was in, but not of, the Graeco-Roman world. Roman law did not run there—except of course as between Roman citizens. The Jewish community had their own courts and their own code of laws. Outside Alexandria, urban life developed on a very limited scale.

It is therefore easy to understand the curious ambivalence in the Roman attitude to Egypt, a mixture of fascination and of hatred. On the one hand there is the interest in the scenery of the Nile Valley, its fascinating animals and birds, and its impressive architecture. This is exemplified in such mosaics as the famous Nile landscape at Palestrina.[53] Some of the Egyptian cults such as those of Isis and Osiris held an attraction for Romans. As against this there was the dislike aroused by the primitive fanaticism of the fellaheen, and the revulsion caused by people who, as Juvenal says, 'are at once the most cowardly and the most cruel of mankind.'[54] At the same time, the squalid and disgusting present of Egypt was overshadowed by its mighty past, so skilfully exploited by the priests who were the guardians of its traditions. Egypt was the land of the exotic and the fabulous. Where else could the Phoenix appear? And then there were the marvels which greeted Germanicus. 'Notable among them the stone statue of Memnon, which gives a singing note when struck by the sun's rays at dawn; the Pyramids, huge as mountains, built among the pathless shifting sands of the desert by the wealth and rivalry of kings; the lakes dug out of the earth to receive the Nile's overflow; elsewhere, the river's gorges, with depths no line can plumb. At last he came to Elephantine and Syene, once the furthest bounds of the Roman empire, which now extends to the Persian Gulf.'[55]

But the greatest impression left on Germanicus was from his visit to the ancient capital, Thebes. 'There, reared on great piles of masonry, inscriptions in Egyptian writing proclaim its former magnificence. One of the senior priests, requested to interpret the language of his forefathers, explained how Egypt had once possessed 700,000 men of military age. With this army, king

Rameses had conquered Libya, Ethiopia, Media, Persia, Bactria and Scythia, and all the lands inhabited by Syrians, Armenians and Cappadocians, reaching as far as Bithynia on one shore of Asia Minor and Lycia on the other. There could still be read the list of tributes assessed on the conquered lands, the payments of gold and silver, the number of weapons and horses, the gifts to the temples of ivory and incense, and all the quantities of grain and raw materials paid by each several nation. The total was as impressive as the revenue now raised by the arbitrary rule of Parthia or the power of Rome.'[56] In showing to Germanicus the list of conquered nations and their tribute, the priests of Thebes proved themselves as good psychologists as they had been five centuries earlier when they were visited by Herodotus[57]—and as good liars too.

The Roman governor of Syria[58] held one of the most exacting posts in the empire. Peace or war, he confronted Parthia, with all that that implied. His was the prime responsibility for dealing with the client kingdoms—Commagene, Ituraea, Judaea and the rest. His own province was wealthy and populous, with some ten million inhabitants. The centre of a great commerce by land and sea, it was also famous for its own products—woollen goods, dyes and glassware. It was a melting pot of hellenic and oriental cultures and religion. Antioch,[59] the capital, was in size the third city of the empire, perhaps its most beautiful, certainly its most licentious.

Some of the ablest imperial administrators held this key post. Such were Lucius Vitellius, brother of the future Emperor, who governed Syria from 35 to 37 under Tiberius, and was praised by Tacitus because 'as a provincial administrator, he showed the virtues of an earlier age.'[60] Certainly he dealt firmly with the threats and pretensions of Artabanus, king of Parthia, and showed sense and flexibility in his dealings with Judaea. Gaius Cassius Longinus (45–59), later famous as a jurist, brought the Syrian legions up to one of their occasional peaks of fitness for action. At other times, however, the governor of Syria was a *fainéant.* Such was Ummidius Quadratus, who allowed his troops to get out of hand, and also the Gaius Cestius who suffered the defeat at the beginning of the Jewish Wars. In any case, in times of special emergency it was necessary to set up an extraordinary command, giving authority over all the provinces of the East. Under the Republic such posts had been held by Pompey and by Antony. A similar command was given to Germanicus, possibly also to Lucius Vitellius, and certainly to Domitius Corbulo after the defeat of Paetus.

There was a certain unity about the Roman East which was capable of asserting itself at moments of crisis. We see it in the mustering of support for Vespasian in the Second Book of the *Histories*.[61] The provinces of Asia had already taken the oath of allegiance. So had the client kings and queens—Sohaemus, king of Sophene, Antiochus, king of Commagene, Agrippa, governor of part of Judaea, and his sister Berenice. 'A supreme council of war was held at Berytus. Mucianus came there with all the legionary commanders and tribunes, as well as the senior centurions and soldiers; from the army in Judaea the best representatives had also been sent. This great assembly of infantry and cavalry, together with the princes who rivalled one another in ostentatious display, made up a gathering well worthy of the fortunes of an Emperor. The first business of war was to hold a levy and to recall the veterans. The strongest towns were selected to manufacture arms. Gold and silver were minted at Antioch. All these preparations were carried on by expert agents, each in his proper place. Vespasian in turn visited each place, encouraging the workmen, spurring on the energetic and stimulating the slow by his own example, and hiding his friends' deficiencies rather than their virtues. Many were rewarded by being made prefect or procurator. Large numbers of men who later had distinguished careers were raised to the rank of senator. Luck sometimes took the place of merit.'[62]

Of provincial life in Syria, Tacitus has little to say. The people of Antioch lament the death of Germanicus, and crowd into the forum to see his naked corpse.[63] In 69 it is in the theatre of

Antioch that Mucianus announces the choice of Vespasian as a contender for the throne, in a display of Greek eloquence. Few Roman governors, it may be supposed, could have spoken acceptably in Greek before that critical audience.[64] Of all the famous shrines of Syria, the only one mentioned is that on Mount Carmel. Here the worship of the ancient war god of the Philistines was still maintained, though the name of the priest was Greek—Basilides. Through him Vespasian received an oracle that relieved his mind at a moment of doubt. 'Whatever it is you are making ready to do, Vespasian, whether to build a house or to extend your estate or to increase your household, you shall have a mighty home, ample bounds, and a huge number of men.'[65] So was fulfilled that ancient prophecy that the ruler of the world would arise in the East.

The people of Antioch belonged, of course, to the hellenised population of the cities. We hear almost nothing of the Aramaic-speaking peoples of the countryside. And of the caravan traffic, of so much interest to the modern world, nothing. More than once Tacitus gives a description of the crossing place at the Euphrates, Zeugma. A Roman army appears at that dramatic point, sometimes confronted by the Parthians.[66] We would gladly exchange at least one of these passages for a description of the great camel trains which crossed the river in times of peace, linking the Roman world with central Asia, with India, and even with China, and bringing riches to the caravan cities of Damascus, Petra and Palmyra.[67]

With Judaea, and its peculiar people, the case is different. Clearly, the Jewish Wars of Vespasian and Titus were for Tacitus a major episode. In them the greatest victories of the Flavian dynasty were won; they were rich in such episodes as Tacitus and his audience loved, desperate battles, sieges like those of Jotopata, Jerusalem, and the last stand of the zealots at Masada.[68] But they fell awkwardly between the *Histories* and the *Annals*. The Jewish war broke out in 66: Jerusalem was captured in 70: Masada fell in 73. The last books of the *Annals*

GT

will have contained the narrative of the exploits of Vespasian in Judaea under Nero. As a prelude to the capture of Jerusalem, the fifth book of the *Histories* contains a fairly long excursus[69] on the geography, ethnography and history of Judaea, and this is what survives. It is longer than the parallel passage on Britain in the *Agricola*, though of course much shorter—twelve chapters as against forty-six—than the *Germania*.

And a very odd concoction it is. The natural features of the land are described with an emphasis on its 'marvels'—the snows of Hermon 'amid all that heat', the course of the river Jordan, the Dead Sea and its strange properties, the blasted region of the Cities of the Plain, the vitreous sand at the mouth of the Naman river near the modern Acre, the balsam tree and the date palm. The story of Roman occupation since Pompey is briefly traced. There are a few sentences—no names—on the lurid history of the native dynasty in Judaea. The odd portion is the account of the history and customs of the Jews. Whatever Tacitus' sources may have been—Manetho, Nicolaus of Damascus, Pompeius Trogus—they did not draw on Hebrew sources, nor were they well disposed to the Jews. Added to Tacitus' own prejudices, this produces a highly distorted picture.

Tacitus' speculations[70] on the origins of the Jewish people stand high among the nonsense written on that subject. There is a rationalising account of the flight from Egypt. 'Moyses' appears as a self-seeking and unscrupulous leader. A herd of wild asses leads them to the discovery of water in the desert. Jewish customs are contrary to those of the rest of mankind. Certain evil customs among them have persisted because of their very depravity. Their exclusiveness extends even to their lusts— promiscuous among themselves, they abstain from intercourse with others. Theirs is, altogether, an obstinate superstition (*pervicacax superstitio*). They are guilty of 'hatred of the human race,' and this, in itself, cuts them off from humanity's pity. So, when under Tiberius, four thousand descendants of freedom of military age and infected with Jewish superstitions are sent to

Sardinia, the feeling is that 'if they fell victim to the climate, they would be little loss.'[71]

This is one of the few glimpses in Tacitus of the Jews of the Diaspora, the Jewish communities scattered throughout the cities of the empire. It was with them especially, that the Jews were so successful in winning proselytes, on whom Tacitus comments: 'the earliest lesson their proselytes receive is to despise the gods, to disown their native land, and to hold cheap their parents, children, and brothers.'[72] How successfully these lessons were learned was to be seen in the great riots provoked by the Jewish communities throughout Egypt, Cyrene and Cyprus at the end of Trajan's reign.[73] They were accompanied by atrocities of many kinds, as is only to be expected when a persecuted people turns on its persecutors. Yet Tacitus does not conceal that Roman persecution and corruption were directly responsible for the outbreak of the Jewish Wars under Nero. After the death of Claudius the Roman province of Judaea was entrusted to Roman knights or freedmen. Antonius Felix, one of these (procurator 52–60), 'indulged in every kind of cruelty and lust, employing the powers of the king to gratify the instincts of a slave.' Gessius Florus (64–66) was also a bad ruler of Judaea.[74]

At the end of the excursus Tacitus moves on to the preparations of Titus to besiege Jerusalem. There is a brief but telling description of the city—its three lines of walls, planned on the most up-to-date methods of fortification, the great Fortress Antonia built by King Herod as a major strong point, and finally the Temple, itself a fortress.[75] The siege is about to begin. Its outcome is preceded by portents of the most unmistakable kind. 'Contending armies were seen to clash in the skies. There was a flash of arms, and the Temple was lit up in the glare of lightning. Of a sudden the doors of the shrine opened and a supernatural voice cried out "the gods are leaving." At the same time there was a huge stir of departure.' The curtain is about to rise on a drama whose conclusion we shall not read in Tacitus. Fortunately, it is accessible in the pages of the Jewish historian, Flavius Josephus.[76]

Josephus could write as a first-hand witness. As governor of
Galilee, he fought on the Jewish side at the siege of Jotopata.
Thereafter, he went over, like the gods, to the Roman side. If one
of the two accounts of the Jewish wars had to disappear, we
must be grateful that it was not that if Josephus. He writes at
much greater length than Tacitus could have done; he has the
authority of an eyewitness; he understood the Jews and their
history. What is cause for regret is that the loss of Tacitus'
account of the Jewish Wars deprives us of the opportunity—so
rare with classical historians—of checking one major author
against another.

Asia[77] proper was a senatorial province, which Tacitus himself governed as proconsul in 112–113. But we shall look in
vain in the *Annals*—where alone they could be—for any passages
which certainly reflect personal experience. By contrast with the
tragic history of Judaea, Asia was rich and prosperous. The city
of Laodicea is made to say in the Apocalypse 'I am rich and
increased with goods and have need of nothing.' Laodicea was
a city of the second rank; opulence was far greater at such places
as Pergamum, Miletus, Ephesus and Smyrna. They enriched—
and occasionally bankrupted—themselves with theatres, aqueducts, baths, temples, gymnasia and other public amenities.
Other than their own extravagance, the only troubles to which
they were exposed were earthquakes (severe but occasional) and
the peculation of Roman governors. Against the latter they were
well able to defend themselves. We hear how, when Gaius
Junius Silanus was accused in 23 of misgovernment, he found it
difficult to defend himself against the most eloquent orators of
Asia, who had been sent to Rome to speak for the prosecution.[78]
Tacitus usually mentions these Asian cities when they send an
embassy to Rome. For example in 26 eleven cities compete for
setting up a temple to Tiberius and Rome. The prize goes to the city
of Smyrna, the clinching argument being the services they rendered to the army of Sulla at a period of distress.[79] Earlier in the
reign there had been the investigation into the rights of sanctuary

claimed by many of the major temples of the province.[80] More than religious issues were at stake; the temples were often enormously wealthy and acted as banks.

It so happens that Tacitus[81] gives unusually full details about one of these Asian embassies, sent by the people of Byzantium to Rome in the year 53 to plead for a reduction of their tax assessment. 'But when the Byzantines complained about the size of their tax assessment, they gave a full review of all their services to Rome. They began with the treaty struck with them at the time of our war with the king of Macedon, known from his doubtful origins as pseudo-Philip. Next they instanced their services against Antiochus, Perseus, and Aristonicus, then the help they had given Antonius in the war against the pirates, also to Sulla, Lucullus, and Pompey, and, more recently, to the Emperors. All this arose from their situation, convenient for the passage of generals and armies by land or sea, and for the procurement of supplies.

'The Greeks had founded Byzantium at the far extremity of Europe, where it approaches most closely to Asia. When they had asked Apollo at Delphi where they should found a city, he had replied, 'Opposite the country of the blind.' This saying referred to the people of Chalcedon, who were the first to survey the advantages of the site, but had then proceeded to choose a worse one. For Byzantium has a fertile soil and a teeming sea: great shoals of fish come out from the Black Sea, and are scared by underwater shoals into the harbours on the European shore, avoiding the inlets of the Asiatic side. This had once been the source of wealth and prosperity for the inhabitants, but now their financial burdens were such that they asked for concessions. The Emperor backed their plea, arguing that their exhaustion in the Thracian and Bosporan wars made them a deserving case. Their taxes were remitted for a period of five years.' Such was the stuff of politics among the cities of Asia.

Further to the south-east, in Asia Minor, a huge new province was organised in Cappadocia[82] after the death of King Arche-

laus in the first year of Tiberius' reign. Scattered references
enable us to reconstruct an outline of its history during the next
fifty years. The transition from a client kingdom to a Roman
province was immediately marked by a reduction of taxes. The
province, sometimes combined with that of Galatia, made an
excellent recruiting ground for the Roman armies, as well as a
military base for campaigns in Armenia. It served as the base for
the campaigns of Corbulo, as well as the disastrous expeditions
of Paetus and of Paelignus. Not all its inhabitants, however,
welcomed their inclusion in the Empire. In particular, the
mountain people of the Cietae in the Anti-Taurus mountains
took to brigandage and had to be subdued.[83]

About Greece proper, now the Roman province of Achaea,
Tacitus has little to say, and that little is usually tart. Tacitus'
admiration for the glory that was Greece fell some way short of
idolatry. He rebukes their historians for their lack of interest in
the annals of other people.[84] He speaks of Nero's freedman
Acratus, 'a self proclaimed admirer of Greek culture, which had
done nothing to improve his morals.'[85] Philhellenism, too, had
marked some of the Emperors Tacitus most detested—Nero and
Domitian. It was also a characteristic of Hadrian. It is a pity we
do not have Tacitus' account of Nero's famous visit to Greece as
a pothunter at the great athletic festivals. He collected 1,808
awards—a record. The comment of Tacitus on such virtuosity is
a sad loss.[86] The truth is that the province of Achaea and its
people were now of very minor importance. The cities of classical Greece were living on their historical memories, which did
not always do them much good.

Tacitus takes a sardonic pleasure in contrasting the reception
in Athens of Germanicus and of Piso in 18. With Germanicus,
as ever, all was sweetness and light. 'Thence he went to Athens;
to that ancient city and ally he made the concession of appearing
with only one lictor. The Greeks provided him with a most
elaborate reception, and by reciting the words and deeds of their
ancestors in the distant past lent a certain impressiveness to their

adulation.'[87] A little later Piso gave the Athenians a much rougher passage. 'He made a violent descent on Athens, alarming that people with a brutal speech. Indirectly he criticised Germanicus, saying that he had praised in indulgent terms, out of keeping with the dignity of Rome, a people no longer true Athenians—now extinct from their many disasters—but the scum of the earth. They had backed Mithridates against Sulla, Antony against the deified Augustus. His reproaches delved far back into Athenian history, including failures against Macedonians and injustices to their own countrymen.'[88] It may be assumed that on neither occasion did the speakers find any shortage of material.

Such, in brief outline, is the picture that Tacitus gives of the provinces of the Roman world. If it omits much, it must be borne in mind that the provinces are treated essentially as they affect the Roman administration in peace or war. But no reader of Tacitus can come away unimpressed with the size and complexity of an empire which stretched from Scotland to the head of the Persian Gulf, from the mouth of the Rhine to the cataracts of the Nile. But Tacitus never falls into the mistake of equating this empire, vast as it was, with the whole of the known world. He is always aware of the forces that pressed in upon the empire on its two most vunerable frontiers. Along the line of the Rhine and the Danube were the powerful and warlike peoples of central Europe, whom he calls collectively the Germans. Beyond the Euphrates was another empire, almost as powerful as that of Rome—Parthia. It is to Germany and to Parthia, to the world beyond the Roman frontiers, that we next turn.

CHAPTER TEN
Beyond the Frontiers of the Roman World

IT IS SAID THAT the Emperors of China were able, over many centuries, to sustain the happy belief that they ruled over the only civilised power in the world, which was surrounded by peoples of varying degrees of barbarism. No such delusion could be entertained by those in charge of the Roman Empire. Only 200 miles east of Antioch, its third greatest city, the Roman frontiers met along the line of the Euphrates those of another great power, which itself extended across Central Asia to the Hindu Kush mountains and the Valley of the Indus. This was the Empire of Parthia,[1] which had arisen as a nationalist reaction against the hellenised Seleucid Empire. The Parthians had extended their power to Mesopotamia about 130 B.C., not very long after the establishment of Roman hegemony in the Mediterranean. History and politics combined to cast the two world empires as rivals. Geography and commerce made them partners—if they wished. Across the Parthian Empire led the main land arteries of trade between India and China and the Mediterranean world.

Roman recognition of Parthian equality was always grudging. If a Parthian King of Kings was ready on occasion to record deference 'out of respect' to a Roman Emperor, we must remember the tendency of these oriental peoples to flattery. On the field of battle, Parthia could assert herself sharply enough if she had to do so. Indeed, in the record of Roman and Parthian warfare in the century and a half between Crassus and Trajan the balance of advantage lay distinctly with Parthia. The Parthian mailed cavalry—the *Cataphractarii*[2]—mounted on their heavy Nisaean horses, and supported by the mobile and lightly armed horse archers, were the masters of the Roman legion in suitable country. Culturally, the two empires were poles apart. Tacitus always speaks of the Parthians themselves as *barbari*, while expressly recognising the difference between them and the Hellenised cities which were the legacy of the Macedonians. Parthia was a feudal state. Its monarch, assuming the old Persian title of King of Kings, exercised a loose overlordship over the great landlords who ruled the vassal kingdoms and governed the satrapies. His was an insecure throne, though his successor could only come from the Royal House of the Arsacids.

Hence the Royal House of Parthia had a record of intrigue, murder and incest that matched that of the rulers of Ottoman Turkey, and constantly shocked Roman historians—who evaded the comparison with the Julio-Claudians. Hunting, feasting and war were the occupations of the great nobles. At first sight, they would seem to differ little from those of the old Persian empire, when the education of a gentleman taught him, according to Herodotus 'to ride, to shoot and to speak the truth.'[3] Two out of these archaic accomplishments were certainly preserved by the Parthian nobles. They were formidable horsemen. Tacitus records of one of them, Vardanes,[4] what must be among the outstanding rides of antiquity—350 miles in two days. Artabanus,[5] deposed as King of Kings, withdrew to Hyrcania and supported himself by his bow. But so far from speaking the truth, the Parthian nobles, as portrayed by Tacitus, had a record of treachery and falsehood that equals the worst said of the Arabs of our own time. What a King of Kings had to remember about his nobles was 'that while their loves are false, their hates are real.'[6]

Sharply differentiated from these great landlords, and from the peasants who worked on their estates, were the Greek cities, the results of Alexander's conquest. The most important of these was Seleuceia on the Tigris, of which more later. The commerce of the Parthian empire was largely in Greek hands, and so was much of its administration. Greek was the official language in the western provinces, Pahlavi in those of the east.

The Parthian provinces of Mesopotamia and Babylonia constituted one world with the Roman provinces of Syria and Palestine—the Hellenised world of western Asia. Across it, east and west, ran the great caravan routes. But, northwards, the rivers Tigris and Euphrates lead into Armenia, where Roman and Parthian interests clashed. This was a harsh and savage land—'cold Niphates peak' of the Roman poets, where winter lasts eight months of the year and armies freeze to death. Rome challenged Parthia in Armenia because she had early determined, rightly or wrongly, that direct Parthian power should not be allowed to extend to the shores of the Black Sea.

Relations between Rome and Parthia went back to the late republic.[7] The campaigns of Lucullus and Pompey against Mithridates, King of Pontus, had brought the Romans into contact with Armenia, and indeed with the peoples of the Caucasus as well. Pompey had organised the Roman provinces and client kingdoms of the East, notably the province of Syria. In 55 B.C. Crassus left Rome to take up what his opponents regarded as an unjust war against Parthia. It had a fearful sequel, the terrible defeat of the Roman Army at Carrhae,[8] which so bedevilled relations between the two powers for the next century. Here a Roman force of 42,000 men was cut to pieces by some 12,000 Parthian cavalry. The Roman casualties were 20,000 killed and 10,000 captured, together with the standards of the legions. Crassus himself was captured, and his head and hands were sent to the Parthian king. They arrived during a performance of the Bacchae of Euripides; the head was—literally—cast as the head of Pentheus, and flung upon the stage to announce the Parthian victory. Such, it is said, was the Hellenisation of the Parthian court!

Here was a stigma to be erased, and for long after the duty of fighting a Great Parthian War lay on each Roman wielder of power. Julius Caesar had assembled 16 legions and 10,000 cavalry for this purpose, but was assassinated before he could take them to the East. The task then fell to Antony,[9] and was aggravated by a Parthian invasion of Syria. Antony is said to have commanded nearly 100,000 troops, but his Parthian campaigns were a fiasco, and he withdrew with the loss of 30,000 men. For nearly a decade Augustus[10] allowed it to be supposed that he would take up the unfinished task that lay before him. In the end, and wisely, the Parthian problem was solved by diplomacy. On May 12th, 20 B.C. Tiberius received the captured standards from the Parthians, and it was agreed that Rome should have the right to confer the crown of Armenia. This was the settlement which began to crumble in the reign of Augustus' successor.

Military disaster at Carrhae, diplomatic success under Augustus—these are the two poles of relations between Rome and Parthia. But, on both sides, older historic memories also played an important part. Heir to the Seleucid empire, Rome was also heir to the heritage of Alexander the Great—the idea, which he briefly realised, of a world empire uniting the Mediterranean and the lands of western and central Asia. Many a Roman Emperor was to fall under the spell of this visionary gleam.[11] None was led further than Trajan, who, while Tacitus was putting the finishing touches on the *Annals*, captured Ctesiphon and Seleuceia, and for a brief time, made Roman provinces out of Mesopotamia and Babylonia.

On the Parthian side, there were memories of the Persian empire as it had been under the Achaemenids, in the spacious times of Darius and Cyrus. They gave rise to the concept of a *Parthia irredenta*, in which at least Syria and Palestine were to be won back from Rome. Indeed, King Artabanus III, late in the reign of Tiberius, even talked about reclaiming Alexander's empire as well as that of the Achaemenids.[12] This would have meant depriving Rome not only of Syria and Egypt, but also of Macedonia and Greece. No Arsacid monarch ever came near the realisation of such imperialist fantasies. Yet *Parthia irredenta* was an idea that had much vitality. From the third century onwards, when under the Sassanian dynasty a stronger Parthia confronted first Rome and then Byzantium, the threat to Syria was constant and real. It culminated in the capture of Antioch by Chosroes in A.D. 540. Only a little later the meteoric rise of Islam was fatal both to Persia and to Byzantium in those lands.

The *res orientis*, or eastern affairs with Parthia at their centre, form a major theme—complex and recurrent—in the *Annals* over fifty years between Tiberius and Nero. Tacitus takes up the narrative of eastern affairs in the second year of Tiberius' reign—16. Germanicus is about to be sent out to the East on a special mission. To explain the circumstances which made this necessary, a brief résumé is given of relations between Rome and Parthia from A.D. 4 to A.D. 16. It centres on the figure of Vonones,[13] the oldest of the four Parthian princes whom King Phraates had sent to be educated in Rome. On the death of Phraates he had been summoned to the Parthian throne, but he found himself in the position, familiar in our own times, of the westernised oriental who is no longer acceptable to his own people. The reaction of the Parthians is vividly expressed.[14] 'We have gone to another world,' they said to each other, 'to find ourselves a King, and we have got one infected with the sophistication of our enemies. The throne of the Arsacids is being bandied about as though it were one of the Roman provinces! Where is the glory we won through butchering Crassus and expelling Antony, if one of Augustus' possessions, inured to years of slavery, now rules in Parthia?'

Vonones himself was personally disliked for his good qualities as well as his bad. 'He seldom hunted, took little interest in horses, was carried in a litter in his progress through cities, and despised the traditional Parthian banquets. Mockery was also directed at his Greek favourites, and his way of keeping even ordinary domestic utensils under lock and key. He was most accessible and of an affable disposition, but such qualities were unknown to the Parthians, who looked on them as a strange new vice.'

He was ousted by another Parthian prince—Artabanus, brought up among the Dahae in the authentic Persian tradition. Vonones therefore went to Armenia, but there again his westernised ways were unacceptable, and he was driven out. Rome refused to back him at the cost of a Parthian war, and the governor of Syria received him as a refugee in Antioch. A refugee in comfortable circumstances, because he had brought the royal treasure with him, and kept up a court. He also intrigued to return to Parthia, and it is at this point in 16 that Artabanus demands his banishment from Syria. Germanicus sent him away to Cilicia, but failed to put a stop to his intrigues. He planned indeed to escape 'to the Albanians, the Heniochi, and finally to his kinsman the King of Scythia.'[15] There was, clearly, another side to this westernised Parthian prince— he had not wholly lost contact with the homeland of his ancestors in the wide lands beyond the Caspian. In mysterious circumstances, he was killed by the centurion appointed to keep guard over him—in modern terms 'shot while trying to escape.' According to Suetonius, Tiberius himself was responsible for this murder, wishing to lay his hands on the treasure of Vonones. It is to be noted that Tacitus does not set down this imputation against Tiberius.

For many years eastern affairs do not obtrude. But later in the reign of Tiberius, there is a dramatic episode. The prestige which the visit of Germanicus had brought to the name of Rome has faded; Tiberius himself has grown old and feeble. The Parthian king, too, has changed for the worse; he has become cruel to his own subjects and insolent towards Rome. He had insulted Tiberius by asking for the return of the treasures of Vonones; sources other than Tacitus say that he had even reproached him for his private life.[16] There was blustering talk about re-conquering the old empires of the Parthians and Macedonians, and invading the lands once held by Cyrus and

Alexander. At this moment a secret mission of Parthian nobles appeared in Rome, asking for the return of Phraates, son of the king of that name, to Parthia: 'all we need,' they argued, 'is the name and backing of Tiberius: then let the scion of the house of Arsaces show himself on the banks of the Euphrates.'[17]

This was exactly what Tiberius wanted. He gave Phraates the insignia of royalty and the means to recover his father's throne, holding fast to his maxim of employing guile and diplomacy in the conduct of foreign affairs, without recourse to arms. Phraates did not last long. The strain of trying to acclimatise himself to the Parthian way of life proved too much, and he died. But Tiberius could still draw from his stockpile of Oriental princes, and he sent out a younger brother, Tiridates, to Parthia, and a certain Mithridates, for the throne of Iberia. Artabanus was driven from his throne and retired to the wilds of Hyrcania; Tiridates was crowned at Ctesiphon.

The Greek cities in Parthia went over to his side, and Tacitus[18] takes the opportunity of giving a description of Seleuceia, the most important of them. It is interesting to see what he says and what he omits. He describes it as a powerful city, still preserving the memory of its founder Seleucus, and faithful to its Greek culture and Greek political forms. There is a senate of 300 members, and also a powerful *demos*. United they can defy the Parthian king; when they are at odds—and in a Greek city that is only too often—he is too much for them. What Tacitus omits is anything on the economic importance of Seleuceia. Situated on the Tigris, it played much the same rôle in commerce as did Babylon in ancient and Baghdad in modern times. It was a nodal point on the great caravan routes. The river Tigris was navigable downstream to the head of the Persian Gulf. With its population of 600,000 people, it was the most important Greek city in the Parthian world.

But the triumph of Tiridates did not last for long. Soon Parthian sympathies had swung back again to Artabanus, and he was successfully restored to the throne. Tiridates did not believe that 'the purple makes a good shroud.' He retired to

Syria, thus, in the words of Tacitus, 'excusing everyone from the charge of treachery.'[19] Among them, presumably, the Romans—they had launched their nominee into the ring once again; if he would not fight, he must take the consequences. From sources other than Tacitus we know that Artabanus was induced to pay some sort of homage to Rome, and allowed to retain his throne until his death. The whole affair had been an impressive demonstration of the power that Rome could exert on the eastern frontiers through diplomacy, and by allowing most of the fighting to be done by her allies, while keeping the Roman army of Syria in being as a threat.

The death of King Artabanus III was followed by civil war in Parthia, Armenia, and several of the lesser kingdoms. This, and the sloth and irresolution of the Roman government, means that relations between Rome and Parthia during the reign of Claudius are exceptionally complex. Moreover, the narrative of Tacitus involves several chronological difficulties. But two episodes of importance stand out. The first[20] is the bid for power of Meherdates, son of Vonones, and the third Roman nominee to attempt to win the throne of Parthia. It begins in 49, when a deputation of Parthian nobles came to Rome to look for a prince who would oust the cruel Gotarzes. Tacitus gives a vivid picture of the reception they met. The Parthians begin by describing the crimes of Gotarzes, and continue 'we have an old, publicly sanctioned pact of friendship with you. Now you must come to the help of allies who are your equals in power, but accord you deference out of respect. It is for precisely this reason that kings' sons are sent to Rome as hostages, so that if we get tired of our rulers at home we can apply to the Emperor and Senate, and obtain a better one, with the advantages of a Roman education.'

This afforded Claudius an excellent opportunity for a statement on high policy, which he did not fail to take. 'Replying to this, and other similar statements, Claudius launched into a speech about Roman pre-eminence and Parthian subservience.

He compared himself to Augustus, who had sent a king to Parthia (Tiberius had sent kings too, but nothing was said about that). From this he turned to giving precepts to Meherdates (who was present) and advising him to think in terms of mentor and citizens, not of despot and slaves. Mercy and justice, he said, were qualities which orientals would accept all the more gladly because they were unknown. Then he turned to the deputation and extolled Rome's fosterling, who had given proof of his good character. Still, they must take kings as they were, frequent changes were unprofitable. Rome had now reached a pinnacle of glory, and desired peace for foreign countries.' These were fine sentiments, indeed, but they do not seem to have been reflected in the conduct of Roman officials in the East.

Gaius Cassius,[21] governor of Syria, conducted Meherdates to the meeting place at Zeugma, where he was received by a deputation of Parthian nobles and by Acbar, king of Edessa. After giving him a salutary caution against the dangers of delay, Cassius left him to make his own way in Parthia. But the young Parthian was now surrounded by false friends. Acbar lured him into spending a long period sampling the delights of Edessa. After that he had to make an exhausting journey through the wintry mountains of Armenia. A further delay was imposed by the king of Adiabene, Izates, who was a secret adherent of Gotarzes.

Tacitus[22] notes, in the course of their journey, the capture of the ancient city of Nineveh, and also the fortress near the site of Alexander's victory over Darius. But, in the meantime, Gotarzes was collecting his forces to win back what he had lost. 'First Izates, with the forces of Adiabene, then Acbar with his Arabs, went over to him. Treachery comes by nature to these peoples, and experience has shown that they would rather invite their kings from Rome than keep them.'[23] A long and bloody battle decided the issue in favour of Gotarzes. Meherdates was captured, but he was not put to death. Instead he was mutilated by the cutting off of his ears, and, thus disgraced, was debarred for ever from the throne of Parthia. Experience, it could also be said, suggests that Rome was more eager to send her candidates into Parthia than to support them. Meherdates' cropped head was a visible proof of the risk they ran.

The second episode[24] concerns the bid of Radamistus, prince of Iberia, for the throne of Armenia. It is of historical importance, because its outcome led to the full-scale military intervention of Rome in Parthian and Armenian affairs under Nero. It is also highly dramatic, and the interest Tacitus takes in its picturesque details means that he gives a fuller picture of Radamistus than of any other eastern prince. The story begins in 51. At this time Vologeses was firmly seated on the throne of Parthia. Radamistus' father, Pharasmenes, was king of the little Trans-Caucasian kingdom of Iberia, with his capital near the modern Tiflis;[25] his uncle, Meherdates, ruled Armenia with Roman support. Iberia was too small a kingdom for the father and his ambitious son, nor did it seem likely that the young prince would willingly wait for his father to die. He was therefore encouraged to insert himself into the kingdom of Armenia. Tall and handsome, with a native education and the good qualities admired by his countrymen, Radamistus appeared as a refugee in Armenia, and soon won favour and support. He returned to Iberia to place himself at the head of an army, which had ostensibly been collected for another purpose. With this he invaded Armenia and drove Meherdates into the fortress of Gorneae. Here was a detachment of Roman troops, under the command of Caelius Pollio, who was camp commandant, and of the centurion Casperius.

Here Meherdates should have been safe. Lacking a knowledge of siege tactics, the Iberian army could not storm the fort. But, as Philip of Macedon used to say, there is always the silver bullet. Caelius Pollio could not resist it; Casperius, failing to keep him to an honourable course, went to inform Pharasmenes and the governor of Syria. Meherdates was induced to leave the fortress to make a treaty with Radamistus. The moment for treachery had come. Radamistus took an oath not to kill him by sword or poison; then they went to exchange the oath of blood

brotherhood, by which the thumbs of the contracting parties
were tied together and blood was exchanged. While his hands
were tied, Meherdates was thrown to the ground and cast in
chains. Radamistus then proved himself a man of his word. 'He
strictly observed his oath not to use sword or poison against his
uncle and his wife. He had them flung to the ground, covered
with layers of heavy clothing, and thus smothered to death.
The children of Meherdates were killed for having shed tears at
their parents' murder.'[26]

Tacitus next takes us to a meeting of the council of Ummidius
Quadratus, governor of Syria. 'He put before the council what
had happened in Armenia, and asked whether they thought
punitive measures were called for. A few members showed
some concern for Roman honour: most played for safety. They
urged that all criminal acts among foreigners should be posi-
tively welcomed, and that discord should actually be fostered.
How often had Roman Emperors bestowed this same Armenia,
outwardly as a token of generosity, but really to unsettle the
minds of the barbarians! So, let Radamistus keep his ill-gotten
gains, so long as he was hated and in bad odour; expediency was
much better served in that way than if he had gained his
kingdom honourably. This was the opinion that prevailed. But
to avoid the risk of seeming to condone the crime—or of receiving imperial instructions to reverse their policy—messengers
were sent to Pharasmenes ordering him to withdraw from Armenia and recall his son.'[27] It could not be said that the council
of the governor of Syria lacked a grasp of *realpolitik*.

But there were limits set to the behaviour of Roman agents in
the East. They were exceeded when Julius Paelignus,[28] imperial
procurator in Cappadocia, after plundering his province, fled
for refuge to Radamistus, and took part in a particularly scandalous ceremony of coronation. This was too much for everyone
concerned. A legion was sent into Armenia under the command
of Helvidius Priscus, but withdrawn when the king of Parthia
invaded that country with Tiridates, a client of his own.

Meanwhile the Armenians themselves were taking a hand against Radamistus. They surrounded the palace with arms, and Radamistus was driven out. 'All that saved Radamistus, and his wife, was that he had a swift horse. But the poor lady was pregnant: at first she endured the journey as best she could because she feared the enemy and loved her husband. But with the continuous galloping her womb and her very entrails were so shaken that she begged for death, to rescue her from the shame of captivity. Radamistus at first embraced her and tried to cheer and encourage her: he was divided between admiration for her courage, and a desperate anxiety that another man should have her if he left her there. But he was frenzied with love, and not unpractised in deeds of violence: drawing his scimitar he ran her through and dragged her, wounded, to the banks of the Araxes, then threw her in, so that even her body should be carried away. He made off at a headlong gallop to his own kingdom of Iberia. Meanwhile Zenobia (that was the lady's name) was found by shepherds in a quiet backwater, still breathing and showing signs of life. They could tell from her beauty and dignity that she was some noble person, so when they heard her name and story, they bound up her wound, used some rustic remedies, and took her to Artaxata. From there she was sent at public expense to Tiridates, who treated her kindly and used her with royal honours.'[29] Eventually Radamistus was killed on the order of his father Pharasmenes on the ground of treachery. There is no reason to suspect the reason given.

In 54, Roman policy in the East lay in ruins. The Roman nominee had been driven off the throne of Armenia. It was now occupied by Tiridates, who had been imposed by Parthia without reference to Rome. In the client kingdoms the prestige of Rome must have been at its lowest ebb since the time of Crassus. These were the circumstances in which Domitius Corbulo[30] was appointed to a special command in the East, leading to the events which take up so large a part of three successive books— XIII to XV. The memoirs of Corbulo are thought to be Tacitus' major source for the tangled narrative of nine years of war and diplomacy. The salient military features have been dealt with in the chapter on the Roman Army. It has been shown how Corbulo's first task was to bring the Roman Army of the East up to standard as a fighting force.[31] Once this had been done, he could employ force or diplomacy as the situation required.

Although it often threatened, there was in fact to be no full-scale conflict between Rome and Parthia. At first the confrontation seemed absolute. 'The year 58 saw a vigorous resumption of the Roman-Parthian war over Armenia, which had been feebly begun and intermittently pursued. The Parthian king, Vologeses, had no mind to allow his brother Tiridates to give up the kingdom he had conferred on him, nor yet to hold it as a gift from a foreign power. Corbulo thought that the dignity of the Roman people demanded the recovery of the lands once conquered by Pompey and Lucullus. The Armenians wavered in their loyalty, and invited in the armies of both sides. Geography, the customs of the country, and frequent inter-marriage made them more akin to the Parthians; they had no conception of freedom, but they preferred a Parthian to a Roman master.'[32]

Yet as early as 58 the ultimate solution had been hinted at by Corbulo—that Tiridates should retain the crown of Armenia, but that it should be conferred by Rome. Much was to happen on both sides before this consummation was achieved. When his proposals had been rejected from the Parthian side, Corbulo conducted a full-scale offensive in Armenia, with brilliant success. Armenian fortresses were besieged and captured; of the two capitals of the country, Artaxata was captured and destroyed, and Tigranocerta surrendered. For a while a Roman nominee, Tigranes, occupied the throne of Armenia. His intransigence and his invasion of Adiabene provoked the Parthians to renewed efforts. It seemed likely that the Parthian king would invade the Roman provinces. But he had trouble in his rear; the half-independent kingdom of Hyrcania was discontented, and disunion in Parthia could be fostered by Rome.

While Corbulo in Syria guarded against the main threat to the Roman provinces from Parthia, Caesennius Paetus[33] pursued

his ill-conceived plan for turning Armenia into a Roman province. The result was the disaster at Randeia—the only major
clash between important Roman and Parthian forces. It was
followed by an armistice, according to which the Romans
destroyed all fortresses held by them east of the Euphrates,
while Parthian forces were to withdraw from Armenia. Even so,
the Parthians were able to negotiate from strength. In the spring
of 63, a Parthian embassy arrived in Rome, bringing messages
from Vologeses. 'The gods,' said the Parthian king,[34] 'are the
judges of affairs of even the mightiest nations, and they have
conferred possession of Armenia on the Parthians, not without
disgrace to Rome. I besieged Tigranes, I could have destroyed
Paetus and his two legions, but I let them go in safety. I have
given sufficient proof of my power; I have also shown a proof of
my clemency. Tiridates would not refuse to come to Rome to
claim the crown of Armenia were there no religious scruples to
forbid him. He will certainly be prepared to go before the
Roman standards and the statues of the Emperor to inaugurate
his reign in the presence of the Roman legions.' As it stood, the
proposal was unacceptable. Further tokens of submission were
required from Tiridates, and again Corbulo prepared forces for
the invasion of Parthia. These were in themselves sufficient to
bring about what was really desired by both sides—a meeting
between Corbulo and Tiridates to arrange the terms of peace.
Both sides, too, were happy that it should take place at Randeia:
'the Parthians asked for that place because it was where Paetus'
legions had recently been besieged, and was associated with
their own success. Corbulo made no objection: contrast in
fortune could only rebound to his glory.'[35]

And so, in 63, there took place one of those confrontations
between the forces of Rome and Parthia which so stirred the
imaginations of contemporaries. We have a description of one
such meeting in the time of Augustus by Velleius Paterculus,[36] a
man of more commonplace mind, but an eyewitness of the
encounter between Gaius Caesar and the Parthian King in A.D. I.
'On an island in the Euphrates, Gaius met the Parthian King, a

man of the most noble bearing. The retinues were equal on either side. This spectacle—of the Roman Army drawn up on the one side, the Parthian on the other, of the meeting of the distinguished leaders of their own empires and indeed of mankind—this splendid and memorable sight I saw as a young officer soon after I entered the service. . . . First the Parthian dined with Gaius on the Roman bank of the river, later Gaius dined with him on the enemy side. . . .' Tacitus, too, describes how behaviour and precedence were carefully noted on both sides.[37] 'On sighting Corbulo, Tiridates at once dismounted. Corbulo followed, and then on foot they clasped hands as a solemn pledge of friendship.

'Corbulo immediately complimented the young prince on his good sense in following wise counsels and avoiding rash actions. Tiridates began with a long disquisition on the nobility of his family, but the rest of his speech was in moderate terms. He said he would go to Rome, and bring to Nero a new distinction—the homage of a Parthian royal prince, although Parthia had suffered no reverse. It was then agreed that Tiridates should lay his crown before the statue of Nero, and should only take it up again from his hand. The interview ended with an embrace. At the meeting which followed a few days later there was a splendid display by both armies. On the Parthian side the cavalry were drawn up regiment by regiment, each with their national ensigns. On the Roman side the legions stood in line, their eagles and standards glittering brightly, and with the images of the gods displayed as in a temple. The chair of state stood in the middle of the tribunal, and on it was placed the statue of the Emperor. Tiridates advanced towards it. After the usual sacrifices had been made, he took the crown from his head and placed it before the statue. On all sides this produced a deep impression. The spectacle of the siege and massacre of a Roman army was fresh before men's eyes; but now it seemed that the tables were turned; if Tiridates was going to make a display of himself before the nations, was he not virtually a prisoner?

'The courtesy and hospitality displayed by Corbulo added

further to his glory. The king wanted an explanation for every novelty he saw—the centurion's announcement of the changing of the guard, the bugle-call at the end of mess, the altar and the torch to light it before the general's tent. All this, explained in colourful terms, aroused his admiration for ancient Roman customs. Next day he asked for permission to visit his mother and brothers before starting on his long journey. Meanwhile he gave his daughter as a hostage, and sent submissive letters to Nero.'

But it was not the intention of the king of Parthia that too much subservience should be inflicted on his brother. 'He sent messengers to Corbulo to request that his brother should not be required to show any outward mark of subjection—he should be allowed to keep his scimitar, be entitled to salute provincial governors with an embrace, and not be kept waiting at their doors. In Rome, he was to have the honours of the consul. Used to oriental ostentation, he did not understand the Roman attachment to the realities of power, and its disdain for the trappings.'[38] But whether Rome or Parthia had gained more of the realities of power, as distinct from its trappings, from the settlement of 63, might be a matter for argument.

In Book XVI of the *Annals* Tacitus breaks off before the journey of Tiridates to Rome, and his elaborate reception there. For this we have to turn to Suetonius'[39] *Life of Nero*, and to the rather lengthier description in Cassius Dio.[40] Since religious scruples made it impossible for him to cross wide stretches of ocean, Tiridates went overland to Rome, riding all the way from the Euphrates. With him were a number of other Parthian princes, his whole retinue of servants and all his royal paraphernalia. There were also three thousand Parthian horsemen and many Romans in his retinue. His wife rode beside him, covering her face with a golden helmet to observe the eastern custom. All the way, says Dio, it was like a triumphal procession. Gaily decorated cities received them, whose inhabitants shouted out many compliments. The entire journey took nine months, and the billeting charges for this magnificent junket were about

£4,000 a day, which was met by the Roman Treasury. The entire journey would therefore have cost over a million pounds.

The main event at Rome was, of course, the coronation ceremony, which took place in the Roman Forum. Dio preserves many details. Nero entered the Forum and took his seat on the Rostra. He was in full triumphal garb, and attended by the Senate and the Praetorians. Tiridates spoke what seems to have been a carefully worded formula. 'Lord and Master, I am a descendant of the line of Arsaces, a brother of the kings Vologeses and Pacorus—and your slave, and I have come to you, as my God, to adore you as I do Mithras. Whatever destiny you spin for me shall be mine; you are my fortune and my fate.' Nero's reply was: 'You have done well to come here in person in order that you should enjoy my bounty face to face. And so what was not left you by your father, nor conferred upon you by your brothers, that I grant you. I declare you King of Armenia, in order that you and they shall learn that it lies in my power to bestow kingships and to take them away.' After these words, he bade him come up by the steps which had been especially built in front of the Rostra for this occasion. Tiridates was made to sit beneath his feet, and he then placed the diadem upon his head. Great shouts arose from every side at this point.'

Both the words of Tiridates and the form of the ceremony seemed to suggest that Nero was appearing in the guise of Mithras presenting the diadem to the Sun God.[41] The coronation was followed by special performances in the Theatre of Pompey, held on so lavish a scale that ever afterwards the occasion was known as The Golden Day. 'The whole interior of the theatre, as well as the stage, had been gilded, and so were all the stage properties introduced. The people therefore gave to the day itself the epithet of "The Golden Day." The curtains stretched overhead to keep off the sun were of purple, and in the centre of them was an embroidered figure of Nero driving a chariot, surrounded by gleaming golden stars.'[42] The display reinforces the parallel. Historic memories as well as religious symbolism must have been evoked, for this theatre had been built from the spoils of war by Pompey, the greatest Roman conqueror of the East.

On his return journey, the Armenian king allowed himself the short sea journey from Brindisi to Dyrrachium, and thence via the cities of Asia 'from which he derived a profound impression of the strength and beauty of the Roman empire.' As for its wealth, he had not only seen that for himself, but brought back with him gifts falling little short of two million pounds in our money. He had also obtained permission to rebuild Artaxata,[43] and took with him a number of Roman craftsmen, 'some of them given to him by Nero, and others bribed by himself with the promise of high wages.' This last is an interesting item, for these workmen must have been engaged on the construction of the New City of Rome after the Great Fire of 64. The rebuilt Artaxata was known 'for a brief while' as Neronia. After that, presumably, as usual in Armenia and Parthia, a native reaction set in against westernised ways. But this Roman city in the heart of Armenia may well have been one of the great architectural wonders of its time. The whole cost to public funds of the journey of the Armenian king can scarcely have been less than five million pounds. No doubt a full-scale war with Parthia would have been more expensive still. For, in fact, the peace thus established lasted for almost fifty years, until it was broken by the offensive of Trajan. When Nero closed the Temple of Janus, 'peace having been established by land and sea,' the claim was less extravagant than many put forward by that Emperor.

Two objects of eastern policy Nero was not destined to attain. He wished to secure control of the great passes across the Caucasus, but a projected expedition never took place.[44] Instead Vespasian built the fort of Harmozica in the modern Georgia, as a protection against raids from outside the Roman-controlled client kingdoms. Nero also failed to induce Vologeses himself to come to Rome, though he made many attempts to do so. The Parthian monarch cleverly pleaded religious scruples as a delaying action, and in the end suggested a meeting with Nero in Asia. But in the first century A.D., at any rate, no Roman Emperor ever met face to face with a Parthian king.

Rome and Parthia—their relations are the closest in antiquity to Great Power Politics. It is therefore surprising to find Tacitus at pains to emphasise that in his judgement the eastern frontier was not the most important. A greater menace lay to the north, where, beyond the Rhine and the Danube, Rome was confronted with the barbarian peoples of central and northern Europe. This is Germania, a term which covered a wider area then than now, for in Tacitus it extends beyond the modern Germany to Czechoslovakia, Poland, the Baltic countries and Scandinavia. Tacitus believed that these people posed to Rome the most serious challenge which had ever confronted her in her history. The most explicit statement of this view is to be found in chapter 37 of the *Germania*. 'Not the Samnites, nor the Carthaginians, neither the Spaniards nor the Gauls—no, not even the Parthians —have taught us harsher lessons. Indeed, the freedom of the Germans strikes with a sharper edge than the despotism of the Parthian king.'[45]

This menace is shown by the protracted nature of the conquest of Germany (which at the accession of Trajan had in Tacitus' view lasted for 210 years), by the many losses incurred on either side, by the disaster of Varus in the time of Augustus, and, in recent experience, by the gaining in Germany of more triumphs than victories. To this important chapter we must return. It is interesting to see that on this topic Tacitus would have been supported by the opinion of Tiberius, who was the greatest German expert in the history of Rome. In Book II of the *Annals*, at the time of the fall of Maroboduus, there is a reference to a speech made by Tiberius to the Senate. In this the Emperor 'took the line that Philip had not posed so great a threat to Athens, nor Pyrrhus and Antiochus to the Roman people. There is still extant the speech of Tiberius on the subject of the greatness of Maroboduus, the fierce spirit of the peoples over whom he ruled, the menace of such an enemy so close to Italy, and his own cleverness in bringing him low.'[46] No wonder, then, that German affairs engrossed so much of Tacitus' attention.

At the beginning of his career as a historian, and in the same year as the *Agricola*, he published a special work on the origins and the customs of the Germans, now commonly known by its short title of the *Germania*. The German wars under Tiberius form an important theme in Books I and II of the *Annals*, full of striking personalities on both the Roman and the German side, abounding in picturesque episodes, such as the Battlefield of Varus, the retreat over the Long Bridges, and the Great Storm on the North Sea coast. We do not know what Tacitus had to say about the abortive German expedition of Gaius. Under Claudius there are a number of campaigns both in western Germany and the Low Countries, though they are on a small scale compared with the great wars of Tiberius. Again, in the year 69, the *Histories* have much about the part played by the tribes of free Germany in the rebellion of Civilis.

Something has already been said on the treatment of German affairs in the first two books of the *Annals*. The *Germania*[47] was published in 98, at a time when Trajan, the new Emperor, was still setting affairs on the German frontier into a satisfactory state before coming to Rome. Tacitus, who had held the consulship in the previous year, would certainly have an exceptionally favourable opportunity of directing public attention to Germany by the publication of the monograph. What other ends it was meant to serve has always been a matter of debate. Unlike the *Agricola*, there is no statement of the author's purpose, nor are any large claims made on behalf of the book. It does not pretend to be a first-hand account, nor to introduce new evidence. Indeed, modern scholarship has shown that Tacitus was not at pains to bring his evidence up to date, and that at several points the account of conditions in Germany omits what was done by the Flavian emperors.[48] But it can be better understood now that we are familiar with the literary conventions of the *genre* to which it belongs. The alternative title—*De origine et situ Ger-*

manorum—proclaims it as an ethnographical treatise, a *genre* which goes back to Hecataeus of Miletus, but for which the *locus classicus* is the famous passage of Herodotus[49] on the Scythian peoples of what is now the Ukraine and south Russia. Herodotus' treatment of the customs of a barbarian people was the model for numerous Greek and Roman writers. By far the most important of these was the great Greek *savant* Posidonius of Apamea,[50] who, early in the first century B.C., travelled extensively in the western provinces of the Roman world, and who wrote not only on the Celts, but also on the Spaniards and the Germans.

It is most unlikely that Tacitus drew direct from Posidonius. But the influence of Posidonius can certainly be proved in what Caesar has to say about the Germans, and it was probably dominant in the books (now lost) which Livy devoted to the same topic.[51] Caesar and Livy will certainly have been among Tacitus' sources. But his most important predecessor is now taken to be the Elder Pliny,[52] whose comprehensive work *On the German Wars* covers the whole period down to the reign of Claudius. Tacitus' dependence on Pliny perhaps explains why his own account of Germany is not always up to date. Non-literary sources must also have been important—the accounts of Roman officers who had served in German campaigns, or of Roman merchants who had penetrated, on a scale greater than Tacitus is willing to allow, into the barbarian world beyond the Roman frontiers. Compiled from these sources, and running to only forty-six chapters, the *Germania* of Tacitus seems to have been no more than a modest tract for the times. The loss of almost all other classical sources for Germany, and the accidents of modern history and modern education, have combined to give it an influence altogether out of proportion to its size.

The *Germania* falls into two main sections. The first twenty-seven chapters give a general survey of the origins, customs, and social organisation of the German peoples, especially those of west Germany, about whom most was known. The last nineteen chapters form a kind of catalogue of nations, mentioning individual features of interest about some seventy barbarian tribes, and extending as far as the shadowy lands of the eastern Baltic and south Scandinavia. Modern scholars have pointed out how early German society, as described by Tacitus, was in fact undergoing a period of rapid change. The growth of private property, the influence of the leaders of the war-bands or *comitatus*, and above all, the presence of Rome on their southern and eastern frontiers for rather more than a century, had gone far to disintegrate the primitive tribal communities described by Julius Caesar.[53]

Tacitus[54] was by no means unaware of social change among the barbarians. But he was more impressed by the survival of archaic virtues that had once characterised Rome, but which had succumbed to the 'progress' of civilisation. These barbarian peoples still had a respect for religion. They preserved the sanctity of marriage and of family ties; their sexual morals were austere. The young men of the *comitatus* were literally loyal to the death to their leaders. A low value was set on slaves and freedmen. The Germans amused themselves with the manly pastime of the sword dance, instead of being mere spectators at mass amusements.

Hence there is in this section a running contrast between the decadence of Roman civilisation and the unspoiled values of barbarian society. It does not, however, as has been claimed, amount to an idealisation of the Noble Savage. Idealisation there certainly is, notably in the passage on German marriages. The wedding customs remind the young bride that 'at the very outset of her marriage she has come to be her husband's partner in toil and danger, and to suffer and to dare with him in peace and war. The yoked oxen, the bridled horses, the gifts of arms, are all symbols of this partnership. So she must live, so she must die: her wedding gifts are to be passed on, worthily preserved, to her children, as her son's wives will receive them in their turn and pass them down to her grandchildren. Thus the German women live in inviolable chastity, with no lascivious shows or provocative banquets to lure them to vice; secret love-letters are unknown to either sex. . . . That is a land where no one has an indulgent smile for immorality or calls seducing or being seduced "the spirit of modern times." '[55]

But sharp limits are set to this idealisation of Germany and the Germans. Tacitus underlines the idleness of the warriors—'they love indolence rather than peace.'[56] They are unproductive, swaggering about and leaving the real work to others. They are much addicted to drunkenness, and this fault can readily be exploited by Rome. And for the land itself, with its swamps and forests, its winds and storms, Tacitus feels all the dislike of Mediterranean man for the north. The reason he gives for the racial purity of the Germanic peoples (a reason not often quoted) is that no one in his senses would wish to go there. 'Apart from the dangers of a turbulent and unknown sea, who would want to change Asia or Africa or Italy for Germany, with its desolate landscape, harsh climate, barbarous way of life and customs— unless he was born there?'[57]

Tacitus' warmest admiration goes out to what may be termed the Unspoiled Barbarian—a people who, like the Chatti of the modern Hessen, have learned something from Roman civilisation without losing their heroic qualities. The commentators have noted the emotional tones in which this people is described:[58] 'beyond the Mattiaci begins the land of the Chatti, from the Hercynian forest onwards: a land not so open and marshy as that of other tribes in the wide expanse of Germany. Indeed the hills continue: only gradually do they break down into gaps: the Hercynian forest, as it were, bears her children the Chatti on her shoulders, and only puts them down on the edge of the plain. This is a people of hardy physique, well-made limbs, threatening visage and a high degree of intelligence. For Germans they have qualities of reason and judgement. They pick leaders, and follow them, when they are in command. They keep rank, have an eye for an opening, hold back their charge till the right moment, organise the day's duties, and entrench themselves at night. They know that fortune is hazardous, but valour is sure. They have another rare quality, usually the product of Roman discipline—they rely more on the general than on the army. Their strength lies in their infantry, who carry trenching tools and rations as well as their weapons. Other tribes march out to battle: the Chatti go on a campaign.'

Here is the picture of a free native people, perfectly adapted to their land, but capable of selecting what is good from their contacts with a higher military organisation. The German wars of Domitian had[59] already rendered this idealised picture out of date; it is highly likely that it originates from the Elder Pliny, who could have observed the Chatti in action during the reign of Claudius. For genuine primitives, Tacitus had little taste. Consider his picture of the Fenni[60]—the ancestors of the modern Finns. 'The Fenni are dreadfully savage and astonishingly poor. They have no weapons, no horses, no homes. They live on plants, clothe themselves in skins, and sleep on the ground. Arrows are their only resource, but, lacking iron, they have to tip them with sharp bones. The hunt feeds men and women alike: the women accompany the men everywhere and claim a share in winning the prey. They can only shelter their babies against wild animals or storms by a miserable kind of network of branches: to this the young men return, but they think it far better than to sweat at the plough or to toil over house-building, or traffic in their own and other people's property in hope and fear. Caring for neither gods nor men, they have achieved a most difficult objective—they have nothing even to pray for.' With the Fenni, mankind proper comes to a stop. 'Beyond them is the realm of myth, the Hellusii and the Oxiones, with human heads and faces, but the bodies of animals. . . . All this is conjecture, and I shall say no more.'

As Homer's Catalogue of Ships served the cities of Greece as a patent of nobility, so does Tacitus' Catalogue of Nations in the *Germania* perform the same functions for the peoples of northern Europe. Many famous peoples and tribes here find their first mention in history. Among them—their names more or less recognisable—are the Angles, Jutes, Lombards, Goths, Swedes,

Finns, Wends, and Quens.[61] The list of names is enlivened by picturesque detail. We hear of the ghostly army of the Harii: 'the Harii are, militarily, the most powerful of the peoples I have listed and they enhance their native ferocity by skill and opportunism. Their shields are black, their bodies dyed: they fight their battles on moonless nights, when the terror of their ghostly army causes panic. No enemy can withstand their grim and hellish aspect, for defeat in battle always begins with what you see.'[62]

Speculation on the origin of amber leads to exotic detail. 'You can perceive that amber is really the juice of a tree, the fact that worms and insects are to be seen shining in it, being caught by the liquid when sticky, and imprisoned as it hardened. My own belief is that—like the secret groves of the orient, where the trees exude frankincense and balsam—so there must be exceptionally fertile woods and groves in the islands of the West, and their juice is drawn out by the rays of their neighbour the sun and flows into the nearest sea. From there storms and tempests wash it up on the coasts opposite.'[63]

J. G. C. Anderson, editor of the best and most modern edition of the *Germania*, points out how often details in Tacitus are confirmed by archaeology.[64] For example, the famous Nydam boat, found in a peat-bog in Schleswig, confirms what he says about the ships of the Suiones: 'their ships have the peculiar feature of a sharp prow at either end, so that they are always ready to put into shore. They are not worked by sails, nor are there oars set in banks along the side. The oarage is loose, as in some rivers, and is reversible as occasion requires.' The sacred wagon of the goddess Nerthus, drawn by oxen, is paralleled by the cult wagon found at Dejbjerg Moor in Jutland. As for what Tacitus says about the punishment on 'shirkers, cowards or perverts, who are drowned in the mud of bogs with hurdles placed over them'—the discovery of no fewer than fifty-five bodies, 'many of them in unnatural postures with limbs tied and pierced and with traces of wounds', attests that this grim punishment survived until the Middle Ages.[65]

Two passages in the *Germania* have always aroused comment, because in them Tacitus speaks in language which is both heart-felt and personal. The first is the famous Chapter 37, already mentioned, on the wars between Rome and Germany. The German scholar, E. Norden,[66] has pointed out how carefully it is introduced and composed. The survey has taken us to the Cimbric peninsula—the modern Jutland. The Cimbri themselves are now only a shadow of their great name: 'they are now but a small people, but they have a great name in history. Many remains attest their former glory, and from the dimensions of the huge camps which are to be seen on either bank of the Rhine you can judge even today the sheer mass and manpower of that nation, indeed, they render credible the size of their great emigration.' The huge camps are, almost certainly, the great Celtic hill forts on either side of the Rhine; here modern archaeology would not support Tacitus.

But the point is the great emigration of the Cimbri at the end of the second century B.C., and the damage which it inflicted on Rome. 'For Rome was in her 640th year when we first heard the clash of Cimbric arms. From then to the second consulship of Trajan will give a period of some 210 years; that is, the duration of the conquest of Germany. In the course of that long period some damaging blows have been exchanged.' The reverses inflicted by the Parthians cannot compare with those of the Germans—'take away the defeat of Crassus (at Carrhae in 53 B.C.) and what else has the East to show?' In the fearful wars against the Cimbri and the Teutones, in the valley of the Rhône and in northern Italy, the Roman people lost five consular armies. Augustus lost Varus and the three legions. Even the Roman victories were won at a heavy price—'it cost something for Gaius Marius to defeat the Germans in Italy, for the Emperor Julius to defeat them in Gaul, and for Drusus Tiberius and Germanicus to win victories on the soil of Germany. Later, too, the immense preparations of Gaius Caesar ended in farce. Peace followed, until our own Civil Wars and dissensions enabled the Germans to capture legionary bases and lay claim to

HT

Gaul. They were defeated: but in more recent times German campaigns have yielded triumphs rather than victories.'

The résumé is exceptionally detailed, and its grim matter goes far to explain the other well-known passage, which concerns a famous episode of Tacitus' own time. In Chapter 33 of the *Germania*, we are told how the Bructeri have been practically annihilated by a confederacy of neighbouring tribes and before the eyes of a Roman army. 'They may have been loathed for their arrogance, or booty may have been the cause, or possibly an act of favour by the gods to Rome. Indeed, we were even allowed to witness the battle, as a kind of show: more than sixty thousand warriors were killed, not by Roman swords or javelins, but more remarkable yet, before the gratified eyes of Roman spectators. Long may the barbarians continue, I hope, not to love us, but at least to hate each other, for the destiny of empire bears hard upon us, and fate has no greater bounties in store than disunion among our enemies.'[67]

Tacitus has incurred censure for the 'terrible inhumanity' of his comment on this massacre, which is probably, but not certainly, dated to 98. But it should be said that the Bructeri were one of the most dangerous of the anti-Roman peoples of western Germany. They had been allies of Arminius, had fought against Germanicus, and had taken part in the Civilis rebellion, incited by their famous prophetess, Veleda. They were certainly what would have been described in the time of the Indian wars in America as 'pesky Indians.' Moreover (though this would have not have pleased Tacitus), their annihilation had been exaggerated—they are heard of again in the second century. The terrible inhumanity of Tacitus' comment is frequently paralleled in reactions to the disasters of enemies. More interesting are the words about 'the destiny of empire bears hard upon us.' What exactly does this mean? Are those scholars[68] right who have seen here a foreboding of the decline and fall of Rome at the hands of the northern barbarians? Such pessimism would seem to be an anachronism at the end of the first century A.D. The destiny of empire may bear hard at times, but better times could come again. And, in any case 'disunion among our enemies' would be a sufficient gift at the hands of fortune. So it was in the disasters at the end of Augustus' reign. The great German leaders Arminius and Maroboduus ended in fighting each other rather than in joining forces against Rome.[69]

'*habent sua fata libelli.*' 'Books, no less than empires, have their destiny.' None more strange than that of the *Germania* of Tacitus. It was natural enough that the high prestige of classical studies in Germany during the nineteenth century should have made it required reading in that country's schools and universities. The great interest in the history of the northern peoples has meant that it has been studied perhaps more intensively than any of Tacitus' other works. And its influence has not always been for the good. At best, it has served to foster one of Germany's besetting weaknesses—that of undue admiration for her heroic past. At worst, it contains passages which give encouragement to racialist theories and the nonsense which has been built up on them. 'I find it credible,' says Tacitus, 'that the people of Germany are indigenous, with a very small mixture of other tribes either as immigrants or friends.'[70] And again, 'I accept the views of those who say that the Germans, uncorrupted by intermarriage with other peoples, form a peculiar, unmixed racial entity, resembling only itself. Even their physical characteristics are the same, although the population is so great—the ferocious appearance, blue eyes, blond hair, large bodies, good only for violent effort. They have little endurance of hard work or exertion, little tolerance of heat or thirst: but their climate and soil have accustomed them to endure cold and hunger.'[71] Leave out the adverse comments, and there is a heady brew, which under Hitler was drunk to the full.

For the great campaigns of Germanicus in Books I and II of the *Annals* the scene is north-west Germany—the stretch of campaigning country between the lower Rhine, with the Roman bases of Vetera (Xanten) and Ara Ubiorum (Cologne), and the rivers Amisia (Ems) and Visurgis (Weser). The campaigns are described—naturally enough—from the Roman point of view, and form one of the most important pieces of military narrative in Tacitus.[72] Some of their main features have already been discussed. But from them we can also learn much about politics and personalities among the west Germans in particular, of what it meant to be pro- or anti-Roman.

The story of Arminius and his kinsmen, by blood and marriage, among the powerful tribe of the Cherusci, is a striking example. Arminius[73] is, of course, the central figure, the embodiment of the struggle for German freedom. Tacitus' dramatic instinct leads him, nearly always, to contrast Arminius with another figure. The major contrast is with Germanicus himself, for whom Arminius is cast as a worthy opponent. The two great adversaries die in the same year 19, in each case by treachery. While Tiberius uses fine words to reject an offer to poison Arminius, he is left under suspicion of having sanctioned its use against Germanicus. Each has his obituary notice from Tacitus. Germanicus[74] is compared with Alexander the Great; Arminius[75] is awarded the less controversial distinction of being described as 'beyond doubt the liberator of Germany.' But Arminius appears in other and more personal confrontations. One is with his father-in-law, Segestes. Both were powerful chieftains among the Cherusci; both had at one time served as auxiliaries in the Roman Army. Segestes had a daughter Thusnelda, and Arminius carried her off and married her, although she was promised to another man. 'So father-in-law hated son-in-law and ties which (Agricola and Tacitus) strengthen the bond between friends'[76] (Caesar and Pompey?) 'here served to enflame animosity between enemies.'

Segestes never varied in his loyalty to Rome, though he paid a high price for it. At the last banquet given by Quintilius Varus to the German chiefs before the fatal rebellion, Segestes had made the remarkable suggestion that Varus should arrest them all, and sort out afterwards the traitors from the loyalists. As always, Quintilius Varus was deaf to good advice. Segestes, against his will, was dragged into war with the Romans. In 15 we find him claiming protection from Germanicus in the second round of campaigns against Arminius. A rescue party was sent out to protect him from his enemies among the Cherusci, and it brought back not only Segestes and a great number of his kindred and dependants, but also women of high rank, 'including that daughter of Segestes who was now the wife of Arminius.' Thusnelda is the subject of a miniature epic of her own. 'She was of her husband's rather than her father's temper. She shed no tears and made no plea for mercy: She folded her hands over her bosom, and looked down upon her pregnant womb.'[77] Here is another example of the fortitude of a pregnant woman to set beside that of Zenobia.

Then Segestes is given a speech by Tacitus. 'There he stood, huge of frame, free from fear because he had been a loyal ally of Rome.' He recites his quarrel with Arminius from the time of the fatal banquet. 'I call that night to witness; I wish I had not survived it! The sequel calls for tears rather than excuses. I imprisoned Arminius in chains; he and his faction did the same for me. Now, meeting you for the first time, let me make it clear that I prefer the old state to the new, peace to restlessness. I want no reward; I am anxious to clear myself of treachery. Also, I am a suitable conciliator for the people of Germany: if they prefer repentance to destruction I ask forgiveness for my son's youthful error. For my daughter, I admit I brought her here against her will. You must decide whether she shall be treated as my daughter, or as one carrying the child of Arminius.'[78]

We are told the sequel. Germanicus made a kind reply. Safety was promised to Segestes' children and his kindred, and for himself residence in the old province of Germany. As for Thusnelda, she had to appear in the triumph of Germanicus, but she was well treated, and gave birth to a male child who was sent to live in Ravenna. 'I shall tell later,' says Tacitus, 'how ironic was the fate that befell him.'[79] Unfortunately, the passage in which he must have done so is now lost. Arminius is also contrasted with his brother Flavus, who bears a Roman name referring to his fair hair. This man had served with the Roman

Army, where he distinguished himself by his loyalty, and had lost an eye serving under Tiberius. In the campaigns of 16 Arminius and Flavus served as spokesmen for the German and the Roman side, hurling insults at each other across the river Weser.[80] 'Where did you get that ugly wound on the face?' was Arminius' opening shot. Flavus named the place and the battle. 'And what reward did they pay you for it?' was the rejoinder. 'Flavus then recounted his increased pay, the torc, the crown, and the other military decorations he had received,' 'The wages of slavery,' jeered Arminius, 'and at a cut rate!' Then began a dispute in good round terms. Flavus spoke of the glory of Rome, the immense resources of the Emperor, the heavy penalties visited on the conquered, the clemency that awaited surrender—even Arminius' wife and child had been received in a friendly fashion. Arminius spoke of their country's claims, ancestral freedom, the household gods of Germany and of their mother, who added her prayers to his. 'Come back, man,' he said, 'to your kith and kin, and your own people: be their leader, not their betrayer!' Then they passed to an exchange of insults, and it would have come to fighting, river or no river, had not a Roman centurion rushed up and held Flavus back, though he was full of anger and shouting for arms and a horse. There on the other bank was Arminius, threatening and challenging to a fight. 'Some of his words were in Latin, for he had once commanded a force of native auxiliaries in the Roman army.' *Libertas*, or freedom, is the slogan of Arminius: it is a handsome tribute when Tacitus calls him *'haud dubie liberator Germaniae.'* But, ironically, his regard for freedom was not absolute. He tried to make himself king among the Cherusci, and was killed by his kinsmen 'as the enemy of the freedom of the people.'

We hear, too, of the next generation among the Cherusci. Segestes' son, Sigismundus,[81] had a chequered record—he had been a priest of the cult of the Augustus at Ara Ubiorum, but then he tore off the sacred fillets and joined Arminius. Perhaps to remove all suspicion of pro-Roman sentiment, he insulted the corpse of Quintilius Varus. No wonder his feelings were mixed

when he surrendered to Germanicus along with his father: but
clementia was extended even to him. What happened to Arminius' son, born at Ravenna, we do not know. But he had a
cousin, the son of Flavus, who bore the name of Italicus[82] and
was brought up in Rome. By the year 47 he was the sole living
representative of the royal house of the Cherusci. When
the Cherusci in that year sought a king from Rome, Claudius
found yet another congenial occasion for the dispensing of
good advice. 'Claudius made Italicus a grant of money, gave
him an escort, and bade him take up his ancestral honours with
good heart: for he was the first man born at Rome as a citizen,
and not a hostage, to win a foreign crown.' The sequel is interesting. Italicus was at first popular amongst the Germans: 'Free
from party feelings, he treated everyone with equal favour: he
won renown and respect at times by amiability and moderation,
qualities universally admired, but even more often by heavy
drinking and lustfulness (he was a handsome man), which
barbarians find congenial.' His popularity became widespread
and began to arouse opposition. 'Men who found profit in civil
strife began to rouse the neighbouring peoples with the cry that
German freedom was in danger, and Roman power on the
increase.'

Italicus had his answer. 'He was able to claim that he had not
come to the Cherusci against their will, but had been invited
because he was of more noble descent than the other claimants.
If they tested his courage, he would show himself worthy of his
uncle Arminius. . . . He had no need to blush for his father, who
had never wavered in a loyalty to Rome which the Germans
had freely assumed. "Freedom" was being falsely bandied about
as a catchword by men of no morals, politically dangerous,
whose only hope lay in civil war. The people applauded this
speech. In a great battle—by German standards—Italicus was
the victor. But his good fortune incited him to arrogance; he
was expelled, and restored again by the help of the Langobardi.
In prosperity and adversity alike he brought trouble to the
Cherusci.' Trouble indeed, for by the time Tacitus wrote the

Germania the Cherusci were no longer a major power. Such was the force of disunion among the barbarian peoples. And clearly Italicus, from the Roman point of view, was a distinct success.

When the *Germania* was published, a new phase was about to open in relations between Rome and the northern peoples. The Danube was to become a more important frontier than the Rhine. Before the *Annals* were completed, the first great Roman territorial expansion in northern Europe since the time of Augustus had been successfully accomplished. The victories of Trajan[83] in his two great wars against Dacia eliminated the most formidable barbarian power which had appeared on Rome's northern frontiers. But Trajan achieved more than that. By turning Dacia into a Roman province, and colonising it by settlers, mostly from the western parts of the empire, he advanced Roman civilisation as far as the line of the Carpathians. Yet the frontiers of the new province were drawn, on the west, without any regard for strategy, and left as a salient in barbarian hands a wide stretch of the Hungarian plain.

A second phase opened in the reign of Marcus Aurelius.[84] This time the initiative came from the barbarians. Impelled by the movements of peoples in northern and eastern Europe, a great confederation of the peoples of the middle and upper Danube assaulted the imperial frontiers. Breaking through the defences at many points, they even penetrated into north Italy. It seemed as though the terrible times of the invasion of the Cimbri had returned. The result was the series of great wars, unfortunately ill-documented, which Marcus Aurelius had to fight on the Danube frontiers against the Marcomanni, the Quadi, the Sarmatians, and the Jazyges. The sources are meagre and the chronology uncertain. But it looks as though Marcus Aurelius was driven to contemplate the formation of two new Roman provinces, Marcomannia and Jazygia. Had he been successful—and at his death he was perhaps not far from it—the northern frontiers would have been able to eliminate the barbarian salient in the valley of the Theiss, and to produce yet another mountain barrier along the line of the Sudeten mountains. All these gains were let slip by the Emperor Commodus, who succeeded him, and the opportunity was not to come again. Looking back, we are able to discern that in the reign of Marcus Aurelius a chain of events was set in motion whose distant culmination was that Christmas day of A.D. 800, when, in the Basilica of St. Peter's, a Pope crowned the German king Charlemagne as Emperor of Rome, and the successor of Augustus.

Conclusion

THE SURVIVAL OF TACITUS' MAJOR WORKS has turned on a narrower margin than any other Latin classic except Catulus—on two manuscripts, to be precise, both now in the Laurentian Library in Florence.[1] Of these, the ones now known as the Second Medicean, which contains *Histories* I to V and *Annals* XI to XVI, was discovered about 1430, while the First Medicean, with *Annals* I–VI, came from Germany about 1510. The *editio princeps* of all his works was that of Beroaldus (Rome 1515), but the first great scholarly edition and commentary was by Lipsius (Antwerp 1574).[2] His impact[3] on the sixteenth century was immediate and far-reaching, notably in Italy. The courts of the Italian despots were like those of imperial Rome in miniature, and they did not look far to find a Sejanus or an Agrippina, a Livia or a Poppaea. Sigismondo Malatesta can attest, as well as any Julio-Claudian Emperor, that absolute power corrupts absolutely. The first six books of the *Annals* were much used by various sovereigns of Europe as a guide to the conduct of affairs, affording as they do lessons in the political arts of simulation and dissimulation, of which Tiberius was so great a master.

The influence of Tacitus was reinforced by that of his admirer Machiavelli, who had himself taken a long hard look at the conflicts that arise between morality and reasons of state, and given precedence to the latter. Cosimo de Medici,[4] first Grand

Duke of Tuscany, used to read and re-read Tacitus, as did the Farnese Pope, Paul III,[5] who preferred him to any other profane author. It is amusing to think of these potentates reading their Tacitus, so to speak, at each other; a major aim of politics must have been to know on what Tacitean maxims an opponent's tactics relied. And surely the practice of so much dissimulation must have set a premium on straight dealing?

The rich dramatic possibilities offered by Tacitus seem to have first been exploited in England, where Ben Jonson produced his *Sejanus His Fall*[6] in 1603, as a rival to the Roman plays of Shakespeare. It was a dangerous theme, concerned with the favour of princes and the intrigues and fall of favourites, and it got him into trouble, for he was 'called before the Council for his *Sejanus*, and accused both of Popery and Treason', the *delator*, it seems, being Lord Northampton. In the age of Louis XIV the monarch was more secure and the dramatists knew their place; we do not hear that Racine was endangered by his *Britannicus*, nor Corneille by his *Otho*.[7]

In the eighteenth century Tacitus was frequently political dynamite. He served as one of the main sources of anti-monarchical propaganda in the American struggle for independence and, even more notably, in the French Revolution—the subject of a well-known passage in Boissier's essay.[8] The revolutionary poet André Chénier was steeped in Tacitus, 'whose name pronounced makes tyrants pale!' Madame Roland read him in prison before her execution, and felt the terrible times of Tiberius had returned again. Camille Desmoulins, in his *Vieux Cordelier*, used Tacitus as a mirror to hold up to the Terror of the Jacobins, showing that the 'river of blood, the sewer of corruption and filth, that had flowed unceasingly through the streets of Rome' was bloodier and filthier yet in those of Paris. The voice of Tacitus, heard through the pen of Desmoulins in the third issue of *Le Vieux Cordelier*, produced a reaction that alarmed Robespierre, who had the journal burned. Later Desmoulins himself was executed by the Revolutionary Tribunal. The whole episode is thoroughly Tacitean, and a notable example of how Tacitus is seen to be especially relevant in dark and troubled times. The arch-betrayer of the Revolution, Napoleon,[9] hated his name. 'Do not speak to me of that pamphleteer!' he once exclaimed, 'he has traduced the emperors!' '*Esprit de corps, Sire?*' was the adroit reply. Professional solidarity was indeed the motive that induced Napoleon to launch his scholars into an attack on Tacitus. Unsuccessfully, for two generations later Victor Hugo used him as ammunition against Napoleon III.[10] Tacitus himself would have found this anti-monarchical rôle congenial.

At no time was more attention paid to the political thought of the classical world, or examples sought more eagerly from ancient history, than during the struggle for American independence, and subsequently during the drafting of the Constitution of the United States.[11] The classical curriculum of the colleges of colonial America—itself deriving from the British universities —had produced a generation of statesmen and political thinkers uniquely adapted to their country's needs. Tacitus played a part in all this intellectual ferment, but, for a variety of reasons, one that was not so important as Aristotle, Polybius, Livy or Cicero. He was always good, of course, for anti-monarchical propaganda, and many a young orator at a college commencement attacked George III in terms borrowed from Tacitus' description of Tiberius or Domitian. But the circumstances in which the thirteen colonies had first to win their freedom from the mother country, and then to found some sort of federal union among themselves, directed attention to the examples of the Achaean, Lycian and Aetolian Leagues of the Hellenistic period. In classical Greece, too, the Greek colonies, almost invariably independent of the mother city, provided an edifying and timely example: those of Rome, conceived as the *parva effigies* of the founder city, and unshakeable in their loyalty to her, exhibited a *pietas* that the American colonies were determined to renounce.

So, on the whole, Greek history was more in favour than Roman, and interest in Roman history leaned rather to the republic than to the Principate, which brought in Livy and

Cicero rather than Tacitus. None the less, political lessons were drawn from at least two important passages of Tacitus. In the *Agricola*[12] he had shown how the Roman conquest of Britain was facilitated by the fact that the British states very seldom consulted together against a common danger, '*rarus duabus tribusve civitatibus ad propulsandum commune periculum conventus: ita singuli pugnant, universi vincuntur.*' 'Seldom do two or three of their state consult together to repulse a common danger; so they fight individually, and are all conquered.' The lesson was not lost on the thirteen colonies who sent their delegate to Philadelphia to sign the Declaration of Independence in 1776. In the debate on the Constitution, and during the early period of trial and error in its working, regard was often had to his warning against the Mixed Constitution. 'All nations and cities must be held either by the people, by the aristocracy, or by a single man. Blends and compounds of these forms of government are easy to commend but hard to establish: if established they seldom last.'[13] The Founding Fathers believed themselves to have established such blends in the Constitution of the United States. The American people have chosen—or believe themselves to have chosen—popular sovereignty. Tacitus would not have commended their choice. But, whether his maxims proved applicable or not to the American situation, Tacitus was widely ready by American statesmen and in the universities. We are told that he was the favourite historian of John Adams and Thomas Jefferson: Jefferson, in old age, declares himself to have 'given up newspapers for Tacitus and Thucydides, Newton and Euclid.'[14] In our own times, the march of progress has established newspapers rather than Tacitus as the required reading for Presidents of the United States.

Tacitus has, of course, had detractors and critics over the centuries. In the late empire, Tertullian took him severely to task for his hostility to the Christians and slanders on the Jews. A persistent vein of criticism of his style has been traced from the Italian humanists of the early Renaissance to French critics of the eighteenth century.[15] It found its most ample expression in the words of Cardinal du Perron,[16] at the beginning of the seventeenth century. 'The style of Tacitus is the worst in the world, and the meanest of all who have ever written history. There are only four or five features of his style . . . one page of Curtius Rufus is worth more than thirty of Tacitus.' Other stylists have objected to his forced brevities, excessive poetical colouring, affectation and artificiality. As an historian, he has often been ranked below Livy and Sallust, though seldom quoted at so low a rate as one-thirtieth of Curtius Rufus! Again, his pessimistic outlook and grim material have often proved too strong to stomach for those who like to take a rosy view of humanity. Not only did Napoleon call him a traducer of mankind, Voltaire described him as '*l'ingénieux et satirique Tacite,*' '*le malin Tacite,*' and tried not to believe his dreadful account of Nero and Agrippina. 'The interests of humanity demand,' he wrote, 'that such horrors *must* be exaggerated: they reflect too much shame on human nature.'[17] There were similar reactions in nineteenth-century England. The terrible uses to which Nazi Germany perverted Tacitus in aid of its campaign for racial purity and its anti-semitic obsessions have been mentioned above. Here was a posterity he could not have foreseen, a depth of human wickedness and degradation before which even he might have recoiled.

But it would be wrong to end on this sour note. Evil men do stand rebuked in his pages, and good ones set on record, as he had intended. Nor has his rebuke to tyrants lost any of its force and relevance. We, too, live in harsh and evil times; it is in such periods that Tacitus' true value appears. And if Hitler, Mussolini and Stalin are gone, tyranny can take new and more subtle forms. Vast and impersonal corporations, public or private, increasingly dominate our lives: they disregard morality for reasons of state more arrogantly and blatantly than any Roman Emperor. As if this were not enough, we allow abstractions to tyrannise over us. Against all this, Tacitus' insistence on the primacy of human nature and the value of human dignity is a wholesome corrective. And at this point in the twentieth century—when the ultimate tyranny of the machine lies perhaps not many years ahead—we should do well to remember the words which Justus Lipsius, the great Dutch editor of Tacitus, wrote in 1574. 'It is an age of disasters. But these histories, I think, do much to make it tolerable, by furnishing comfort, advice and examples to follow.' *Solatio, consilium, exemplum*— it is for these that one turns to Tacitus, and for his record of human experience in one of the great ages of mankind.

Notes to the Text

A.—*Annals*, H.—*Histories*, Agr.—*Agricola*, G.—*Germania*

CHAPTER ONE: *Life and Writings*

1. A. XI, 11, 1.
2. A. II, 61, 2: *cf.* Syme *Tacitus* II, 470ff.
3. Agr. 6, 1.
4. Agr. 4, 3.
5. Agr. 45, 5. He may have held a legionary command for three years, and then have been sent to govern one of the minor provinces—see Ogilvie and Richmond, *De Vita Agricolae*, 9.
6. Pliny, *Letters*, 2, 1, 6.
7. Pliny, *Letters*, 4, 13, 10.
8. Pliny, *Letters*, 6, 16, 4.
9. The inscription was found at Mylasa. See further Syme, *Tacitus* II, 664f.
10. For the rise of *novi homines* in the late Republic and early Empire, see Syme, *Tacitus* II, 566–84.
11. See note 5 above.
12. Agr. 44, 5.
13. Agr. 3, 3.
14. Pliny, *Letters*, 7, 33, 1.
15. H. I, 1.
16. For the likely date of his death, see Syme, *Tacitus* II, 473.
17. Historia Augusta, *Tacitus* X, 3. In addition, ten copies were to be made each year in the official copying establishments.
18. Ammianus' sub-title was *a fine Taciti historiarum.*

19. For the structure of the *Histories*, see Syme *Tacitus* 211ff: for the Annals, *id.* 253ff.

20. Jerome, *Comment. ad Zach.*, 3, 14. 'Cornelius Tacitus, who wrote the lives of the Caesars (from the death) of Augustus to that of Domitian, in thirty books.'

CHAPTER TWO: *The Writing of History*

1. A. III, 65, 1.

2. Herodotus, *Histories*, I, 1.

3. According to Suetonius, 'Next to the gods themselves, Augustus honoured the memory of those great men who had raised the empire of the Roman people from obscurity to greatness. So it was that he restored the works of these men, with their original inscriptions, and dedicated statues in triumphal dress of them all in the two colonnades of his Forum, issuing at the same time a proclamation: "This I have done to bind the Roman people to require me, while I am alive, and also the princes of ages yet to come, to live by the standards set by these great men." ' (Suetonius, *Augustus*, 31.)

For what is known of the statues and their inscriptions, see D. R. Dudley, *Urbs Roma*, 128f.

4. Agr. 46, 4.

5. H. III, 9.

6. H. I, 3. 'non esse curae deis securitatem nostram, esse ultionem.'

7. F. W. Walbank, *Polybius*, in *Latin Historians* (ed. T. A. Dorey), 46f.

8. H. I, 2.

9. A. IV, 32.

10. H. I, 1.

11. A. I, 1.

12. 'The discipline and evolution of a modern battalion gave me a clearer notion of the Phalanx and Legion, and the Captain of the Hampshire Grenadiers (the reader may smile) has not been useless to the historian of the Roman Empire' (Gibbon, *Memoirs of My Life*, ed. G. A. Bonnard, 117). The historian also claimed to have profited from his eight years as a backbencher in the House of Commons—a much shorter and slighter experience than that of Tacitus in the Senate.

13. A. IV, 33.

14. For the careers of provincial senators, see Syme, *Tacitus* II, 589ff.

15. Horace, *Odes*, III, 3, 57–60.

16. Pliny, *Letters*, 2, 11, 17.

17. H. I, 69.

18. Agr. 10.

19. A. III, 30.

20. Quintilian, X, 1, 101.

21. See B. Walker, *The Annals of Tacitus*, 71–4, 155–6: Syme, *Tacitus* I, 196–9, 353–6 (Sallust), 200–1 (Livy), 357–8 (Virgil).

22. H. IV, 62: 72, and Livy, IX, 5, 11ff.

23. A. I. 61. 1, and Virgil, *Aeneid*, VI, 198ff.

24. Julia 'omnis spei egenam inopia ac tabe longa peremit'—A. I., 53.

25. On sources for the *Histories*, see Syme, *Tacitus* I, 176ff.: for the Annals, *id. ib.* 271ff.

26. On this question, see Syme, *Tacitus* I, 272 f.

27. Also called the *commentarii Senatus* (A. XV, 74, 3). For the use Tacitus made of them, see Syme, *Tacitus* I, 186–8, 278–85.

28. For the *acta diurna*, see Suetonius, *Julius*, 20. For its circulation, see Tacitus, A. XVI, 22, where it carries the news of Thrasea Paetus' obstinacy 'per provincias per exercitus.' In A. III, 3, it is quoted for details about the funeral of Germanicus. Besides the official acts of emperors and magistrates, it contained items about the imperial family, births and deaths, Roman society, public disasters, etc.

29. Pliny. *Letters*, VI, 16 and 20.

30. For the Palatine Library, see D. R. Dudley, *Urbs Roma*, 157ff.

31. Pliny. *Letters*, IX, 10, 2.

CHAPTER THREE: *Narrative*

1. Augustine, *Frang.*, 2, 4.

2. On this, see E. Löfstedt, 'On the Style of Tacitus,' *Journal of Roman Studies* (1948), 1ff.: Syme, *Tacitus* I, 340ff.; II, 710–45.

3. Sir Henry Savile (1549–1622), then Warden of Merton College, Oxford, published his translation of the *Agricola* and the *Histories* in 1591. In 1595 he was appointed Provost of Eton, and embarked on his major work of scholarship, the edition of St. John Chrysostom (8 vols., 1610–1613).

4. Bernardo Davanzati (1529–1606). The quarto edition of his translation of Tacitus was published in Venice in 1658. It met with a critical reception for its brevity and obscurity.

5. H. IV, 81.

6. A. IV, 67.

7. A. I, 61. There may also be a parallel with stories told of Alexander (Syme, *Tacitus* II, 770); *cf.* also Vitellius' visit to the battlefield of Bedriacum in H. II, 70.

8. Savile, *op. cit.* Preface.

9. Syme, *Tacitus* I, 168.

10. This is convincingly argued by Syme, *Tacitus* II, 762ff. For a general account of the rebellion, see Donald R. Dudley and Graham Webster, *The Rebellion of Boudicca* (1962).

11. Suetonius gives only a short account of the Messalina–Silius affair (*Claudius*, 29); Tacitus makes it the climax of Book Eleven. (B. Walker, *The Annals of Tacitus*, 22.)

12. Juvenal has two passages on Messalina. The first (VI, 115–35)—some of the most terrible and graphic lines in Latin—shows her nymphomania. The second (X, 329–35) is on the Silius affair—with Silius in the rôle of victim. The language suggests that Juvenal had read the account of Tacitus.

13. B. Walker, *The Annals of Tacitus*, Appendix I, 259–62.

14. Agr. 29–32.

15. A. XIV, 53–6.

16. Bruce Catton, *Never Call Retreat*, 284f. (Gettysburg); 430ff. (Second Inaugural).

CHAPTER FOUR: *Characters*

1. A. XVI, 18–20. This Petronius is almost certainly the author of the famous *Satyricon*, a novel of low life unique in ancient literature, to judge from the substantial fragment which survives. It has been recently translated by J. P. Sullivan (1967).

2. His governorship of Bithynia is now dated 59/60.

3. A. XIV, 32.

4. H. III, 79.

5. H. IV, 71.

6. H. IV, 73–4.

7. H. V, 22. Tacitus can give her name, Claudia Sacrata.

8. For these men, see D. R. Dudley, *A History of Cynicism*, Chapter VII, p. 125ff.: H. H. Scullard, *From the Gracchi to Nero*, 332ff.

9. Agr. 42, 4.

10. Pliny, *Letters* I, 5. Q. Arulenus Junius Rusticus, tribune in A.D. 66, consul in 92, was put to death by Domitian in 93.

11. C. Helvidius Priscus, praetor 70, exiled and then put to death by Vespasian 74.

12. Suetonius, *Vespasian*, 15.

13. Dio Cassius, 66, 12.

14. See above, note 13.

15. On him, see further Syme, *Tacitus* II, 556–61.

16. P. Clodius Thrasea Paetus, consul *suffectus* 56, died 66.

17. A. XIII, 49.

18. A. XIV, 12.

19. A. XV, 20.

20. A. XVI, 22.

21. Suetonius, *Nero*, 37.

22. A. XVI, 23.

23. A. XVI, 27.

24. A. XVI, 31.

25. A. XVI, 34f.

26. Dio, 61, 15.

27. H. III, 81.

28. A. XVI. 32.

29. Aulus Caecina Alienus, quaestor in Baetica 68, placed by Galba in command of a legion (IV Macedonica?) in Germany, joins Vitellius, consul *suffectus* 69, put to death 78–9. One of the cleverest intriguers of the Civil Wars, he enjoyed in turn the favours of Galba, Vitellius and Vespasian.

30. H. II, 20. Not only did he appear improperly dressed, but on a formal occasion—an address to the citizens of Placentia.

31. H. II, 92.

32. Suetonius, *Titus*, 6.

33. Fabius Valens, consul *suffectus*, 69. It was he who denounced Verginius Rufus to Galba, and who engineered the murder of Fonteius Capito, Governor of Lower Germany.

34. H. I, 66. Tacitus says of him: 'He had long been poor: now suddenly rich, he made no attempt to hide the change of fortune. . . . After a youth passed in poverty, he became a debauched old man.'

35. H. III, 40.

36. H. III, 62.

37. M. Antonius Primus, born *c.* A.D. 20, and one of the few leading figures of the Civil Wars to reach a ripe old age and a peaceful death (some time after 95).

38. H. II, 86.

39. Martial 9, 99, where he is called 'the glory of Tolosa, dear to Pallas.' In 10, 23, he is portrayed as 75 years of age, 'with no regretful memories' (not even of Cremona?).

40. On the *Dialogus*, see Syme, *Tacitus* I, 104–7; on the date of composition, *id. ib.* 112–13.

41. H. III, 9.

42. Shakespeare, *Macbeth*, Act V, Scene III.

43. A. XVI, 1. The story of Dido's Treasure also appears in Suetonius, *Nero*, 31.

44. A. XV, 51f.

45. A. XV, 54.

CHAPTER FIVE: *Emperors and Court*

1. On the inception of the *Annals*, see Syme, *Tacitus* I, 369, 427.

2. A. I, 2.

3. A. I, 3, 7.

4. Suetonius, *Augustus*, 28.

5. A. I, 4. igitur verso civitatis statu nihil usquam prisci et integri moris: omnes exuta aequalitate iussa principis aspectare. . . . The words contain an echo of Sallust.

6. A. I, 1, 2.

7. A. III, 25.

8. A. I, 10, 4. Outrageous as this charge may seem, it is recorded in Suetonius, *Tiberius*, 212, and Dio, XLVI, 45, 3.

9. On Tacitus' portrayal of Tiberius see Syme, *Tacitus* I, 420–30: F. B. Marsh, *The Reign of Tiberius*, chapter 1, and also Appendices III and IV.

10. A. I, 73, 1.

11. A. VI, 19. B. Walker, *The Annals of Tacitus*, 83, points out that, according to Suetonius, fewer than twenty people were involved (Suetonius, *Tiberius*, 61).

12. On this, see especially F. B. Marsh, *The Reign of Tiberius*, Appendices IV and V; and also B. Walker, *The Annals of Tacitus*, Appendix II— a convenient summary of the known treason trials and their results.

13. Suetonius, *Domitian*, 20.

14. See Syme, *Tacitus* I, 345f., 420–30.

15. A. I, 6, 1.

16. A. IV, 8, 2.

17. A. IV, 11, 3.

18. A. VI, 50.

19. A. VI, 51. The obituary notice is given as the verdict of the historian, not—as with Augustus—derived from contemporaries.

20. This letter is also quoted by Suetonius, *Tiberius*, 67.

21. See especially F. B. Marsh, *The Reign of Tiberius*, and M. P. Charlesworth, *Cambridge Ancient History* X, chapter 19.

22. A. VI, 46, 4.

23. A. VI, 48, 2.

24. See especially A. Momigliano, *Claudius*; V. M. Scramuzza, *The Emperor Claudius*.

25. Suetonius, *Nero*, 49.

26. H. I, 18.

27. H. II, 47–9.

28. 'ut ignava animalia, quibus si cibum suggeras, iacent torpentque.' (H. III, 36.)

29. 'egregium principatus temperamentum, si demptis utriusque vitiis solae virtutes miscerentur.' (H. II, 5.)

30. A. I, 69, 2.

31. A. I, 69, 5.

32. A. 5, 1. The rumour is also found in Dio 56, 30, I, see further Syme, *Tacitus* II, 692ff.

33. A. I, 10.

34. A. V, 1, 3. 'cum artibus mariti, simulatione filii bene composita.' The Emperor Gaius, who could turn a good phrase, used to call her 'a female Ulysses.' (Suetonius, *Gaius*, 23.)

35. Vipsania Agrippina (the Elder) (14 B.C.–A.D. 33) was the daughter of Marcus Agrippa and Julia.

36. A. II, 72.

37. A. II, 75.

38. A. III, 4.

39. A. IV, 52.

40. A. IV, 53. Agrippina was then 40.

41. A. IV, 54.

42. A. VI, 25, 2.

43. Valeria Messalina, daughter of Barbatus Messalla and Lepida, third wife of Claudius, mother of Britannicus and Octavia.

44. A. XI, 1–3.

45. A. XI, 2.

46. Juvenal, *Satires*, 115–32.

47. Julia Agrippina (the younger), A.D. 15–59.

48. A. IV, 75.

49. Suetonius, *Nero*, 5.

50. Dio, 59, 22; see also J. P. V. D. Balsdon, *The Emperor Gaius*, 75, 87.

51. A. XII, 7.

52. A. XII, 64.

53. A. XIII, 13, 5.

54. A. XIII, 14, 6.

55. A. XIII, 19, 1.

56. A. XIV, 1–13. For a fine appreciation of these chapters, see K. Quinn, 'Tacitus' Narrative Technique' in *Latin Explorations*, 114ff.

57. K. Quinn, *op. cit.* 124.

58. The Misenus episode is described in two phases (*Aeneid* VI, 156–82 and 211–35) separated by Aeneas' discovery of the Golden Bough.

59. Virgil, *Aeneid*, VI, 231–5.

60. A. XIV, 10, 5.

61. A. XIV, 64, 4.

62. A. II, 41, 3. 'breves et infaustos populi Romani amores.' They had in mind Marcellus, who died at 20, and Drusus, who died at 30. A later example was the Emperor Titus.

63. The comparison is in A. II, 73, 1. *Cf.* Suetonius, *Caligula*, 3 (who credits Germanicus with 'outstanding physical and moral excellence'); Dio 57, 18, 7ff.

64. A. II, 13. 'Some spoke of their general's noble birth, others of his physical beauty: all agreed about his endurance, his charm of manner, the level temper he kept in jest or earnest. . . . They said, "We must butcher these German traitors and breakers of the peace, for glory or for revenge."'

65. A. I, 3, 6.

66. A. IV, 1, 3. 'deum ira in rem Romanam.'

67. A. I, 24.

68. A. I, 69.

69. A. III, 16.

70. A. IV, 1. For the parallel with Catiline, see Syme, *Tacitus* I, 353.

71. A. IV, 3.

72. A. IV, 40.

73. On the discoveries at Sperlonga see G. Iacopi, *I ritrovamenti dell' antro cosidetto 'di Tiberio' a Sperlonga* (Rome 1958). For a short account see Paul MacKendrick, *The Mute Stones Speak* (1960), 172ff.

74. A. IV, 2, 3.

75. On the fall of Sejanus, see Juvenal, X, 56–107; Suetonius, *Tiberius*, 65, 1: Dio, 58, 10, 2 and 12, 3. Also F. B. Marsh, *The Reign of Tiberius*, Appendix VII.

76. For the trap Sejanus prepared for Gaius see A. VI, 3.

77. Philo, *Leg.*, 53f.: on this passage, see J. P. V. D. Balsdon, *The Emperor Gaius*, 38f.

78. In an inscription from Vasio (C I L XII 5482) he appears as the *patronus* of that city: his own career advanced under the patronage of Livia, Agrippina and Claudius. Where his soldierly qualities were displayed is not stated: a recent suggestion is in Thrace (H. G. Pflaum, *Les carrières procuratoriennes équestres*, Paris 1960, 30ff.).

79. A. XIV, 15.

80. A. XIV, 51. The other, Faenius Rufus, was 'innocent, but idle.'

81. Ofonius Tigellinus, said to have been of Sicilian origin, was banished from Italy in 39 on the charge of adultery with Agrippina. Later he made money through horse-breeding in Apulia, and at the time of Great Fire of 64 owned extensive property. Syme, *Tacitus* I, 263, rightly says that he is cast as the Sejanus of Nero's reign.

82. H. I, 72.

83. *Cf.* Suetonius, *Claudius*, 28, 29.

84. A. XII, 53. Pallas was originally the freedman of Antonia, and took the name M. Antonius Pallas. His career is discussed in detail by S. I. Oost, *American Journal of Philology*, 79 (1958), 113ff.

85. A. XIII, 14.

86. On his mission at the time of the British expedition, see Dio, 60,

34, 5. Pliny, *Nat. hist.*, 33, 134, speaks of his great wealth. His death is noted in A. XIII, 1.

87. Dio, 59, 29.

88. A. XIV. 39. 'Polycleitus . . . burdened Italy and Gaul with a huge retinue, and after crossing the ocean, struck terror even into a Roman army. The barbarians only thought him ridiculous: liberty still prevailed with them, and they had as yet no acquaintance with the power of a freedman. They could not understand how an army and general who could complete so great a war should obey the commands of slaves.'

89. Dio, 63, 12, 1ff.

90. A. XV, 45—not only the temple treasures but the very images of the gods were plundered by Nero's two commissioners.

91. H. II. 95. Galba's freedman Icelus was granted equestrian status, and took the name of Marcianus Icelus. One of Otho's first acts was to have him publicly executed.

92. On this, see J. R. Crook, *Law and the Life of Rome* (London 1967).

93. A. I, 72. 'exercendas leges esse.' *Cf.* Suetonius, *Tiberius*. On the treason trials see B. Walker, *The Annals of Tacitus*, 83–110.

94. Dial, 5, 7.

95. A. II, 28.

96. A. III, 66.

97. A. III, 66.

98. T. Clodius Eprius Marcellus, praetor 48, governor of Lycia 56?, consul *suffectus* 62, governor of Asia 70–73. For his oratory, see Dial., 5. 7; A. XVI, 22. 29.

99. Q. Vibius Crispus: for him see Quintilian, *Inst. Or.*, 10. 1. 119; 12, 10, 11; Juvenal, IV, 80–93.

100. Suetonius, *Domitian*, 3, 1.

101. Agr. 45, 1.

102. Seneca de Ben., 3, 26.

CHAPTER SIX: *The Senate*

1. A. I, 3, 5. 'quotusquisque reliquus qui rem publicam vidisset?'

2. A. I, 11–14. The debate took place on Sept. 17, A.D. 14. See further Syme, *Tacitus* I, 389, 410f.

3. Suetonius, *Tiberius*, 24. Another senator said to Tiberius 'Some are slow to do what you have promised: you are slow to promise what you have done!' Suetonius also makes Tiberius, in accepting the title of Emperor, hint that he might resign it with the words 'Until my age is such that you are kind enough to grant me release.'

4. Suetonius, *Tiberius*, 26 and 31.

5. A. I, 74, 5.

6. A. 79, 2.

7. A. III, 60. The source here is (presumably) the *Acta Senatus*.

8. A. III, 65. In fact, he used the phrase, we are told, whenever he lef the Senate.

9. A. IV, 7.

10. A. III, 75.

11. A. IV, 34. Tacitus sees his own precursor in Cremutius Cordus senator and historian, firm in the defence of free speech, compunctious i his narrative of civil war. See Syme, *Tacitus* I, 339 and II, 546.

12. A. VI, 26.

13. A. II, 34.

14. A. VI, 8.

15. This took place on January 24th, A.D. 41. For the speech of Sentiu Saturninus see J. P. V. D. Balsdon, *The Emperor Gaius*. On January 25th the Senate recognised Claudius as Emperor.

16. A. XII, 38. Comparisons were freely drawn with the capture o Syphax by Scipio Africanus, of Perseus by Aemilius Paulus, 'or indeed with that of any other generals who had displayed captured kings to the Roman people.' But Tacitus is at pains to conceal the point of the comparisons—that these triumphs were notable for the display of clemency to a beaten enemy.

17. A. XII, 7.

18. A. XII, 53.

19. A. XI, 23ff.

20. CIL XIII 1668—Dessau 212. For the Tablet, see Ph. Fabia, *La table Claudienne de Lyon* (1929). For the comparison between the text of the tablet and the speech of Claudius in Tacitus, see B. Walker, *The Annals o Tacitus*, 147, and Syme, *Tacitus* I, 317f. and II, 707. The Tablet itself, one of the noblest of Roman inscriptions, is preserved in the Museum in the Roman Theatre in Lyon: no visitor to that city should fail to see it.

21. Dio, 61, 3, 1.

22. A. XIII, 26.

23. A. XIII, 50.

24. A. XIV, 12.

25. A. XIV, 64.

26. A. XV, 36. 'senatus et primores in incerto erant procul an coram atrocior haberetur: dehinc, quae natura magnis timoribus, deterius credebant quod evenerat.'

27. A. XVI, 9.

28. A. XIV, 47.

29. H. I, 17. 'imperaturus es hominibus, qui nec totam servitutem pati possunt nec totam libertatem.'

30. H. I, 50. 'deteriorem fore qui vicisset.'
31. H. I, 84.
32. H. II, 53.
33. H. II, 89.
34. H. II, 91.
35. H. IV, 4.
36. H. IV, 4 and 6.
37. Dessau, 244.
38. H. IV, 4, 3.
39. H. IV, 5.
40. H. IV, 7 and 8.
41. Suetonius, *Titus*, 8.
42. Martial, I, 33.
43. Agr. 2, 3.
44. *Id.* 45.
45. Pliny, *Letters*, I, 12, 8.

CHAPTER SEVEN: *The Army*

1. Dio, LXXVI, 15, 2.
2. For instances, see Syme, *Tacitus*, I, 412, n. 5.
3. H. I, 4.
4. Agr. 14, 'uterque bello egregius.'
5. Agr. 16. Petronius, sent to Britain after the Boudicca rebellion, settled the previous disorders, but attempted nothing further. Trebellius was 'rather indolent and devoid of military experience: he ran the province by a kind of geniality.'
6. Sextus Julius Frontinus. Governor of Britain 74–78, the effective Roman conqueror of Wales. Under Trajan he was made *curator aquarum*, in charge of Rome's water supply: in that capacity he wrote a book *De aquaeductu urbis Romae*. He died *c.* 104.
7. This campaign in the Snowdon mountains and Anglesey is given a brief notice in Agr. 18. The Twentieth Legion and the Batavian auxiliaries formed the main part of his striking force.
8. Tacitus reports that he 'had often heard Agricola say that a single legion and a moderate force of auxiliaries would be enough to complete the conquest of Ireland.' (Agr. 24, 3.) No Roman general was ever to put this exercise in logistics to the test.
9. Agr. 10. 5. This was not, of course, the first circumnavigation of Britain by a Greek or Roman expedition. As early as 325 B.C. Pytheas of Massilia had circumnavigated the island (of which he made the first recorded map) and sighted Thule and the 'sluggish waters' of the northern ocean. His discoveries are recorded, in a tone of scepticism, by

the geographer Strabo (4, 5, 4), who wrote in the time of Augustus

10. On the voyage of the Usipi, see now Ogilvie and Richmond, *D. Vita Agricolae*, 321f.

11. Agr. 22. For these *castella*, see now Ogilvie and Richmond, *op. cit.* 57

12. The great unfinished legionary fortress at Inchtuthil (Pinnat: Castra) has been excavated by the late Sir Ian Richmond and J. K. St Joseph. A final report is expected. For a brief account see Ogilvie an Richmond, *op. cit.* 69f. and Fig. 9.

13. Agr. 25.

14. When Scotland had been conquered, the problem arose as to how i was to be occupied. For reasons of geography—chief among them the indented coastline of the West Highlands—the formula that had bee applied to Wales was not practicable. Once it had been decided to abando the Highlands, it was necessary to provide a northern frontier for the pro vince of Britain. Hence the Walls of Hadrian (Tyne–Solway) and o Antoninus (Forth–Clyde). On these, see now Sheppard Frere, *Britannie* (1967), 125ff. ('Hadrian's Frontier') and 141ff. ('The Antonine Wall').

15. A. I, 16–52 and 55–71.

16. In Lower Germany, the First, Fifth, Twentieth and Twenty-firs Legions. In Upper Germany, the Second, Third, Fourteenth and Sixteenth

17. These were the Fourth, Ninth, and Fifteenth Legions.

18. In fact, either on the marshes of the 'sea of Ljubljana (Ljubljanskd Barje), or on the Karst plateau.'

19. A. 16, 3.

20. A. 20, 2.

21. A. 23, 2.

22. A. 28, 2.

23. A. 30, 2.

24. See note 16 above.

25. A. I, 32, 7. 'pariter ardescerent, pariter silerent, tanta aequalitate e constantia, ut regi crederes.'

26. A. I, 31, 4.

27. A. I, 31, 5.

28. A. I, 32, 1.

29. A. I, 35, 1; Dio, 57, 5, 28, gives a somewhat different account.

30. A. I, 39.

31. A. I, 44.

32. A. I, 49, 4. 'non medicinam illud plurimis cum lacrimis sed cladem appellans.'

33. A. I, 50, 7.

34. A. II, 22, 1. This would seem to be the only official Roman inscrip-tion quoted by Tacitus. Its wording recalls that on the trophy erected by

Drusus on the banks of the Elbe (Dio, 55, 1, 3). Such a *tropaeum*, or trophy of arms, was not of course a permanent construction, nor was it ever possible to erect a commemorative monument in Germany. Instead an arch was dedicated close to the Temple of Saturn in the Forum at Rome to commemorate the recovery of the eagles of Varus under the leadership of Germanicus and the auspices of Tiberius (A. I, 41).

35. A. I, 61, 2: see above, p. 37.

36. Dessau, ILS 2244. Now in the museum at Bonn.

37. A. I, 63. The *pontes longi*, wooden causeways over the morass, had been built by Lucius Domitius Ahenobarbus about 2 B.C. Their site is not known, but must lie to the west of the river Ems.

38. A. I, 23, 24.

39. Note the feeling of the troops that they have passed 'beyond the edge of the world' on these North Sea islands. Such fears played powerfully on the nerves of Claudius' invading army in 43, and actually delayed its embarkation.

40. A. 68, 5.

41. A. XIII, 35, 1.

42. *Id. ib.* 35, 4.

43. A. XIV, 24, 1.

44. A. XV, 6.

45. A. XV, 13. Tacitus does not give the name of the besieged Roman fort: it is from Dio (62, 21, 1) that we get the name Randeia. This and the other fort Arsamosata are now located on the river Murad, a tributary of the Euphrates, not far from the modern Kharput. (See *Cambridge Ancient History* X, Map 9.)

46. A. XV, 16.

47. A. XV, 25.

48. H. I, 25. 'suscepere duo manipulares imperium populi Romani transferendum et transtulerunt.'

49. H. I, 63.

50. H. I, 65. The rivalry between Vienna in Gallia Narbonensis, the capital of the Allobroges, and Lugdunum, capital of Lugdunensis and the chief city of the Three Gauls, was bitter and permanent. It was exacerbated because Vienna had supported Galba, while Lugdunum favoured Vitellius.

51. H. I, 66. Lucus, the modern Luc, was a town of the Vocontii.

52. H. I, 67, 69, 70. The tribal name survives in Helvetia, the Latin name for Switzerland.

53. H. II, 56.

54. Virgil, *Georgics*, I, 505–6.

55. H. III, 25.

56. Shakespeare, *King Henry VI*, Part III, Act III, Scene 3.

57. H. III, 32, 34.
58. H. III, 33, 34.
59. H. I, 88.
60. H. I, 93.
61. H. I, 99.
62. Dillius Vocula, commander of the Twenty-second Legion, wa
placed by the elderly and incompetent Hordeonius Flaccus in command o
a force to take the field against Civilis. The disaster which overwhelmec
them is offset only by his personal courage. Syme, *Tacitus* II, App. 8o
points out that Dillius Vocula came from Corduba in Spain.
63. H. IV, 59.
64. H. IV, 59.
65. Virgil, *Aeneid*, IV, 170-1.
66. H. IV, 62.
67. H. IV, 72.

CHAPTER EIGHT: *Rome—City and People*

1. Pliny, *Natural History*, III, 66-7.
2. In the absence of contemporary and reliable statistics, all attempt:
to estimate population in the ancient world can only be approximate. The
population of the city of Rome was considered by L. G. Friedlander
Roman Life and Manners under the Early Empire (sixth edition 1913)
Appendix V; his estimate is that given here. More modern investigation:
have placed it as low as 750,000 and as high as 2,000,000, but have no
been widely accepted.
3. Pliny, *Natural History*, XXXVI, 121-2.
4. Notably in the Third Satire (imitated in Johnson's *London*).
5. 'hic ultra vires habitus nitor hic aliquid plus
    quam satis est interdum aliena sumitur arca
    commune id vitium est, hic vivimus ambitiosa
    paupertate omnes, quid te moror? omnia Romae
    cum pretio.'
'Here we all dress beyond our means, and the something extra often come:
from another's pocket. It's a fault common to all: we're all living in pre-
tentious poverty. In short, there's a price-tag on everything at Rome.'
(Juvenal, III, 180-4.)
6. A. I, 79, 2.
7. A. IV, 65. Caeles Vibenna was also alluded to by Claudius in the
speech recorded on the Tablet of Lyon.
8. A. XII, 24, 1. Claudius enlarged the *pomoerium* because he extendec
the empire to include Britain and Mauretania.
9. A. III, 9.

10. The Great Fire is described in A. XV, 38. 41. See also Donald R. Dudley, *Urbs Roma*, 17–21.

11. H. III, 71–72.

12. Thucydides, II, 47–54.

13. On the Great Fire see further A. Profumo, *Fonti e tempi dell'incendio neroniano* (1905).

14. CIL VI. 826. See Donald R. Dudley, *Urbs Roma*, 20; also plate 11.

15. Pliny (*Natural History*, 17, 1, 5) and Suetonius (*Nero*, 31) both attribute the blame to Nero.

16. On the Domus Aurea, see A. Boethius, *The Golden House of Nero* (1960); J. B. Ward-Perkins, *Antiquity* XXX (1956), 209–19.

17. Recorded in Suetonius, *Nero*, 39.

18. On this, see M. Scherer, *Marvels of Ancient Rome* (1955), 91.

19. A. XV, 44.

20. There is a contemporary description of the siege of Masada in Josephus, *Bellum Judaicum*, VII, 280–406. See also *The World of Josephus* in this series.

21. See J. M. C. Toynbee and J. B. Ward-Perkins, *The Shrine of St. Peter* (1956).

22. A. XV, 43, 1. On the rebuilding, see A. Boethius, 'The Neronian Nova Urbs' in *Corolla Archaeologica*, 84–97.

23. H. III, 71–72.

24. For the Capitol, see T. Ashby and W. Dougill, *The Capitol* (1927); for the Temple of Jupiter Capitolinus, see A. Zadoks Jitta, *Journal of Roman Studies* (1938), 50ff.

25. H. IV, 54.

26. H. IV, 53.

27. Suetonius, *Augustus*, 30.

28. Juvenal, X, 80–1.

29. A. XVI, 4.

30. A. V, 4, 2.

31. A. VI, 13.

32. H. I, 32, 1.

33. H. I, 88 and 2, 3.

34. H. I, 88.

35. Not only in the Third Satire, but also in the Fifth (the humiliations inflicted by a rich patron), and Seventh (the plight of the intellectual).

CHAPTER NINE: *The Provinces*

1. Pliny, *Nat. Hist.*, XXVII, 3.

2. Agr. 21.

3. *Cf.* the comment in Ogilvie and Richmond (*De Vita Agricolae*, 228)

on this passage: the attitude of Tacitus, himself an administrator, towards the policy of assimilation is remarkable.

4. For Spain as a Roman province, see C. H. V. Sutherland, *The Romans in Spain* (1939).

5. Pliny. For further details, see O. Davies, *Roman Mines in Europe* (1935).

6. A. VI, 19.

7. A. XIV, 45; IV, 13; VI, 27.

8. A. III, 44.

9. Suetonius, *Galba*, 9, 10. The *Annals* as we have them break off before the proclamation of Galba in Spain. Tacitus' lost account may well have contained something about his notably successful administration of Tarraconensis.

10. Known only through Pliny, *Nat. Hist.*, V, 14.

11. The Tacfarinas affair is mentioned in A. II, 52; III, 20, 21, 32, 73-4; IV, 13, 23-5. Tacitus prefaces his account of its final phase with the remark 'By now (A.D. 23) there were three triumphal statues in Rome, and still Tacfarinas was plundering Africa.'

12. The war against Caratacus is described in A. XII, 31-40. There are two accounts of the rebellion of Boudicca: Agr. 14, 4-16, 2 and a longer one in A. XIV, 29-39. (See above, pp. 41-44.)

13. Agr. 10, 4-5 (the northern ocean); 12, 3-4 (the long days of summer).

14. Agr. 10, 6. 'unum addiderim, nusquam latius dominari mare, multum fluminum huc atque illuc ferre, nec litore tenus adcrescere ac resorberi, sed influere penitus atque ambire, et iugis etiam ac montibus inseri velut in suo.'

15. A. XII, 37.

16. Agr. 30-2. See above, pp. 50, 51.

17. On this see D. R. Dudley and Graham Webster, *The Rebellion of Boudicca* (1962), 84ff.

18. On the work of Augustus in Gaul, see C. Jullien, *Histoires de la Gaule* IV, chapter II; *Cambridge Ancient History* Vol. X, 585ff.

19. A. IV, 5, 1.

20. Agr. 9.

21. The poems of Ausonius (died *c.* A.D. 395) contain many references to the prosperity of Burdigala and its countryside, and to the personalities of its university.

22. On these rebellions, see now L. Harmond in *Rome et l'Occident* (1960), chapter IV.

23. A. III, 40-6.

24. This famous school—founded as a potent instrument for the Romanisation of Gaul—was still in existence three hundred years later—

when it was known as the 'Schola Maeniana.' Agricola perhaps founded such a school in Britain. (Agr. 21, 2.)

25. A. III, 43, 5. They were called *crupellarii*.

26. On the rebellion of Vindex, see Syme, *Tacitus* I, 461–3.

27. The rebellion of Civilis is a major theme of Books IV and V of the *Histories*.

28. See further on Civilis, Syme, *Tacitus* I, 172–5.

29. H. IV, 61.

30. H. II, 61.

31. H. IV, 61 and V, 22. Veleda was one of the prophetic wise women honoured among the Germans (G. 8). Petilius Cerialis used her services to persuade the German rebels to lay down their arms.

32. H. IV, 55.

33. H. IV, 68, 69.

34. The advice was disregarded, at the instance of Valentinus: but Tacitus says that he was not as active in preparing for war as for haranguing the people. As a result, both the Treviri and the Lingones made inadequate efforts to prepare for the crisis.

35. H. IV, 71. 'proniores ad officia quod spernebantur.'

36. See above, pp. 151ff.

37. For Lugdunum, see C. Jullian, *Histoire de la Gaule* VI, 515–27.

38. See above, p. 121,

39. Agr. 4, 2. On Massilia in the time of Augustus see Strabo, 4, 179–81.

40. See above, p. 151.

41. On Cologne see A. Grenier, *Archéologie gallo-romaine* (1931), 345ff.

42. H. IV, 54 and 65.

43. G. 41.

44. A. IV, 46–51. On this passage, see Syme, *Tacitus* I, 354.

45. H. I, 79.

46. Dio, 71, 8–10.

47. H. I, 11.

48. This man had an interesting career. A nephew of Philo, head of the Jewish community in Alexandria, he was *procurator* of Judaea (46–48), and was then admitted to the equestrian order. In A. XV, 28, we find him on the staff of Corbulo, and employed on a diplomatic mission to the King of Parthia. Shortly after he became Prefect of Egypt: his edict on the accession of Galba is preserved, and he was the first provincial governor to declare for Vespasian.

49. On Cornelius Gallus, see *Cambridge Ancient History* X, 240ff.

50. H. III, 8.

51. The rivalry between Greeks and Jews in Alexandria was endemic, and drew some admonitions from the Emperor Claudius, but to little purpose.

IT

52. On the fifteenth Satire, see Gilbert Highet, *Juvenal the Satirist* (Oxford 1954).

53. On the Palestrina mosaic, see F. Fasolo & G. Guilini in *Il Santuario della Fortune Primigenia in Palestrina* (1953).

54. Juvenal, XV, 126.

55. A. II, 61. Elephantine and Syene (Asswan) lie below the First Cataract of the Nile.

56. A. II, 60.

57. Herodotus devoted his second book to Egypt, and frequently quotes priests as the source of his information, e.g. those of the temple of Hephaestus at Memphis, of the temple at Heliopolis, 'the scribe who kept the register of the treasure of Athene at Sais, etc.' It was this person who told him that 'between Syene and Elephantine there were two mountains of conical shape called Crophi and Mophi: and that the springs of the Nile, of fabulous depth, flowed out between them.'

58. On Roman Syria, see A. H. M. Jones, *Eastern Cities*, 227–95 and *Cambridge Ancient History* XI, 15.

59. On Antioch see now G. Downey, *A History of Antioch in Syria* (Princeton 1961).

60. A. VI, 28.

61. H. II, 81.

62. H. II.

63. A. II, 73.

64. H. II, 80. 'satis decorus etiam Graeca facundia' (of Mucianus).

65. H. II, 78.

66. A. XII, 12.

67. On the caravan traffic see Freya Stark, *Rome and Parthia on the Euphrates*.

68. These are all described in the *Jewish War* of Josephus.

69. H. V, 2–13.

70. H. V, 2–3.

71. A. II, 85. 'si ob gravitatem caeli interissent, vile damnus.'

72. H. V, 5.

73. See the account of the Jewish rebellion in B. W. Henderson, *Life and Principate of the Emperor Hadrian* (1923).

74. H. V, 10.

75. H. V, 12. Tacitus notes that the Temple itself (rebuilt by Herod) had its own system of walls, that its colonnades formed excellent outworks, and that it possessed an ever-flowing spring, with pools and cisterns to supplement the supply of water.

76. Josephus, *Jewish War*, VI, 71ff., 250–80. See also A. de Sélincourt, *The World of Josephus*.

77. On Roman Asia, see David Magie, *Roman Rule in Asia Minor* (2 vols., Princeton 1950)—a splendid documentation.

78. A. III, 67.

79. A. IV, 56.

80. A. III, 60–3. See above p. 118.

81. A. XII, 62–3.

82. A. II, 42, 56; XII, 49; XIII, 8, 35.

83. For Cappadocia as a Roman province see David Magie, *Roman Rule in Asia Minor*, 495 and 1355.

84. A. II, 88. Tacitus is recording the death of Arminius, 'who lives today in the songs of the barbarians. Greek historians know nothing of him'—*qui sua tantum mirantur. . . .*

85. A. XV, 45.

86. Nero's tour of Greece is recorded in Suetonius, *Nero*, 22–4.

87. A. II, 53.

88. A. II, 55.

CHAPTER TEN: *Beyond the Frontiers*

1. On Parthia, see N. C. Debevoise, *A Political History of Parthia* (1938). On Roman policy towards Parthia, see David Magie, *Roman Rule in Asia Minor*, chapter XXIII.

2. The *Cataphractarii* were the models for the armed cavalry of the Late Roman Empire, from whom in their turn derived the medieval knights.

3. Herodotus I, 135.

4. A. XI, 8. Vardanes was King of Parthia 42–6.

5. A. VI, 43. Artabanus III, King of Parthia 16–42.

6. A. VI, 44.

7. On wars between Rome and Parthia, see David Magie, *Roman Rule in Asia Minor*, 436–7, 558–9, 608–9, 661–2.

8. On the battle of Carrhae, see *Cambridge Ancient History* IX, 606ff.

9. On Antony's eastern campaigns, see *Cambridge Ancient History* X, 71ff.

10. On Augustus' policy towards Parthia, *id. ib.* 223ff., 260ff.

11. For the Alexander idea in Rome, see Syme, *Tacitus* II, 770f. Among Roman emperors affected by it were Caligula, Caracalla and Julian.

12. A. VI, 31.

13. Vonones I, King of Parthia 5–16. For the story of his murder by Tiberius, see Suetonius, *Tiberius*, 49.

14. A. II, 2.

15. A. II, 68.

16. On the episode, see N. C. Debevoise, *A political history of Parthia*, 155f.

17. A. VI, 31.

18. A. VI, 42. For further details on Seleuceia, see Strabo, 16, 1, 5 and Pliny, *Nat. Hist.*, 6, 122.

19. A. VI, 43.

20. A. XI, 10 and XII, 10–14.

21. On Tacitus' account of Gaius Cassius, see Syme, *Tacitus* II, 730.

22. A. XII, 13.

23. A. XII, 14.

24. A. XII, 44–51.

25. Iberia.

26. A. XII, 47.

27. A. XII, 48.

28. A. XII, 49. 'The imperial agent in Cappadocia was a certain Julius Paelignus, a man as contemptible for the meanness of his mind as for the absurdity of his person.' He was the first imperial procurator to govern Cappadocia.

29. A. XII, 51, 4.

30. Cn. Domitius Corbulo had already shown himself a capable general and a strict disciplinarian in Lower Germany under Claudius (A. XI, 18 and 19). His record in the East established him as the best Roman general since Tiberius. Tacitus, while stressing the merits of Corbulo, is careful not to let him overshadow Germanicus.

31. A. XIII, 55. See above, pp. 147f.

32. A. II, 3.

33. Caesennius Paetus had held the consulship in 61. Despite his failures in Armenia, Vespasian later appointed him to be governor of Syria, and he was responsible for the annexation of Commagene. He may be one of the 'less worthy persons' whom Tacitus mentions as benefiting from Vespasian's favours (H. II, 82).

34. A. XV, 24.

35. A. XV, 28. Tacitus says that Corbulo was so little moved by Paetus' disgrace, 'that he ordered Paetus' son, then a military tribune, to take his men and bury the dead of that shameful battle.'

36. Velleius Paterculus, II, 101f.

37. A. XV, 28–31.

38. A. XV, 31. 'scilicet externae superbiae sueto non erat notitia nostri apud quos vis imperii valet, inania tramittuntur.'

39. Suetonius, *Nero*, 13.

40. Dio, LXIII, 6, 5f.

41. Cumont (*Riv. Fil.*, LXI (1933), 145f. has pointed out that the coronation ceremony as described resembles reliefs in which Mithras removes a tiara from the head of a kneeling Helios and replaces it with a

radiate-crown, the inference being that Nero was now the incarnation of Mithras. (See David Magie, *Roman Rule in Asia Minor*, 1417, n. 61.) The colossal statue of Nero as the Sun-God, erected for the Domus Aurea in Rome, is another manifestation of these ideas.

42. Dio, LXIII, 6, 2–4.

43. Dio, LXIII, 6, 5.

44. Tacitus, H. I, 6, speaks of the *claustra Caspiarum* needed for a war in preparation against the Albani; which Caucasian passes are meant has been much debated. On the whole problem, see David Magie, *Roman Rule in Asia Minor*, 1418, n. 63.

45. 'quippe regno Arsacis acrior est Germanorum libertas.'

46. A. II, 63.

47. The proper title is *De Origine et Situ Germanorum*. On its date, see Syme, *Tacitus* I, 46–8.

48. On the anachronisms, see Syme, *Tacitus* I, 127–8.

49. Herodotus, IV, 5–15.

50. On Posidonius, see E. Norden, *Die Germanische Urgeschichte in Tacitus' Germania* (1923), chapter 2. The thirtieth book of Posidonius appears to have contained an account of the Germans.

51. Book 104 of Livy is known to have described Germany.

52. On the *Bella Germaniae* of Pliny, see J. G. C. Anderson's edition of the *Germania*, XXIVf.

53. See E. A. Thompson, *The Early Germans* (Oxford 1965).

54. e.g. G. 33, 42, etc.

55. G. 19, 3. 'nemo enim illic vitia ridet, nec corrumpere et corrumpi saeculum vocatur.' In A. XIV, 20, 5, we are told that everything that is seduction or being seduced is to be seen in Nero's Roma. 'ut quod usquam corrumpi et corrumpere queat in urbe visatur.'

56. G. 15.

57. G. 2.

58. G. 30–1.

59. On Domitian's German Wars, see *Cambridge Ancient History* XI (1936), 162ff.

60. G. 46.

61. The names as given by Tacitus are the Anglii, Eudoses, Langobardi, Gotones, Suiones, Fenni, Venethi.

62. G. 43, 3, 5.

63. G. 45.

64. J. G. C. Anderson, *Tacitus' Germania*, XXVIIIf.

65. *Id. ib.* 88, for the *Moorleichen* or bog-corpses.

66. E. Norden, *Die Urgeschichte Germaniens*, 220, 2.

67. G. 33, 1.

68. On this, see the note of J. G. C. Anderson, *op. cit.* p. 163.

69. A. II, 26 and 62.

70. G. 2, 1.

71. G. 4, 1, 2.

72. A. I, 55–71, and II, 5–26.

73. On Arminius, see also Velleius Peterculus, 2, 118f. Of the (understandably) numerous German works on their national hero I cite only E. Hohl, *Um Arminius, Biographie oder Legende?* (Ak. Verl., Berlin 1951).

74. A. II, 73.

75. A. II, 88. 'liberator haud dubie Germaniae.'

76. A. I, 55.

77. A. I, 57.

78. A. I, 58.

79. A. I, 58, 5.

80. A. II, 9.

81. Or Segimundus, A. I, 57.

82. A. III, 5.

83. On the Dacian wars of Trajan, see Dio, LXVIII, 6–14. Trajan's Column in Rome commemorates these great wars and the army that fought them.

84. On the northern wars of Marcus Aurelius see now Anthony Birley, *Marcus Aurelius* (1966), chapter VIII.

CONCLUSION

1. On the survival of Tacitus' manuscripts, see the section in Clarence W. Mendell, *Tacitus, The Man and His Work* (New Haven, 1957).

2. Lipsius commends Tacitus as 'an excellent author for these times,' and 'a theatre, as it were, of modern life.' He was the first to separate the *Histories* and the *Annals*.

3. On this see J. von Stackelberg, *Tacitus in der Romania* (Tübingen, 1960), especially chapters 4 (Machiavelli) and 8 (Boccalini).

4. *Id. ib.* 10, 11, 95, 260.

5. *Id. ib.* 10, 95.

6. In the Second Preface to *Britannicus* Racine described Tacitus as 'Le plus grande peintre de l'antiquité.'

7. Corneille, *Otho*, in Pléiade, II, ed. Caillois (1957); Racine, *Britannicus*, Pléiade I, ed. Picard (1950).

8. G. Boissier, *Tacite* (Paris 1912), 153ff.

9. 'Tacite! Ne me parlez pas de ce pamphlétaire! Il a calomnié les empereurs!' On Napoleon's views of Tacitus, see J. von Stackelberg, *op. cit.* 242, 243.

10. On Victor Hugo and Napoleon III, see G. Highet, *The Classical Tradition*, 406.

11. On the classical background of the American constitution see Richard M. Gummere, *The American Colonial Mind and the Classical Tradition*, 173ff. (Boston 1963).

12. Agr. 12, 2.

13. A. IV, 33, 1.

14. For the anti-Tacitean tradition, see J. von Stackelberg, *op. cit.* 239ff.

15. On their reading of Tacitus see Richard M. Gummere, *op. cit.* 192f.

16. Quoted *id. ib.* 240.

17. Quoted *id. ib.* 225, 226.

Bibliographical Note

A number of works have already been cited in the Notes. I append a brief list of some useful commentaries, translations, and general works.

EDITIONS WITH COMMENTARY

GERMANIA. J. G. C. Anderson, *Tacitus, Germania* (Oxford 1938), remains the best English edition. Well illustrated, it is especially good on archaeology.

AGRICOLA. R. M. Ogilvie and the late Sir Ian Richmond, *Cornelii Taciti De Vita Agricolae* (Oxford 1967) now supersedes all earlier editions. It takes account of advances in Romano-British archaeology, and of recent work on the language and style of Tacitus.

HISTORIES. The edition of W. A. Spooner (London 1891) remains useful, but a modern English edition is needed.

ANNALS. Here again English readers depend on a Victorian edition, that of H. Furneaux (vol. I, 1896, vol. II, 1891), of which books XI–XVI were revised by H. Pelham and C. D. Fisher (1907). By contrast, Germany has the splendid modern edition of Erich Koestermann (Heidelberg 1963).

TRANSLATIONS

In the Penguin series: *Tacitus on Britain and Germany*, by H. Mattingly (1948); *Tacitus on Imperial Rome*, by M. Grant (1956); *Histories*, by K. Wellesley (1965).

In the New American Library (Mentor Series), *The Annals of Tacitus*, by Donald R. Dudley (1966): *The Agricola, Germania, and Histories*, by Donald R. Dudley (forthcoming).

GENERAL WORKS

I mention yet again R. Syme, *Tacitus* (2 vols., Oxford 1958) to emphasise that it is fundamental for the whole range of Tacitean scholarship. M. L. W. Laistner, *The Greater Roman Historians* (Berkeley 1947), sets Tacitus in the tradition of Roman historiography. E. Lofstedt, *Roman Literary Portraits* (Oxford 1958), 142ff., is excellent on Tacitus' literary style. C. Questa, *Studi sulle fonte degli Annales di Tacito* (Rome 1963) is a recent study of sources. On persons and places mentioned by Tacitus, the invaluable handbook by P. Fabia, *Onomasticon Taciteum*, is now available in an Olms reprint (Hildesheim 1964).

Finally, modern scholarship on Tacitus is usefully surveyed in *Classical Weekly* 48 (1954), 5–121 (for 1948–53); 58 (1964), 5–69 (for 1954–63).

Index

Roman personal names, other than those of Emperors, are indexed under the *nomen* (middle name). Thus Agricola appears as Julius Agricola, Gn.